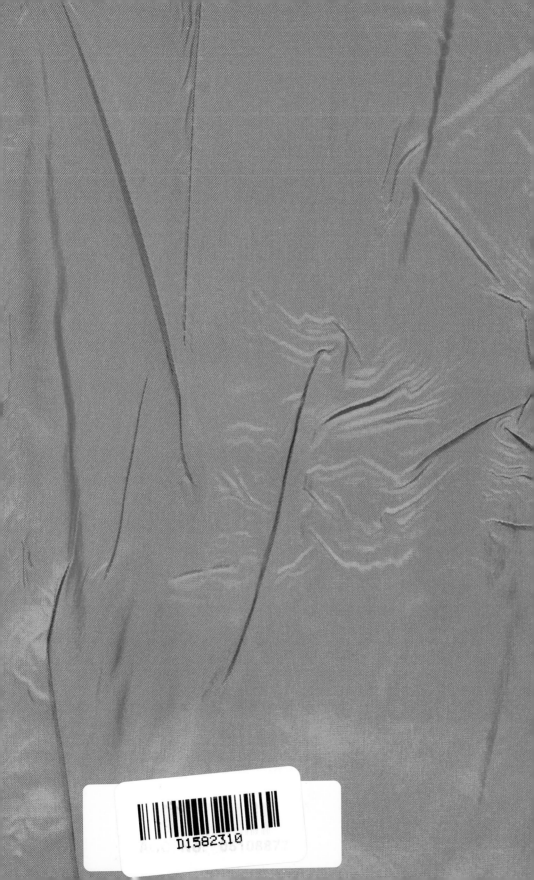

Llyfrgelloedd Caerdydd
www.caerdydd.gov.uk/llyfrgelloedd
Cardiff Libraries
www.cardiff.gov.uk/libraries

CAERDYDD
CARDIFF

LANCE
RICHARDSON

HOUSE OF
NUTTER

THE
REBEL
TAILOR
OF
SAVILE ROW

1 3 5 7 9 10 8 6 4 2

Chatto & Windus, an imprint of Vintage,
20 Vauxhall Bridge Road,
London SW1V 2SA

Chatto & Windus is part of the Penguin Random House group of companies whose
addresses can be found at global.penguinrandomhouse.com.

Penguin
Random House
UK

First published in the US by Crown Archetype in 2018
First published in the UK by Chatto & Windus in 2018

penguin.co.uk/vintage

A CIP catalogue record for this book is available from the British Library

ISBN 9781784741242

Printed and bound by Clays Ltd, St Ives Plc

Penguin Random House is committed to a sustainable future
for our business, our readers and our planet. This book is made
from Forest Stewardship Council® certified paper.

for

Rebecca Cubitt

because it was your idea

&

Dawn Black

because it is your life

CONTENTS

Tommy Nutter in New York, 1974.

PREFACE

You may not recognise the name of Tommy Nutter, but you almost certainly know his clothes. Picture Elton John in the 1980s, playing the piano on a vast arena stage while wearing a heavily padded suit that is half black, half white, like a yin and yang symbol. Or imagine Bianca Jagger sometime in the 1970s, languorous and grumpy in a pistachio-coloured men's suit as she fiddles with her Malacca cane. Or – a sure bet – recall the album cover of *Abbey Road*: four Beatles marching across the street in north-west London, with John Lennon, Ringo Starr and Paul McCartney dressed in immaculate bespoke.

Tommy Nutter was just twenty-six years old when, in 1969, he opened Nutters of Savile Row. He had no formal education as a fashion designer, and no advanced training as a tailor – nothing, really, except what he once described as an 'in-built feeling for clothes'. And yet almost immediately he found himself outfitting everyone from rock stars to Members of Parliament, Twiggy to Diana Ross. Within a few years, the *Evening Standard* pronounced Tommy 'as established and as important as any British tailor or designer'. He accrued an avid following in America that stretched from New York to Los Angeles. People raved about his Savile Row suits, describing them as nothing short of art. In the words of one former client, wearing one made you feel like 'an honoured custodian of something spectacular'. Today, his trailblazing legacy can be sensed in the work of contemporary tailor-designers like Richard James, Ozwald Boateng and Timothy Everest. Tommy Hilfiger recently credited his 'irreverent approach' as an enduring inspiration.

Even Tom Ford, arguably the most important figure working in menswear today, has acknowledged his influence.

I first heard about Tommy Nutter several years ago, when a friend told me the story of a young man who once, after being denied entry into a party at the Tate, threw himself into the River Thames. It sounded so outlandish, so extreme and operatic, that my curiosity was piqued. What intrigued me once I did further research, however, was not so much his burnished image as the 'Tailor to the Stars' – an iconoclast who shook the foundations of a hallowed industry – but the tension between his vaunted reputation and the realities of his private life.

Here was a man whose suits are now safeguarded in the Victoria & Albert Museum and New York's Metropolitan Museum of Art, though he could barely manage a backstitch. Here was a man who comported himself with grace and hobnobbed with Princess Margaret at galas in Venice and Munich, yet had grown up above a humble cafe that catered to truck drivers. A man who'd managed to pull himself out of the working class using nothing more than the strength of his own imagination, an imagination so boundless, it seemed, that it could overcome all reason and even prove ruinous.

Tommy Nutter was obsessed with his public image. He was also gay, coming of age in the oppressive censoriousness of the 1950s. Indeed, his life vividly personalised forty years of critical gay history. From the underground queer clubs of Soho to the unbridled freedom of New York bathhouses to the terrifying nightmare of Aids – Tommy was there, both witness and participant. As a gay man myself, it occurred to me that Tommy's focus on outward appearances might have been a way for him to take control and overcome the more challenging aspects of his lived experience. After all, one way gay men mitigate the perennial pressure to conform to societal norms of masculinity is by striving for perfection (in body, in clothes, in career), overcompensating until that which sets us apart – our taste, say – becomes so impressive it assumes its own power.

Tommy ultimately died from Aids-related pneumonia in August 1992. The lives of many artists, performers and designers were lost prematurely to the plague and have since been unfairly marginalised in the collective memory. This, finally, was the strongest motivation for me writing this book: I saw an opportunity to rescue one person's story from the drift of oblivion.

———

Of course, when you go rummaging around in the past there is a good chance you'll stumble across something you never dreamed of finding. It happened to me early in the research phase, when I arranged to meet Tommy Nutter's brother in a cafe on New York's Upper West Side. Seventy-seven years old, David Nutter turned up wearing a crumpled Rolling Stones T-shirt and clutching a tote bag stuffed with the kind of original photographs usually exhibited in a gallery. He had taken them all himself, he said; they were just sitting in his apartment in stacks of cardboard boxes. Over coffee, he made a range of passing references that seemed inscrutable in the moment – to an obscenity trial, to the birth of disco, to *Starship 1*, to Michael Jackson, to Mick Jagger. It would take me many months to untangle everything, and years before I understood exactly how kaleidoscopic the Nutter saga really was. But I quickly intuited that I was writing a book about two people here, two gay brothers, two halves of a larger, stranger whole.

To discuss a man's wardrobe is really to discuss a man's life. For the kind of clothes he has in it reveals his way of life; and their condition and degree of fashionableness will show his character.

HARDY AMIES, *ABC of Men's Fashion*

Grace / to be born and live as variously as possible.

FRANK O'HARA, *'In Memory of My Feelings'*

HOUSE OF NUTTER

PART I

1939–1968

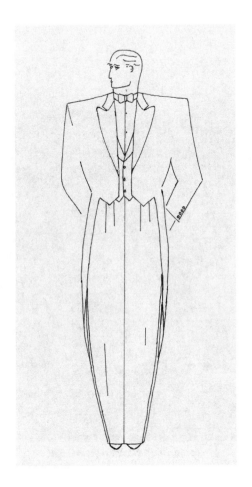

*Fashion, indeed, is born only in social struggle, and it is
typical of new and struggling societies and times of violent
social change which give birth to new social orders that
styles change with equal violence.*

PEARL BINDER, *The Peacock's Tail*

Tommy and David Nutter, 1946

1

ESCAPE ARTISTS

In the mid-1970s, rapidly approaching middle age, David Nutter began to shake the family tree to see who might fall out. He wanted to understand his pedigree, to know how far the name had roamed, so he poked through genealogical records, immigration logs, birth and death certificates. He found it everywhere: a whole diaspora of Nutters. Then he considered etymology, trying to trace the name back to its source. Was 'Nutter' Norman-French, or was it Danish – *notar*, a kind of professional notary? The Danish path led David to history books, which led him to Cnut the Great, also known as King Canute, a Viking warrior who once ruled over a vast Anglo-Scandinavian empire. David liked the sound of that; he noted it down. But as he rifled further through library archives, the figure who really piqued his interest turned up a little closer to home: Lancashire, England, in the early 1600s. David had always had a great deal of fondness for the era of King James ('all his boyfriends running the country, sending him letters'), and now he alighted on a wealthy widow from Roughlee – one Alice Nutter, who had been tried and hanged during the trials of the Pendle witches.

Witches in the Nutter bloodline?

Thrilled by the possibility, David dashed off a letter to his brother. Tommy soon replied: 'Somebody told me the other day that I have strange eyes. Do you think I could be one? Please tell all. It would make a great story for the papers.'

In many ways, David and Tommy Nutter were a case study in familial disparity. As the elder, David was on the shorter side, fair-skinned, with sharply defined features and a blond widow's peak. He was emotionally volatile, often careering one way into depression or the other into euphoria. Tommy, by contrast, was statuesque and dark; he would one day be described as resembling 'a Botticelli youth', and the 'living, breathing embodiment of Peter Pan'. Four years younger than David, he mostly floated along, a little aloof, unflappable, out to have a good time.

What the brothers did share in common, though, was a way of looking at the world – what could be called a Nutter *sensibility*. Both tended to fixate on peripheral, decorative details, often at the expense of more fundamental concerns (like remaining solvent). Both disdained pretension, and would come to treat royalty and rock stars with a generous dose of irreverence. Both spoke a private language rich in double meanings, loaded code, Polari and camp. And both liked to pose questions about themselves (who were they? where did they come from? what did they deserve out of life?) and then embroider their theories so extravagantly that truth, in their hands, could take on the texture of a personal mythology.

Nothing sparked Tommy's and David's imaginations more than their relationship with one another. Why was Tommy olive-skinned but David pale? Why was Tommy introverted while David had such an easy rapport with strangers? Why was Tommy even-keeled (most of the time), and David susceptible to wild, unpredictable mood swings that could strike him down like a sickness?

How were they *brothers*?

The elaborate explanations they dreamed up, or wove together, from thin threads of fact and rumour, invariably began with a single crucial figure: their mother.

Dorothy Lucy Banister was born on 14 July 1916, in Kilburn, a modestly prosperous if overcrowded area of north-west London then known for industry and manufacturing. Dorothy's mother, Lily Tribe, worked in Kilburn as a milliner. Her father, Albert Banister, worked as a labourer for the railway at Camden Town. Unless, that is, her father was Bruno Brunieri, in which case he worked as an attaché for the Italian government down in the West End. 'We can't prove *anything*,' says David, describing his mother's paternity as 'an enigma'.

Lily and Albert lived in a plain but comfortable brick terrace house on Eresby Road, which connected the Kilburn High Road with Kingsgate Road. Lily's father – Dorothy's grandfather – had built the entire row sometime in the 1880s, after his mother begged him to stop sailing off to China and the Far East as a cabin boy on clipper ships. The house he gave Lily was the last in the row, bordered on the left by a cobblestone lane; on the right by the next terrace, where Lily's brother lived with his own burgeoning family; and out front by a sad-looking privet hedge that afforded scant privacy for a bulging bay window. Lily and Albert occupied the first two floors. To earn extra income, they leased out the third to international lodgers, like Bruno Brunieri.

By all accounts, Lily Banister was an unusual woman, manicured but mercurial. Some called her 'Creampot Lil' for her habit of putting so much cream on her scones that they all but disappeared beneath the avalanche. In Kilburn, she was divisive for her aggressive animal-rights activism; she would berate the milkman for mistreating his horses and cut up stale loaves with a pair of scissors to feed the birds. 'I remember pulling away from the front gate in a black cab and seeing a flock of pigeons hovering by the side of the house,' says one relative. 'The window was open, and Lily was tossing out handful after handful of bread. She was almost the double, visually speaking, of a Miss Marple character.'

Lily Banister feeding the Kilburn wildlife near her house.

Later, when Tommy and David finally arrived on the scene, they came to see 'Nanny Banister' as a figure of exquisite camp, like a Victorian Bette Davis. Once, during a sightseeing trip to Clacton, Lily was overcome with light-headedness and declared that she was probably about to die. Turning to Dorothy, she whispered, in front of her grandsons, 'I'm going, Doll.' Decades hence, Tommy would flummox a newspaper journalist by saying the same thing as he went off to retrieve a white sailor suit for a fitting: 'I'm goin', doll.' Lily Banister, the journalist discovered, had 'made such an impact upon the young Nutter that even to this day he rarely leaves anywhere for anywhere else without employing the phrase'.

Lily was ridiculous, but she was also sanctimonious, imposing her version of propriety with ruthless determination. One story has her doctoring photo albums to erase all traces of a daughter's ex-husband, as though he and the divorce had simply never occurred. Could a woman capable of that kind of behaviour really conduct a short-lived affair with her Italian lodger, then return to Albert and pass a love child off as his own?

'It's all quite likely,' Tommy wrote to David in the same letter where he entertained his brother's theory about the witches.

Dorothy, her daughter, did look vaguely Mediterranean. When she was a child, her family mocked her olive complexion; like Tommy with David, she struck a remarkable contrast if placed next to her older sister,

Dorothy Lucy Banister

Gladys, who was as white as salt and unapologetically bourgeois. Dorothy was a carefree bon vivant; she liked to go dancing with her friends at the Cricklewood Palais. For short, people called her Dolly, which suited her better anyway, capturing something of her abiding youthfulness and playful style.

Dolly was not afraid to wear make-up. She adored high heels and floaty cotton dresses, and for several years she kept her hair cut short with a sharp fringe – something like Louise Brooks, the famous American flapper. By the time she was a young woman, capable of making some of her own decisions, she'd become sufficiently self-aware to sense that her complexion, though setting her apart from her family, was also an asset, the distinction that made her beautiful enough to (for example) model in a newspaper advertisement for a secretarial school. And so, to emphasise her colouring, making herself even darker – and more Mediterranean-looking – Dolly began to spend long hours worshipping the sun, relentlessly, recklessly.

Like Lily, Dolly was governed by a powerful moral compass, though perhaps hers pointed more accurately in the direction of empathy. She liked to say, 'I take people as I find them,' almost as a kind of personal mantra. But no matter how open-minded or inclined to independence she may have been, a woman of the working class had limited options in 1930s London: marriage and children were a given, particularly under the coolly expectant eye of Lily Banister. How Dolly first encountered Christopher Nutter, a seating upholsterer for the de Havilland Aircraft Company; how he penetrated her social milieu of close friends and dance halls, of tea gowns and chaperones; what she made of his stiff reticence, so different from her own easy volubility; how their courtship unfolded and how he ultimately proposed – all these details are lost to history.

David describes his parents' marriage as 'a leftover from the Victorian era'. There were no public displays of affection, no hugging or indulgent expressions of warmth. The power structure was traditional, non-negotiable from the first: Christopher would lead, Dolly would follow – plus, of course, raise any children that might appear in the future. 'He was of that old mindset that the woman had to do everything.'

Sometime after the wedding, Christopher left de Havilland and assumed the management of a cafe owned by his sister's husband, John 'Jack' Cross, who had his hands full running another establishment on the Holloway Road. John's Cafe, as it continued to be called, appealed to a blue-collar clientele – plumbers, binmen and lorry drivers. Thus appointed regent ruler of a tiny empire of eggs and chips, Christopher moved his new wife to a modest flat built directly above the cafe in the semi-rural suburb of Edgware. Dolly soon resigned from a secretarial job in the City; work now became cups of tea served from a hefty Stotts of Oldham urn.

Christopher with his mother, Constance Nutter,
who sometimes helped at the cafe.

In the years before Neville Chamberlain's radio declaration that the United Kingdom was, once again, at war with Germany, government ministries began making speculative calculations about how many civilians might die during a theoretical aerial attack on British cities. If Hitler launched an all-out raid, the Home Office estimated that the demand for coffins might become so great – 20 million square feet of timber each month – that mass graves and the incineration of bodies might become necessary. Worst-case predictions foresaw the spread of typhoid fever, unchecked civil disorder, and so much material damage that the assessments were quietly withheld, perhaps to avoid inciting public panic. By late 1937, gas masks were being assembled at a rate of 150,000 units per week. Then, with Nazi movements looking increasingly ominous, planning began for precautionary evacuations that were intended to reduce the projected casualty toll. This scheme would scoop up schoolchildren, elderly and blind people, infirm and invalids, expectant mothers, and mothers with children under five years of age. Because it would lead them out of urban centres into the countryside, the evacuation plan was code-named Operation Pied Piper – a curious choice given the fabled Pied Piper of Hamelin lures children away to their doom.

On 1 September 1939, people mobilised as the operation began to play out. The first day of evacuations focused solely on schoolchildren, many of whom had name-and-address tags pinned to their coats that made them resemble luggage on the railway platforms. Overhead, as the trains shuddered off to safety, giant barrage balloons bobbed in the sky. On 2 September and 3 September (the day Britain officially went to war), mothers with young children became a priority, and they crammed the carriages with their luggage and government-issued General Civilian Respirators. David Christopher Nutter, born on 10 May 1939, was less than four months old at the time. Family lore has Dolly joining the voluntary exodus of 1.47 million people, boarding a train bound for Scotland that was so overcrowded David had to be handed aboard through an open carriage window.

But if Dolly did escape to Scotland, she also quickly returned. Perhaps, like the 80 per cent of evacuated mothers who'd come home by Christmas, she was deceived by a protracted calm on the Western Front that soon became known, somewhat ironically, as the Phoney War.

After the Phoney War, the Luftwaffe began the very real Blitz. As London began to burn in 1940, Christopher turned John's Cafe over to his elderly parents and enlisted in the army for DOW – 'duration of war'. He travelled to Bulford Camp on the Salisbury Plain to fill his first posting as Private Nutter in the Royal Army Service Corps. Dolly, back in London, faced falling bombs no matter where she stayed; both Edgware and Kilburn would be hit repeatedly by the Germans. So she rejoined the government's evacuation scheme and fled with her son into the country again; this time they washed up in Fairbourne, a tiny village on the coast of Cardigan Bay, in North Wales.

Fairbourne is an unusual place. Houses are small and exposed, like dice tipped from a tumbler onto a tabletop of green felt. Dense forest is girdled by drystone walls of Welsh slate. Behind the village, hills begin a punishing climb towards the heights of Cadair Idris. Along the shore, beyond a miniature train that has chugged back and forth for more than a century, gulls populate a shingle beach, and a slither of sand plays hide-and-seek with the tide. The beach feeds into the mouth of the River Mawddach in a wide, changeable estuary that divides Fairbourne from the larger settlement of Barmouth, just to the north. Tennyson wrote part of 'In Memoriam' in Barmouth ('Sweet after showers, ambrosial air . . .'), and, seen in a certain magic-hour light, the entire area looks something like a prelapsarian Eden.

At least, that's how David describes it, having spent his formative years there. 'We lived in a boarding house, in a room right at the top,' he recalls. 'When I was old enough, I'd go and ring the church bells on Sundays, because I was friends with the vicar's daughter. And the stationmaster used to let me into the signal box to pull the huge levers that shunted the rails between Fairbourne and Barmouth. I loved the smell of steam trains.'

What it meant to the urbane, twenty-four-year-old Dolly is more opaque. Although she was far from solitary in her new home – marked as a 'Safe Area' by the military, Fairbourne had been flooded with evacuees – there would not have been much to occupy the time, and even less in the way of employment. It is not hard to imagine Dolly walking down the shingle beach as she wondered how she'd ended up in a place like this, and what with another child on the way.

Thomas Albert Nutter: when he was conceived, Christopher was stationed just several hours north-east of Fairbourne, repairing army equipment in the workshops at Overton-on-Dee. When Tommy was born, Christopher was right there in the Barmouth maternity hospital, signing his second son's birth certificate on 17 April 1943.

The bedlam of wartime Wales, though, with its bell-jar isolation and suspension of familiar social rules, had been bizarre enough to roil some ambiguity around Tommy's origin. Besides evacuees, Fairbourne and Barmouth saw many unfamiliar faces during the war: 'a polyglot assembly', as a local historian has described it, of Brits, Norwegians, Lithuanians and 'at least one Russian lady'. American GIs passed through the area, while Crete Camp in Barmouth was used by the Royal Marines. Polish Commandos billeted with residents, ran mysterious night manoeuvres, and finished punishing training exercises by marching down the road singing 'You Are My Sunshine'. In the town's pavilion, they threw rowdy public dances and flirted with the local girls, who flirted back.

When he was a teenager, David whispered an idea into Tommy's ear that would prove intractable: What if their mother had paramours out there in the wild west of Wales?

What if Christopher Nutter was *not* his biological father?

This was pure hokum, one teenager goading another with a fantasy that diagnosed the differences between them as symptoms of illegitimacy. Still, Tommy seemed to run with it. 'He liked the idea that his real father was an American GI,' David says. Tommy told the story to cousins, friends and even Dolly herself – who, far from being scandalised by the insinuation of her wartime promiscuity, apparently found it compelling enough to share with several *more* people. 'She told me the story,' recalls one family acquaintance, 'but it was only a joke. Although, I don't know. It might not have been a joke?'

Tommy, Dolly and David sunbathing together on the beach.

Just one month after Tommy voiced his first scream in Barmouth, Christopher left the home forces and headed for North Africa, where he would draw on his experience as an aircraft seating upholsterer to provide maintenance support for the 1st Airborne Division. Africa was 'filthy, with flies everywhere', he later complained, though he also refused a vaccination against typhus while he was there. Towards the end of the war, after the invasion of Normandy, he headed to Norway as a member of the British Liberation Army. Scandinavia, by contrast, was to him 'beautiful, wonderful' – particularly the ski jumps.

Christopher Nutter, with his perpetual grimace, was not a bad person. His main shortcoming was a lack of imagination: he knew what he knew and had only minimal interest in knowing anything more. With a few exceptions – science; the 'Dome of Discovery' at the Festival of Britain, which seemed to intrigue him – horizons were there to be fortified, not expanded. Like many men of his generation, Christopher grabbed hold of easy prejudices and built a barrier of abrasive pessimism around himself. Black people were lesser people; the new South Asian migrants to Britain were a cause for alarm; and America (New York particularly) was 'a hellhole', even though he'd never been there and would never go. Why anyone might voluntarily seek out somewhere other than one's own comfortable abode was beyond his understanding.

Christopher was discharged from service on 15 February 1946. He immediately reinstalled his expanded family in the Edgware flat and Dolly back behind the tea urn. This was the natural order of things, as he saw it: an obedient wife, pints at the pub, the occasional game of football. 'Chris just went to work, made some money,' a relative recalls. 'He didn't expect anything else out of life.'

What he expected of his sons was just as banal. When he went off to war he was following an example set by his own father, also Christopher, who'd fought in the Great War and Second Boer War before that. In other words, Christopher Jr had taken the torch of traditional British masculinity and relayed it through to the 1950s with minimal disruption. And now his own sons were expected to start carrying.

'He used to take me to the Edgware Football Club and Lord's Cricket Ground,' David recalls. 'I think he was trying to encourage that sort of thing. He always wanted me to get into boxing, too, so he bought me boxing gloves. But I didn't like it.'

David lasted four days in the British Boy Scouts; Tommy never pretended to try. Instead of communal sports, they both preferred big Hollywood spectacles, viewed for free because their parents had agreed to display Odeon advertisements in the cafe. They also liked to spend time with their mother, whom they'd call Dolly, sunbathing together on the back stairs by the apple trees and accompanying her to live performances (Ethel Merman, Marlene Dietrich) at the Golders Green Hippodrome. Dolly, the brothers soon decided, was 'almost like a slave' to her husband. Though she never spoke to them openly about being dissatisfied, they sensed Christopher got under her skin with his endless grousing – that he was, in effect, holding her back from reaching her full potential.

As payback for the tyrannical atmosphere Christopher created at home, Tommy and David liked to play pranks on their father. One involved positioning an object atop a slightly open door: when their father

The Nutters on holiday in Broadstairs, Kent.

pushed into the room carrying several plates of food, the object fell on his head, causing him to drop everything. Christopher was incensed; their arguments could be explosive. But the brothers were unperturbed and vowed to do it all over again. 'We used to call him names because he got on our nerves,' David says. 'And he was racist. All the things that we weren't.'

Though Christopher struggled to make any headway in toughening up his sons, there was always the hope the school system could do the job for him. By the time the boys came of age, the Education Act of 1944 had divided secondary schools into three distinct types and implemented an exam known as the eleven-plus to sort students among them. Doing well in the eleven-plus would grant a child access to one of the country's coveted grammar schools, which opened a pathway to university and white-collar comfort. Doing poorly, on the other hand, diverted a child to a technical school, or one of the secondary moderns, which were looked upon by some with a dread bordering on horror. Capturing a widely shared opinion, the journalist Peter Laurie once wrote, 'To have been consigned to the limbo of the secondary modern is to have failed disastrously, and very early in life.' Keith Richards summed up the secondary modern as 'the school for kids that don't stand much of a chance of doing anything except unskilled or semi-skilled labour'. Simon Doonan, the writer and window-dresser, is even more blunt: 'If, like me, you failed your eleven-plus, you were left with this horrible sinking feeling that society had essentially written you off already.'

David failed the eleven-plus.

Three years later, Tommy also failed – 'desperately' – joining the other 75 to 80 per cent of students who did the same.

Prospects for escaping the working class now looked dim for both of them. David was given a reprieve, however, when Christopher and Dolly decided to send him to a private preparatory school instead. This was followed by Clark's College, a secretarial school, where the Dickensian-named Mr Savage would hold communal canings like public executions.

Following in David's wake, Tommy received no such boost. 'My parents put me on to a council school, which was very rough,' he later recalled. 'Rough' to Tommy was, in fact, a horticultural school, Camrose Secondary Modern, where students were taught how to grow vegetables and could elect to join the pig club.

Camrose Secondary Modern was not to Tommy's taste.

In 1956, Tommy got another chance to safeguard his future, this one called the thirteen-plus. Doing well this time round would allow him to transfer to a building school, an engineering school, or even an art school, once vividly described by George Melly as a refuge for 'the bright but the unacademic, the talented, the non-conformist, the lazy, the inventive and the indecisive' – essentially, a character sketch of T. A. Nutter. Over the 1950s and 60s, art schools would develop into bastions of fashion and modernist jazz, Sartre and duffel coats, the Campaign for Nuclear Disarmament. All of the imaginative people seemed to be art students, and Tommy was desperate to join the party; indeed, when he passed the thirteen-plus – 'to everybody's amazement' – art school was his first and only choice.

However, as Tommy later acknowledged, 'Art in those days was looked upon as a bit odd, a little bit funny, the Beatniks, all that sort of thing.' Christopher believed his sons were already funny enough. 'My parents, bless them, just wouldn't allow me to go to art school,' Tommy recalled. 'They didn't know what "art" was.'

At Christopher's behest, Tommy was shunted instead into Willesden Technical College. There, he was condemned to a three-year building trade course that covered the rudiments of plumbing and bricklaying – or, as Tommy preferred to put it, 'all those butch things I couldn't bear'.

In part to inoculate themselves against the unbearable expectations of their father, Tommy and David combined their powers of invention. They treated the walls of their shared bedroom with shocks of coloured paint. They built a faux fireplace from scavenged bricks and sculptures out of tin film containers threaded with wire. They sliced out pages from *Marie Claire*, *Paris Match*, and made a giant photo mural that juxtaposed Brigitte Bardot with African tribal dancers. They collected the entire back catalogue of Leonard Bernstein, which they blared on a portable radiogram.

One of David's early multiple-exposure experiments.

David also took up amateur photography.

While stationed in Norway, Christopher had developed a taste for taking pictures, a taste he'd then passed on to his firstborn son (one of the few things they had in common). Christopher was content to just take snaps on summer holidays, but David was more inclined to pursue such hobbies to their creative extremes. In Edgware, he converted a cupboard into a makeshift darkroom, filling the tiny space with sloshing liquids, strips of film, and a cheap enlarger he could use to make experimental exposures. Over time, with the help of Tommy, who performed

Tommy, taking inspiration from the classic Hollywood portraits of George Hurrell.

the role of artist's muse, his work became increasingly sophisticated – and glamorous.

'Glamour', today, is most often used as a synonym for beauty or celebrity, but it also has another meaning. As the writer Virginia Postrel has argued, glamour has to do with illusion – an illusion that masks certain details of reality and arouses longing for something better: 'It leads us to feel that the life we dream of exists, and to desire it even more.' Glamour is part performance, part seduction. For Tommy and David, it also became a guiding life principle.

Perhaps the starkest exposition of glamour is the modern American musical, where messy lives are streamlined through the grace of staging, and where inarticulable emotions are effortlessly expressed through a medium of song and dance. Unsurprisingly, young Tommy

Making the matinee at Her Majesty's Theatre.

and David were musical 'groupies' (as David describes it), catching the train down to the West End for standing-room tickets in the big theatres. It began with *Guys and Dolls* in the mid-1950s. *My Fair Lady* opened in 1958. *Candide* in 1959. *Bye Bye Birdie* would premiere in 1961. But their abiding favourite was – and remained, for much of their lives – *West Side Story*, which felt transgressive and true, somehow, though they struggled to put their finger on exactly what spoke to them.

Tommy and David framed a picture of Chita Rivera in their bedroom. When they received word that George Chakiris was playing tennis near their house, they stalked him like paparazzi. Between the two of them, they saw *West Side Story* at least a dozen times, over and over, Tommy even skipping classes to make the matinees at Her Majesty's Theatre.

Tommy finally escaped Willesden Technical College in the summer of 1959 with a Pass standard in English language and geometrical drawing – which qualified him for almost nothing. His teachers and parents despaired of his ever landing 'a decent job'.

Now sixteen years old, Tommy had just missed conscription under the National Service Act, which was finally ending. Just the previous December, David had stood before a medical board in Acton and been rejected for his asthma. ('And I don't think my eyesight was that good either,' David recalls with relief. 'It would have finished me off, you know, because I don't like being told what to do by anyone.')

Tommy got piecemeal employment at a variety of places, including a plumbing firm that forced him to transport ceramic toilet bowls on the Tube. 'It really wasn't me,' he later said. And then Christopher interceded once more on his son's behalf. 'My parents, thinking of a nice, safe job for their little boy, suggested I take the Civil Service exams,' Tommy recalled. A government position would mean a respectable, dependable career for life. He took the exams in October 1959.

Four months later, a letter from the Ministry of Works arrived at the cafe advising 'T. A. Nutter, Esq.' that he was now a clerical assistant.

'Your starting pay will be £4 17s. 0d. per week, rising to £5 10s. 6d. per week on your birthday in April, 1960,' the letter informed him. 'Up to the age of 18 you will be entitled to a meal voucher valued ⅛d. and purchasable for 10d. You will also be allowed time off (a day each week) to attend school, if you wish, until you are 18.'

What this actually meant was that Tommy had essentially become an office *chai wallah*. Fetching tea left him 'practically insane with boredom', and he spent most of his time staring at the scratched surface of his wooden desk. During Tommy's tenure, the Ministry of Works was finalising designs for the Post Office Tower (now the BT Tower), a centrepiece of the country's modern telecommunications network that would dramatically alter the London skyline with its bulbous figure. If Tommy took any notice of what was happening around him, though, he never gave any indication. Instead, his attention seemed focused elsewhere – on himself, on what he was wearing. 'I shall never forget my first suit,' he later recalled, and he would recall it so often and with such wistfulness that the suit came to seem almost talismanic, a glorified relic for which he'd paid £8. Bought from Burtons, it featured a short, square jacket in brown worsted, narrow lapels, three covered buttons, and tapered trousers with slits up the ankles: what was called 'the Italian Look'.

Tommy loathed the Ministry of Works. Administrative bureaucracy was, he decided, tedious and 'dismal'. He endured it for nine months, got his pay raise. And then, on 8 November 1960, he bought a copy of the *Evening Standard*, turned to Situations Vacant, and alighted on an advertisement.

> **SAVILE ROW TAILORS** have vacancy for youth to learn trimming, packing and general shop duties. Little knowledge of tailoring preferred, but not essential. Good appearance and manner important. Apply in writing. G. Ward & Co., 35 Savile-row. W.1.

Tommy would later claim that he'd always had a natural flair for dressing well. At the technical college he'd woken up to the idea of personal style, had kept his little white shirt carefully well ironed ('or at least my mother did'), and his hair parted, creamed and combed into a peak. The advertisement now spoke to him, and it seemed to say, 'Come on, if you don't do it now you'll never do it.'

The following day, Tommy wrote an application letter using his most painstaking penmanship.

> *. . . Unfortunately I have no experience of the tailoring trade, but I am sure I will pick it up very quickly, because I am very interested in it.*
>
> *Should you be so good as to offer me the vacancy I would use every effort to fill the post to your satisfaction.*
>
> *Yours faithfully,*
> *Thomas A. Nutter*

Tommy posted the letter without telling his parents. When they found out, 'their feeling was one of amazement', Tommy recalled. 'They had always wanted me to find a steady, secure job. Tailoring did not fit into that category.' Christopher, for his part, was 'not exactly pleased about the idea'.

But Tommy didn't much care about his father's opinion, and he was through with blindly following convention for the sake of security. He'd tried things their way, Dolly and Christopher's; now it was his turn. 'I knew from a little boy what I wanted to do,' he once told a journalist, glamorising the facts only a little. 'And I went against everything to do it.'

Chelsea Bridge and the Battersea Power Station

2

THE GOLDEN AGE

A regular workday, 1960: Tommy is dodging men in black bowlers, traffic conductors, scooters and women whose skirts seem to be getting shorter these days; past tobacconists and newsagents, florists, hair salons, cosmetics shops, immigrant-run restaurants selling foods that he's never heard of, let alone eaten; past dank, unpaved alleyways, seedy cellar spaces and low-slung windows coated in grime; and past narrow espresso bars with those newfangled Gaggia machines, where the kids are 'packed tight', just as Colin MacInnes wrote, 'whispering, like bees inside the hive waiting for a glorious queen bee to appear'. This labyrinth – Soho – unfurls all the way to Charing Cross Road, a gauntlet populated by boys much like Tommy rushing cans of celluloid from one production house to the next, by drunkards and prostitutes, by people cruising down around Piccadilly for anonymous sex.

As an 'errand boy-trotter', or deliveryman, Tommy has a bag on his back filled with toiles and valuable cloth. He comes to a door and pushes inside, then climbs a staircase to a cramped workroom, where men sit cross-legged, squinting, beneath lighting that will probably destroy their eyesight before the end. These men, called outworkers, look up from their boards at the new arrival, who promptly distributes his cargo: cloth to be assembled into coats go to the coat makers (a popular saying: 'Gentlemen wear *coats*, potatoes wear *jackets*'); and trouser pieces go to the trouser makers. Everyone has his specific role, an area of expertise. Some have callused ridges on their fingers from years of repetitive exertion.

Tommy collects any garments the outworkers have completed and folds them gingerly into his bag. Then, mission accomplished, he dashes down the stairs and retraces his path back through the squalidness to Regent Street.

A canyon carved from grey-white Portland stone, Regent Street divides this part of London into two distinct realms: louche Soho in the east; genteel Mayfair in the west. A river of black cabs and red buses rushes in between. Tommy bridges the canyon at the traffic lights, adjusts his pace, and begins a respectable stroll towards the famous stretch of Savile Row.

Say, today, that you have some serious money in your pocket, £3,000 to £6,000, and an overwhelming desire to buy a suit so finely made it will immediately diminish everything else in your wardrobe to the level of rags. On Savile Row, do you go to the tailor's your father has gone to (and grandfather before him, for his military uniforms), Dege & Skinner? Or is your primary interest a signature house style: the slim-looking single-button coats at Huntsman, perhaps, as skilfully balanced as a samurai sword? If old Hollywood is an influence, you might follow Rudolph Valentino into Anderson & Sheppard, just round the corner on Old Burlington Street. Of course, Henry Poole & Co. is always a safe bet too, having been favoured by everyone from tsars and shahs to Charles de Gaulle, who led the Free French during the Second World War while looking immaculate.

Whichever firm you choose to patronise, the process of bespoke is largely the same. During a first consultation, a salesman, attentive but not obsequious, will begin by peppering you lightly with questions. What suits do you already own? And what is the intended event for this one: a wedding, a law office, a film premiere? What's the weather like where you plan to wear it, because that will influence the cloth selection (worsted wool, linen, mohair, tweed, flannel . . .). And then, of course, there is the matter of design: pinstripes, windowpane, Glenurquhart check? Single- or double-breasted? If you happen to be the indecisive type, this step alone might take several hours, which is exactly why alcohol is often on standby.

Eventually a cutter will be summoned to the front, a star employee, confident and persuasive, who is supremely educated in all aspects of the craft. The cutter usually has at least seven to eight years of experience; in the past, tailors have been known to claim, with proud exaggeration, that training a cutter 'takes longer than to train a brain surgeon'.

The cutter's first charge is sizing you up. Accompanied by one or more assistants, sometimes called strikers, he (or she, if the firm is particularly progressive) will wrap and poke a tape measure in up to two dozen different ways, charting the topography of your body with unnerving precision. He will also observe your figuration – the way you hold yourself, the way you move. Physical measurements are recorded as a list of numbers; figuration, however, might become a series of covert abbreviations, meaningless to all but those in the know.

> DR: Sloping down on the right shoulder
> RB: Rounded back
> FS: Flat seat; no backside

The cutter will ask his own questions. With tact and subtlety, for example, he may enquire whether you 'dress left' or 'dress right' – which way your manhood tends to fall in your underpants.* Unsurprisingly, this intimate collaboration between client and cutter has assumed a special status in tailoring lore, a status that a *Playboy* fashion director once summed up like this: 'They used to say that the relationship of a man to his tailor was like a woman and her gynaecologist – all private.'

The cutter combines technical skill with subjective interpretation; mathematics with art. This becomes particularly true once you've played your part and vacated the premises. Standing at a workbench

---

* According to Stephen Howarth, a historian who has examined ledger notes from across the decades and centuries at Henry Poole & Co., more than 95 per cent of men 'dress left'. One notable exception was 'Buffalo Bill' Cody, who was first measured at Poole in 1892, and always did things his own way.

before a wide expanse of clean manila paper, the cutter looks over your details and, using a piece of chalk, sets about translating them into an original pattern. He may do this using a draughting square and French curves, jotting down equations based on long-held principles of scale, proportion and balance.

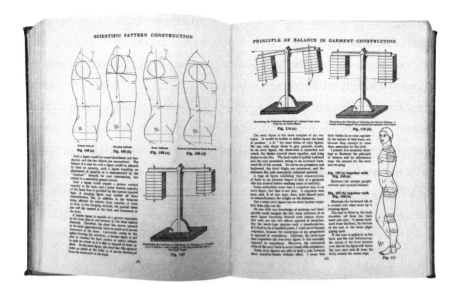

'A corpulent man may, and, if of true type, does, hold himself erect to counterbalance the weight of his abdomen.'

Or he may just wing it. If complex geometry is second nature, his preferred cutting system will be 'rock of eye', or the rule of thumb, meaning he'll sketch out your coat freehand, using almost nothing but a refined instinct for graceful lines. All details of the suit – angle of the gorge, sweep of the lapel – will then be inflected by those idiosyncrasies of hand that make some cutters good and others astounding.

Once finished, your pattern will be safeguarded in the firm's store-room for decades. In the future, whenever you visit for a new suit, alteration lines will be added to reflect the passage of time, until the pattern becomes, in effect, a palimpsest of your life. Many years ago, Poole employed a man who acted as an in-house librarian, his primary job to maintain thousands of numbered patterns on shelving in a vast basement. His secondary job was to read *The Times* obituaries every morning: if a client's name happened to appear, he would locate their pattern and 'get rid of it', effectively closing the record.

Eventually your pattern is transferred to approximately three and a half yards of cloth. Extra lines are added for pockets and vents. Then the cutter (perhaps running shears through his hair to ever-so-lightly oil the blades) strikes out each of the requisite panels, or has an able assistant do it for him. There is no room for sloppiness here. 'Cutting bespoke suits is almost the hardest thing in the world if you're really into it,' explains Rupert Lycett Green, who ran a tailoring firm near Savile Row from 1962 until the early 1980s. 'You're trying to create things of beauty. If you're Michelangelo, you can take a bit of stone and keep at it until it's perfect. But if you do that with a suit – well, then the man goes on holiday and comes back eight pounds heavier, or takes up marathon running and comes back eight pounds lighter. You've got to alter it. There's *tremendous* pressure.'

The first fitting is a subdued affair. You return to the showroom and pull on a ragged-looking 'skeleton baste', tacked together with white cotton thread. The cutter dances around, slashing you with more chalk marks to refine your silhouette. This is generally done away from a mirror: people who gaze at themselves tend to stiffen their posture in an unconscious act of self-magnification.

Following the fitting, the baste suit is unstitched, ripped flat, recut if necessary, and then built, on average, for eighty hours. Give or take a dozen.

If you're of the rare breed able to appraise your own body honestly, then by the second or third fitting you will begin to understand what makes these suits so exceptional. The materials and feel, of course, as well as the way it makes *you* feel, like you're wearing a carapace. But there is also something more: what could be called the sartorial airbrushing.

A master tailor 'must be able not only to cut for the handsome and well-shaped, but bestow a good shape where nature has not granted it; he must make the clothes sit easy in spite of a stiff gait or awkward air . . .' So decreed the *Dictionary of English Trades* in 1804, and the principle remains true more than two hundred years later. Take, for instance, a man with a slight frame, sloping shoulders and an abnormally large head: a Savile Row suit can pad up his shoulders by multiple inches, and be draped to emphasise his chest and hips, thereby making his head seem more flatteringly proportioned. Just look at Archibald Leach: this is precisely what the consummate experts at Kilgour, French & Stanbury did to help turn him into Cary Grant.

On Savile Row, this magic trick is executed with a particular attitude that only enhances the effect. Hardy Amies, the couturier and fashion designer, once wrote, 'A man should look as if he had bought his clothes with intelligence, put them on with care and then forgotten all about them.' The Italians call this idea *sprezzatura*: studied carelessness, artifice concealed behind an appearance of casual ease. A good suit is not really supposed to draw attention when you wear it; it should, in fact, be all but invisible as it corrects for your deficiencies, the implication being that *no corrections are even taking place*. Archie Leach was not transformed through the tireless effort of a team of craftsmen; he was simply Cary Grant, already perfect, who just happened to be wearing a suit he picked up somewhere in London.

The magic of a Savile Row suit, which rarely looks new in the conventional sense, is that it enhances your real self into heightened fantasy, then presents this fantasy as your real self.

'I started off picking up pins,' Tommy once recalled of his first job at G. Ward & Co. He landed the position after skipping a day of work at the Civil Service, which docked his pay in penalty. 'I think they were rather desperate to have somebody sweep the floor,' he said, though in truth he was experienced for G. Ward in exactly the right ways: processing mail, running parcels around town, delivering tea to more senior employees. The pay was just as abysmal as in the Civil Service – £5 10s. per week – and yet it hardly seemed to smart this time round: 'I was so keen I loved every minute of it.'

G. Ward occupied a modest showroom at No. 35 Savile Row, with space behind it and below for cutters and storage. All traditional tailors at the time refrained from window displays or outward flourishes of any kind. The sole concession, perhaps, would have been a small brass nameplate that recalled the sign on a law office or funeral parlour. Window glass was heavily frosted, admitting light from the street, but not curiosity: either you knew what was there or you would never know, were not *meant* to know. The hoi polloi was carefully segregated from an esteemed clientele that included the English conductor Sir Adrian Boult; Hugh Gaitskell, leader of the Labour Party; and the Grand Ducal Family of Luxembourg.

Later in life, Tommy would describe G. Ward as 'rather an old-fashioned company', even 'a bit stuffy'. But he was an attentive observer who absorbed everything he could about the tailoring trade: the variations of button (horn, corozo nut), the proper number for a coat, how many should be fastened when the coat was being worn. Rules of dress fascinated Tommy in the same way that some people are fascinated by feng shui. He learned, for example, how to measure quality by scrunching cloth and reading the creases. He trained his eye to spot one suit sleeve two millimetres longer than the other. He practised the tailor's lingo until he was fluent, acquiring the full arsenal of obscure (and devastating) abbreviations.

SLABC: Stands like a broken-down cab horse

Tommy's attentiveness soon got him promoted out of the broom cupboard and into the cutting room, where he assumed a new role as trimmer, meaning he was responsible for organising interlinings, buttons and thread – all those trimmings (thus the name) that go into making up a single garment beyond the cloth.

In the cutting room, Tommy was exposed to the customs and traditions of Savile Row tailoring, many of which could be traced back to George 'Beau' Brummell, a Regency-era dandy who'd effectively become (and remains today) the patron saint of bespoke tailors, for reasons enumerated by Virginia Woolf: 'His clothes seemed to melt into each other with the perfection of their cut and the quiet harmony of their colour. Without a single point of emphasis everything was distinguished – from his bow to the way he opened his snuff-box, with his left hand invariably.' Tommy would come to trust in the gospel of Brummell so completely that he would one day preach it authoritatively on BBC Radio.

By 1961, Tommy had enrolled in night classes at the Tailor & Cutter Academy on Gerrard Street, in Soho. Under the tutelage of A. A. Whife, he completed the six-month cutter's course; later, he would credit it with teaching him 'how to actually make a jacket and properly fit a sleeve', which may have been something of an overstatement. According to Andrew Ramroop, a tailor who once considered attending the school himself, Tommy 'learned pattern drafting, he learned the rudiments of translating measurements onto paper'. If a cutter can be likened to a brain surgeon, the academy taught Tommy just enough to be a nurse.

While Tommy went about his studies, the West End continued to change all around him. The city of London had never seen so many cars on its roads. Post-war prosperity meant Ford Anglias, Morris Minors and, most recently, the fabulous, head-turning Mini. Parallel parking was a particularly vexing issue in areas like Mayfair, the lanes of which had never been envisaged to accommodate automobiles.

In March 1962, *The Times* published a notice that sent a grumble of discontent through the workrooms of Savile Row.

FROM OUR ESTATES CORRESPONDENT

Westminster City Council are to be recommended by their Car Parking Committee to approve a scheme for a multi-storey garage in a building to be erected on the site of 33–39, Savile Row, and 3–9, Old Burlington Street. The building would also provide shops, showrooms, offices, and flats.

. . . A compulsory purchase order for the site awaits confirmation by the Minister of Transport.

None of the tailors seemed to go out of business because of the compulsory purchase order, or not exactly. Samuel Cundey, the owner of Henry Poole & Co., was deeply shocked and never quite the same afterwards. 'To see the family inheritance being bulldozed . . . upset him no end,' his son and heir, Angus Cundey, once recalled. But the company gathered its stock and employees and shifted slightly over to Cork Street, where it soon resumed a nimble trade. Meanwhile, G. Ward & Co., also slated for demolition, combined its resources with another tailor's to become Donaldson, Williams & G. Ward, which popped up so quickly in the stately Burlington Arcade (just 370 feet from Savile Row) that there was barely a hiccup in trading.

Donaldson, Williams & G. Ward was located in the north end of Burlington Arcade.

And yet it is difficult not to read the parking-garage imbroglio as a kind of sign – a sign of the industry's decline, perhaps, that had been creeping on since before the war. Savile Row was succumbing to senescence in a furiously modernising world, figuratively and now literally. Later, Tommy would describe the brief flash he spent at No. 35 as 'the very end of the Golden Age', adding, because he could rarely help himself: 'Either I finished it off or it was already in its death throes.'

The so-called golden age of Savile Row arguably began in 1860, exactly a hundred years before Tommy turned up on the doorstep asking for a job. One evening in London, the Prince of Wales attended the performance of a play about Robert Macaire, an archetypal villain and con man. While sitting in the audience, the prince noticed that the actor playing Macaire was wearing 'a mass of rents and patches' that seemed, the closer he looked, to be an incredibly well-cut mass of rents and patches.

The prince was Prince Edward, son of Victoria and Albert, later King Edward VII, though his family just called him Bertie. He had a discriminating eye, and at the end of the play he summoned the actor, Charles Fechter, to enquire which tailor happened to be responsible for producing his raffish adventurer's coat. Fechter said it was 'Poole'.

Before Bertie elevated Henry Poole to the position of his chief tailor, fine British tailoring had subsisted since the days of Beau Brummell on a trade of aristocratic dress and military uniforms. James Gieves and Thomas Hawkes, for example, had once kitted out Admiral Lord Nelson and Arthur Wellesley, 1st Duke of Wellington; during the recent Crimean War, Gieves had even filled a yacht with tailoring supplies and sailed off to the Black Sea to make a fortune dressing British naval officers between battles.

But the Prince of Wales's patronage represented something new for bespoke tailoring, and for Savile Row particularly. Here was a young man who adored clothes – *too* much, in the opinion of his father, who allegedly complained that 'even when out shooting, he is more occupied with his trousers than with the game!' When he travelled abroad, Prince Edward packed more than forty suits and twenty pairs of shoes. He took two valets to keep everything in order and left more behind to tend to the rest of a wardrobe that was, by some accounts, the largest in the world: 'the robes of nine British and fifty foreign orders of chivalry, a complete set of uniforms of every British regiment and plenty of foreign ones besides, plus enough civilian wear to satisfy a man who was pleased to change his dress five or six times a day'.

The prince was not afraid of ordering novelties when he visited the Row. In 1865, he decided he was tired of changing every night into full tails at Sandringham, so asked Henry Poole to contrive an easier alternative. The result – a short celestial-blue smoking jacket with silk-satin facings – would one day become known as the dinner jacket, and later 'tuxedo', after a copy (or so the popular theory goes) caused a stir at the Tuxedo Club in New York in 1886.

Among numerous other design follies, Bertie introduced two-piece velvet suits for wear in country houses. He took to wearing loose, waist-banded Norfolk jackets, homburg felt hats and Tyrolean hats with a feather. He had an Inverness cape – the kind now associated with Sherlock Holmes – crafted in silk-lined black, which he wore like an opera cloak, thereby breaching the age-old boundary between sportswear and more decorous kinds of dress. He also popularised white waistcoats for wear with dark dress coats: the penguin look. One story has him spilling spinach down his starched front during a dinner at Buckingham Palace; instead of exploding with anger, he just laughed, let Queen Alexandra have a go at scraping it off, then dipped a napkin in the green purée and proceeded to develop the blotch into a fully realised illustration. Clothing, for Bertie, was both a serious fixation and a delightful game.

It is because of him that no gentleman today fastens the bottom button on a waistcoat. He once forgot, and soon everybody began 'forgetting'. Indeed, Prince Edward's innovations, deliberate or otherwise, were duly adopted by refined society across the Continent. In Marienbad, which he enjoyed visiting annually, tailors from Paris and Vienna would trail him like journalists, taking notes on his new outfits so they could report back to their rich clientele. In this way, he became an international arbiter of men's style; as King Edward VII, he would become an icon, lending his name to a whole era.

Because Edwardian style was largely realised on Savile Row, the reputation of its tailors soared for several decades. Edward would bespeak it; Savile Row would make it; everybody else would follow, flocking to Mayfair in a long line of Russian luminaries, American magnates, maharajas, entrepreneurs, lords, hoteliers and politicians. As the Duke of Windsor once wrote, 'He was a good friend to the tailors of Savile Row, consolidating the position of London as the international sartorial shrine for men, as already Paris was for women.'

King Edward VII died in 1910. Then the First World War took its toll, which included many from the next generation of wealthy gentlemen. For Savile Row, the short-term rush of military orders kept them afloat – some tailors were stretched beyond capacity during the conflict – and then afterwards, at least in part, by the earnest efforts of yet another Prince of Wales.

Prince Edward Albert Christian George Andrew Patrick David shared his grandfather's almost fetishistic attraction to clothes. (King George V, coming in between them, not so much.) Like Bertie before him, Edward was said to travel with an astonishing number of trunks: at least forty, carefully guarded by his devoted valet. When it came to Savile Row, he was not afraid of innovation either, bespeaking new and dazzling things in response to what he saw as grotesque 'constrictions of dress' thrust upon him by 'rigid social convention'. Edward's preference was for comfort and freedom. He had zips installed in his trousers – a controversial development in the history of royal trousers. When he was alone, he peeled off layers and rolled up his shirtsleeves, a process the future duchess would come to describe as his 'striptease act'. He tried unlined jackets and sports coats, and lounge suits in a new drape cut devised by his genius, mercurial tailor, Frederick Scholte. He rebelled against 'the tyranny of starch', then wrote about it in his book, as though a great evil had finally been eradicated from the British Isles.

Edward was acutely aware of what his stature meant for the international pre-eminence of Savile Row. 'I was in fact "produced" as a leader of fashion,' he later explained,

> with the clothiers as my showmen and the world as my audience. The middle-man in this process was the photographer, employed not only by the Press but by the trade, whose task it was to photograph me on every possible occasion, public or private,

with an especial eye for what I happened to be wearing. A selection of these photographs, together with patterns of materials and samples of collars, ties, socks, waistcoats, and so forth, was immediately rushed to America, where overnight a new fashion might well be born – to the considerable advantage of the British export trade.

Also in America, Hollywood had begun dressing its idols (see: Clark Gable) in Savile Row bespoke, thereby offering the tailors another boost through association with the romantic silver screen. Indeed, between Hollywood and Edward, it could have gone on for years in an endless procession of backless waistcoats, soft shirts and tailcoats so brilliantly made you could tap-dance across a soundstage in them. But then came two inconvenient twists.

In January 1936, upon the death of his father, Edward ascended the throne to become King Edward VIII. Eleven months later, following a constitutional crisis, he abdicated to marry a divorcee from Pennsylvania named Wallis Simpson. This decision scandalised the country, and Edward immediately lost his lustre as a sartorial standard-bearer. Prince Charming had strayed, suddenly and irretrievably, into the wilderness.

Then, of course, there was the Second World War.

Savile Row workshops were incinerated during the Blitz; a landmine vaporised ten entire firms. Tailors scattered, seeking shelter under one another's roof, but the general attitude was resilience. The historian Richard Walker tells the tale of one secretary who 'placed her typewriter on some debris and tapped out orders on her knees in the street'.

The shakiness set in afterwards, like post-traumatic stress disorder. The causes for this were myriad: a government-mandated rationing of cloth, which made it illegal to order things like pleats, cuffs or decorative buttons; 'demob' suits issued to all demobilising servicemen, many of whom decided to make do with what they were given; the further annihilation of an aristocratic class; and a generational break between fathers and sons, who once would have inherited their tailors as a family tradition.

Like everyone else, Savile Row tailors turned to the Americans for salvation. 'During the war,' explains Angus Cundey, 'American servicemen used to come and order from us [at Henry Poole], and afterwards they would come and order civilian suits while they were waiting to return home from the RAF or army camps. Subsequent to that, we used to go over [to] visit them to encourage repeat business, steaming across the Atlantic on the *Queen Mary*, sometimes for five weeks at a time.'

Tailors on the Row began to search for a new champion closer to home, a man who could conjure up fresh styles and then incite longing for them on the world stage: that is the next Prince Edward. (No contenders were forthcoming.) Savile Row also took the unprecedented step of forming a Men's Fashion Council, made up of representatives from a handful of the most powerful firms: something like the UN Security Council, but for menswear. If no ideal spokesman could be found, Savile Row would perform the role by committee. 'We'd get round a table and say, "This year we're going to do turn-ups; next year will be waistcoats,"' recalls Angus Cundey. 'We'd be determining the fashion, effectively. Then you'd get headlines in *The Times*: SAVILE ROW SAYS TURN-UPS ARE IN.' The Men's Fashion Council was criticised for 'sitting in secret', though its suggestions were dutifully adopted by the middle-class shops along the high streets.

Eventually the council went so far as to begin hosting fashion shows at the Savoy, each single-breasted suit revealed to journalists 'as though it came from Chanel or Molyneux'. However, because many tailors had developed an almost pathological aversion to publicity – they saw publicity as *vulgar* – these parades remained largely self-defeating, though they went on for years. 'The exasperating thing about these shows is the group insistence on total anonymity,' one journalist would complain. 'You may admire a suit, topcoat or jacket, but nobody will disclose who made it.'

Still, the Men's Fashion Council did experience at least one success at playing tastemaker in the years after the war. At the start of the 1950s, some upper-class youngsters began to sense the privilege eroding from beneath their feet and responded by adopting a distinctive style that evoked the halcyon days of King Edward VII, when supremacy of the aristocracy seemed all but assured. Savile Row was only too happy to assist in what amounted to a grand act of wishful thinking, and the product was neo-Edwardian brocade waistcoats, slim-cut overcoats with velvet collars and cuffs. Steeped in nostalgia, these clothes were popular among ex-Guards officers and members of the elite – the kind, say, who dreamed of valets to accompany their own extensive luggage on a tour of the Continent.

Sometime around 1953, a small but conspicuous gang of British working-class youths hijacked the neo-Edwardian look and car-crashed it into an American zoot suit, 'the garb of ghetto rebellion'. The product, handcrafted by less discerning (and less expensive) tailors than those on Savile Row, was deranged. The youths became known as Teddy boys (from Edwardian), and they took their new uniforms very seriously. Those slim-cut overcoats suddenly appeared on the streets in maroon, black or pale blue, now even longer and paired with tight, suggestive drainpipe trousers. Slim Jim ties were held in place by medallions, skulls-and-crossbones, tiny Texas longhorns, or maybe a silver dollar. Bright-coloured socks were worn high on the ankles and left exposed above crêpe-soled shoes called 'brothel creepers'. Meanwhile, the Teds massaged so much Brylcreem into their hair that it became almost sculptural, funnelling down over the forehead like an elephant's trunk or swept back and peaked like the tail of a duck. For maintenance, they used steel-toothed combs, channelling Elvis or James Dean by way of south London.

Where had they come from, these disgruntled young men? ('The lack of parental authority during the war?' asked George Melly, who was still mystified more than a decade later. 'The breakdown of the working-class family as a strong social unit . . . ? The effect of the bombing? Regret that the war was over too early to allow them to release their aggression under risk?') Whatever the catalyst for the Teds, the moralistic media quickly affiliated them with delinquency and violence, even murder. And in this hysterical narrative the neo-Edwardian style now came to function as an unsettling set of semaphore flags: the look signalled sexual energy, an aggressive hunger for change. Teds had kidnapped a benign (if conceited) bespoke style, vandalised its meaning, and then made their vision fashionable among a group of marginalised kids who shared an open disdain for the Establishment. In doing so, they signalled the emergence of an entirely new demographic in Britain, otherwise known as the modern teenager.

Savile Row was appalled.

Instantly, the neo-Edwardian look was abandoned, as were most other attempts at fashionable innovation. Instead of setting the agenda, tailors retreated to conservatism; they dug their heels even harder into the past. Determined to survive by avoiding risk, they closely adhered to what Pearl Binder, writing in 1958, would call 'the exquisitely prosaic city suit' – a sober, anonymous outfit of grey or navy blue that could 'press to perfection the man whose mission in life is to make money'.

On Savile Row, almost anything flamboyant became taboo.

―――――――

In the handful of years after Tommy migrated with Donaldson, Williams & G. Ward into the Burlington Arcade and diggers set upon a great swathe of Savile Row's western flank, articles began to appear in the popular press that added up to a kind of eulogy.

'As far as setting men's fashion goes,' the *Daily Mail* declared in one characteristic example, 'the mods have taken over.' The paper continued, 'There's been no violence. Savile-row [*sic*] hasn't been put to fire and sword, just quietly elbowed aside by a lot of under-20's with tiny pointed heads and suede bootees. Savile-row goes on producing beautiful clothes, timeless and built to last for ever. But the gimmicks, the bright ideas and new styles which make fashion fizz are produced by and for the mods . . .'

A similar sentiment was soon expressed by Cecil Beaton in the pages of *Vogue*: 'It is ridiculous that they go on turning out clothes that make men look like characters from P. G. Wodehouse. I'm terribly bored with their styling – so behind the times. They really should pay attention to the fashion produced by the young mods . . . the barriers are down and everything goes. Savile Row has got to reorganize itself and, to coin a banal phrase, get with it.' Soon enough the journalist Nik Cohn would be likening Savile Row to 'some deposed Slavic princeling, once despotic but now made humble, reduced to chauffeur or cinema commissionaire'. It was something to be humoured, Cohn suggested – 'cherished' was the word he used – with all the condescension of a young man talking to his friends about an embarrassing uncle.

Tommy sympathised with these kinds of sentiments at the time they were written. Now a few years into his apprenticeship, he was beginning to feel ambivalent, even frustrated, by Savile Row's insistent close-mindedness. 'Although I actually loved the clothing and the tradition,' he later explained, 'I was always a bit of a rebel.' On several occasions, he tested the boundaries of acceptability by turning up to work wearing a bright tie or outrageous pocket handkerchief, only to find himself banished from public view by an apoplectic boss.

There is no question that Tommy respected his tailoring colleagues. Yet in the early 1960s, he was also one of those 'under-20's with tiny pointed heads and suede bootees'. London had started to move with a strange new rhythm, as seductive as it was seemingly democratic; if Savile Row refused to move an inch in Mayfair – well, Tommy would dance on the sly in the dingy maze of Soho.

This created a sharp tension in his life. During the day, he went about his duties in the Burlington Arcade, remaining respectful and attentive except for the occasional outburst of insolent playfulness. At night and on weekends, however, he joined those teenage insurrectionists who were supposedly undermining the very place where he'd staked his future prosperity. He was like a double agent, working at cross-purposes, and the outcome was probably inevitable, as Tommy would be the first to recognise: 'I was moving right away from all the stiffness of Savile Row.'

'I'd rebel when I wasn't actually at work,' Tommy once said.
'I'd be wearing things that were quite different.'

3

YOUNG METEORS

One day, seemingly out of the blue, Christopher Nutter threw down the hand towel at John's Cafe and closed up shop. Dolly's father had recently died, and Lily, her mother, was living all alone in her spacious Kilburn terrace. The Nutters and their two sons now moved into the bottom two floors, while Lily kept the one above. Christopher returned to work as a seating upholsterer; Dolly found work serving meals at a community hospital. Each evening on Eresby Road, the couple would come home and convene in front of the television, and Lily would shuffle downstairs to join them for the 'lovely murders', as she liked to call her favourite crime dramas.

Tommy and David went out. Often, they didn't have to go very far: a short stroll up the street to the Gaumont State, a theatre that loomed 120 feet over the neighbourhood like a miniature Empire State Building. In the ornate foyer, filled with huge mirrors and glass chandeliers, they would buy two tickets for the cheapest of cheap seats. Ascending the grand stairways in the auditorium, which seated 4,004 people, they would continue to the top back. Then they would peer down across a rapt audience and the orchestra pit at an illuminated stage. Louis Armstrong would appear, clutching his trumpet. Or Bill Haley and the Comets in matching dinner jackets. Once, Ella Fitzgerald came out to perform, and after she was finished, during her standing ovation, Tommy yelled that she was 'awful!' for no reason other than to aggravate the people around them.

In truth, Tommy loved Ella Fitzgerald. He loved most American music, from Sarah Vaughan to the Modern Jazz Quartet. For his older

brother, though, these concerts and the vinyl LPs represented something almost life-sustaining. To David, good music offered a thrill, an
escape, and, most important, a medium for coping with the despon-
dency that had pummelled him mercilessly from a young age.

Depression wasn't something most people talked about in the
1950s. In the Nutter household, there was no understanding of how to
navigate its mysterious shoals. Tommy was rarely afflicted with lingering sadness, and as far as Christopher or Dolly knew, bipolar disorder didn't exist, and therefore didn't need to be treated in their elder
child. Back in Edgware, before the move, David would sometimes be
too stricken with ill-defined anxiety to even leave the flat. When that
happened, he would put on a record and find solace in the rhythm,
curling up in a chair by the window. From there, he often watched the
same scene recurring on the street below: Long John Baldry, a friend
and neighbour, lumbering – he was six foot seven – to the Tube station
with his duffel coat and guitar case, heading off to jam somewhere in
a darkened room.

Soon enough, David began to seek out the clubs himself. In 1960, he
was twenty-one years old – mature enough to explore all the salacious
nooks of Soho, including the Flamingo, known for its all-nighters, and
the Marquee Jazz Club, just to the north on Oxford Street, which was
damp and salty, tucked away in a basement ballroom beneath a cinema.
David would arrive early and stay late.

Some nights, Dudley Moore would come out to play the piano, or
Johnny Dankworth would blow on a saxophone with his wife, Cleo
Laine, who'd rightfully earned a reputation for her virtuosic vocal
scatting. 'Long John Baldry would sing in a group with Charlie Watts,'
David says, 'and I remember Mick' – as in Jagger – 'coming in to play
with them.' The band was Alexis Korner's Blues Incorporated; 'Mick'
contributed vocals and harmonica over a string of Thursday evenings,
after he'd finished up a day of study at the London School of Economics.

On 12 July 1962, Long John Baldry played at the Marquee the
same night as the debut public performance of a new band: the Rolling
Stones. David failed to make it down to the club that night, though he

heard about the set, and the band's sound of joyful, defiant screaming soon became impossible to miss.

By the time Tommy moved with G. Ward into the Burlington Arcade, David had already flitted through several forgettable jobs and arrived in the employ of Robert Horner, a photograph printer who had contracts developing the portraiture and fashion spreads for magazines such as *Queen*. Horner was Scottish, well respected in the industry, and, in David's recollection, impossible to work with. 'He and his wife used to get drunk and go out and come back and start fighting,' David says. 'Then he would throw the photographs in her face.'

David found this kind of behaviour unusual, though he tried to keep to himself in the studio. As Horner's darkroom technician, he was being exposed to some of the best photographers in the world: Irving Penn, Guy Bourdin, David Bailey and (his favourite) Frank Horvat. He also had incredible facilities at his disposal, which he was not inclined to disregard; though Horner was a cheapskate, he was also inattentive, so David could freely print his own stuff on the side without getting caught.

To earn extra income, he accepted a slate of freelance jobs around town. Some of the more interesting assignments came via a man named Mike McGrath, a journalist (in the loosest sense of the term) who churned out entertainment and fashion columns advising kids on the hottest trends and where to find them: 'The up-to-the-minute mod wear for the mods – by a mod who knows!'

McGrath had a system: he would offer work to young photographers who wanted to take pictures of celebrities but lacked the know-how to make it happen. Seeing himself as a kind of benevolent fixer, he would tell them he had 'no problem' with access because his features were coming out in *She* and *Woman's Own* every month, 'as well as all the teenage market magazines, such as fashion articles for *Rave*'. McGrath would then head off to conduct his interviews and take a photographer along to illustrate the articles. In this way, David found himself snapping an entire line-up of young wannabes all clamouring for the big time. Some, like Cliff Richard, would actually make it; most would not. Not Paul & Paula, an American pop duo who'd sell more than a million records before vanishing into obscurity seemingly overnight. Nor Neil Christian, a pointy-chinned fop who'd become a one-hit wonder for an uninspired track titled 'That's Nice'.

Neil Christian and Tommy modelling the latest fashions, photographed by David.

Sometime around 1963, Tommy felt suddenly compelled to try his own luck with McGrath, who seemed, through his articles, to be capable of bestowing fame as he pleased. David was baffled, but he took his brother to pay the journalist a visit.

Without a hint of irony, Tommy told McGrath: 'I think I've got a voice.'

'Tommy did not have a voice,' David says. He could barely hold a tune.

McGrath saw something else he could use, though, and engaged Tommy on the spot.

By then McGrath had another position, which today would be considered an egregious conflict of interest. While writing for the fashion magazines, he was also working with a fashion producer, John Stephen, who was already being touted as 'Apostle of the Mods'.

Stephen was a shy, eccentric Glaswegian who chewed his fingernails and liked to take his white German shepherd to lunch at the Ivy. A brilliant entrepreneur, Stephen had noticed the tsunami of youth created by a post-war baby boom, and he understood what the youth wanted, what made their hearts flutter. In 1957, when he was just twenty-three years old, he'd opened a small Soho boutique on Carnaby Street, painting the shopfront canary yellow to make it pop from the grey, and set to selling a range of affordable fast fashions aimed specifically at young people: pony-skin coats, striped lilac oxford shirts, low-riding hipster trousers in flame red or orange cotton that would advertise the wearer's backside like a neon sign. This gamble proved so exactly in tune with the shifting zeitgeist that Stephen soon owned nearly a dozen shops – Mod Male, Domino Male, Male W1 – and a sleek £6,000 Rolls-Royce, though he didn't know how to drive.

Pinpointing the source of his success, Stephen, who was gay, once told a newspaper: 'Man is asserting his masculinity by choosing for himself and feeling free enough not to go for the old stereotyped clothes.' On Carnaby Street, a man was a man for dressing how he *pleased*, even if the older generation condemned his choices as sexually ambiguous. 'There was no fashion for men,' Stephen declared, 'and then we came along.'

Mike McGrath spied the 'new and exciting world' Stephen was creating in Soho and wrote about it approvingly in one of his columns. Stephen had been 'very pleased' with the press – so much so that he then hired McGrath to handle all his publicity.

Part of McGrath's job in the John Stephen Organisation was to exploit his access to beautiful people. Stephen wanted Carnaby Street to be associated with the best and brightest – to, in effect, borrow the starlight of bands like the Kinks. And so McGrath would conduct his interviews for the magazines, then have some of his subjects wear Stephen's clothes in the accompanying photographs (taken by those young protégés). McGrath later claimed that his biggest success was getting

Billy Walker, the 'red hot boxer of the Sixties' and 'epitome of masculinity', to wear skintight trousers more commonly associated with fey homosexuals. The provocative shots of Walker were blown up and placed in Stephen's boutique windows. 'Afterwards,' McGrath boasted, 'the clothes almost ran out of the shops.'

Tommy was about as far from a famous pugilist as he was from a pop singer destined for the hit parade. But he had something else going for him.

'The coolest man you've ever seen,' recalls Carol Drinkwater.

By the age of twenty, Tommy resembled a matinee idol. He was six foot two, with a twenty-eight-inch waist: as ideally proportioned as a wooden artist's model. He wielded his long limbs slowly, deliberately, like a praying mantis. His complexion could be spotty, but a carefully cultivated tan helped disguise any redness, and he had curious, attention-drawing eyes that could shift from guileless to suggestive in less than a blink. Tommy struck one friend who met him around then as 'the coolest man you've ever seen', somebody whom 'nothing would ever bother'. This apparent equanimity was part of a little-boy quality that would linger his entire life, making him appear open, innocent, even a touch naive. Yet also corruptible. Which was an ideal combination for a fashionable clothes horse.

One day that summer, with the blessing of Stephen and McGrath, the Nutters raided Carnaby Street. They caught the Tube back to Kilburn with bags full of clothes. David loaded film into a Mamiya camera. Tommy coordinated outfits and pouffed his hair. For vivid backdrops, they scouted local playgrounds, a cobblestone lane. Inspiration for the shoot was *West Side Story* ('our religion', David recalls), rough urban streetscapes contrasting with Jerome Robbins's fluid ballet movements. Or Tommy's version of them, anyway.

West Side Story, Carnaby Street edition

David snapped several dozen frames of his brother, all of them radiating earnestness. The next morning, he developed contact sheets on the sly in Horner's darkroom. These were passed along to McGrath, who passed them along to Stephen, who approved of the work. And soon enough blow-ups appeared in several of Stephen's boutique windows, each one surrounded by pieces of the outfit Tommy was modelling.

Tommy's audacity (or lunacy) in approaching McGrath had paid an unexpected dividend. Never mind that a talent scout would never walk down Carnaby Street and say to himself, upon glimpsing these tableaus, 'There's my next leading man.' These model shots would come and go just as lightning-fast as the fashions they were ostensibly promoting. But that was hardly the point. The important thing was the precedent being set, the fact that, for the first time in his life, David was seeing his work published in a professional context beyond some niche magazines. And for the first time in *his* life, Tommy was being presented to the public as someone with style, somebody aspirational, worth emulating through the purchase of unconventional clothes.

Every Sunday, with the dutiful regularity of church sermons, Tommy and David would meet up in a pub near Leicester Square and begin drinking.

Michael Long would inevitably be there, a well-dressed chap from Luton who worked on the window displays at Jaeger. And Carol Drinkwater, an Essex 'dolly bird' Tommy had met one night while dancing to Blue Beat records at La Douce. As the sun began to set, the rest of the crowd – pretty, young, up to a dozen in total – would become increasingly rowdy, egged on by Tommy, who was silly and impossible after a few too many rounds.

When it was dark, the carousers would empty their glasses, grab their coats, and decamp to an unassuming lane in Soho called Archer Street. At No. 9, they would knock on a discreet door, which opened onto a steep staircase, then a reception desk, where one was required to flash a membership card for further access.

NAME .... **T. A. NUTTER.** ....

EXPIRY DATE ..**April...1965** *No.* ....**4755.**...

SECRETARY ....

This card must be produced on request

A Rockingham Club membership card

Stuart Hopps, a choreographer and friend of the Nutters, knew there was something odd about the Rockingham Club the first time he went there. 'I was very naive,' he recalls, 'but it didn't take me too long to work out it was a gentlemen's club.' That is, a *queer* gentlemen's club, which it had been since Toby Roe bought the place in 1947 and named it after a porcelain vase.

Roe filled the Rockingham with flocked Regency wallpaper, leather armchairs and a large white piano. He implemented a strict dress code and oversaw the membership list himself. During the 1950s, well-heeled homosexuals would frequent the club wearing their own take on the neo-Edwardian look (before the Teddy boys ruined everything). This posh formality, the stiff collars and cravats, led some people to roll their eyes and dismiss Roe's establishment as 'piss-elegant and full of queens' who think they're in 'the Athenaeum' (a grand members' club on Pall Mall). The pomp and performance, however, was partly a defence mechanism: the more respectable something appeared, the less attention it would draw from the outside world. 'Top drawer queers' like Francis Bacon used to mingle at the Rockingham, a fact that led Quentin Crisp to anoint it the 'closet of closets'.

By the time Tommy and David talked their way onto Roe's list, Sunday night at the Rockingham had become Ladies' Night – yet another strategic decision by the wary management. 'You would have gay politicians there who didn't want it known that they were gay, as well as other professional men and quite a few designers,' recalls Kim Grossman, a frequent visitor. 'They wanted girls to dance with them because, of course, it was illegal for them to dance with each other.'

Despite its provenance, the Rockingham attracted many ladies on Sunday – and at least one entire family. Jack and Violet Aron were a Jewish couple who set an extraordinarily liberal example for their teenage children. Louise, their daughter, recalls, 'My mother would cook a big Sunday lunch for a bunch of guests, and afterwards one of our gay friends would do my hair and make-up. We'd all prepare ourselves and then go down to the Rockingham together. I guess I was fourteen or fifteen years old when it started. My family was very camp.'

Jack Aron played penny whistle with the West Indian band. Violet Aron played unofficial club hostess, greeting everybody with a high-pitched 'Darling!' Meanwhile, petite Louise, flouncing around in feather boas as though she'd just broken into a costume store and pilfered all the stock, danced with the gay men, including Tommy.

Louise fell hard for the enigmatic boy in his fine Savile Row suit. He began visiting her house for dinner, while she, in turn, began helping him pick up trade in the Rockingham.

'He's rather nice,' Tommy would say, loitering shyly with a drink in his hand. Louise would nod, accepting her mission, then drift off across the dance floor, up to the chosen one, and announce, with all the flinty bravery of a young girl who has literally nothing to lose in this scenario (though perhaps she wished things were otherwise, because he was *very* good-looking): 'My friend really likes you.'

But even with the willing complicity of a young girl, behaviour like this put Tommy at considerable personal risk. During his childhood, the British Medical Association had regarded homosexuality as a serious condition. Men were subjected to brutal aversion therapies – electroshock treatment; doses of Antabuse, which induces headaches and vomiting when mixed with alcohol – in what amounted to Pavlovian experiments to make them associate gay sex with horrendous pain. In 1953, as Tommy, ten years old, marched in a street parade dressed as Charlie Chaplin to celebrate the queen's coronation, Alan Turing was undergoing chemical castration after being put on trial for homosexual acts. The judge had understood what would happen (gynaecomastia: the growth of breast tissue) but ordered the oestrogen anyway. In 1954, Turing committed suicide by eating an apple laced with cyanide.

As Tommy was failing his eleven-plus, Sir David Maxwell Fyfe, the Home Secretary and a former prosecutor at the Nuremberg trials, was calling for a 'new drive against male vice' – a drive, incidentally, that was strongly sanctioned by the Americans, who were carrying out their own government purges across the Atlantic. In the first year after Maxwell Fyfe's appointment, 670 men were prosecuted for sodomy, 1,686 for gross indecency, and 3,087 for indecent assault or 'attempted sodomy'. The smallest suspicion could result in aggressive police harassment as authorities questioned friends and rifled through private correspondence in search of a smoking gun. The specious rationale behind this witch-hunt was captured, in part, by an editorial published in the *Sunday Times* on 1 November 1953: 'In public terms, a society with a high or growing proportion of unnaturalness is a weakened and perhaps a decadent society.' One so-called decadent society was the Weimar Republic, many readers would have recalled – and look how that turned out.

In 1954, the biggest news story in Britain concerned the youngest member of the House of Lords: the twenty-eight-year-old Edward John Barrington Douglas-Scott-Montagu, 3rd Baron Montagu of Beaulieu. The 'wretched business', as Montagu called it, had begun the previous year, when a Boy Scout accused him of sexual assault while camping on his estate in Hampshire.

Montagu denied the accusation, but the police sniffed blood and began a chase, trailed by a pack of pressmen. Eventually Montagu was put on trial in Winchester ('the same place that Sir Walter Raleigh had once been sentenced to be beheaded', Montagu wryly noted) and subjected to confused proceedings ('I felt bemused and helpless, like the accused in a Kafka novel') during which a graphic testimony provided by the Boy Scout struck the jury as extremely improbable. They dismissed all charges. Montagu was reassured, but he'd underestimated the determination of the authorities to get a man they suspected was a pervert.

On the night of 9 January 1954, officers stormed Montagu's house and pulled him from his bed. They also arrested his second cousin, Michael Pitt-Rivers, and a *Daily Mail* correspondent named Peter Wildeblood. This time round the allegations concerned two airmen. According to the prosecution, after a series of events involving, among other things, a bottle of champagne and tickets to a West End production of *Dial M for Murder*, the five men had convened at a Beaulieu beach hut for a party that would become more notorious 'than any other since the days of Nero', as Wildeblood once sarcastically phrased it.

To incriminate their suspects, the police ransacked their homes without legal warrants and seized letters that proved Wildeblood was indeed in love with one of the airmen. (On being an 'invert', Wildeblood would later write: 'I am no more proud of my condition than I would be of having a glass eye or a hare-lip. On the other hand, I am no more ashamed of it than I would be of being colour-blind or of writing with my left hand.') Everything else about the case was, however, circumstantial. Montagu again denied the charges against him – to no avail this time. The lord was sentenced to twelve months in prison, while Pitt-Rivers and Wildeblood each got eighteen months for 'Serious Offences'. From start to finish, the entire affair, Montagu would write nearly fifty years later, was 'a searing episode that taught me much about my fellow human beings'.

For its relentless persecution of inherently decent men, the Montagu Case, as it came to be known, proved one step too far for many people in positions of power. Sure, homosexuality was an abomination of nature; that much was widely assumed. But this double trial was like a public hanging transposed from the Middle Ages: prurient, ethically indefensible. A backlash arose against the government's 'caricature of justice', its shameless invasion of privacy. In the words of one taxi driver, it was all a lot of 'bleeding nonsense': 'If two chaps carry on like that and don't do no harm to no one, what business is it of anybody else's?'

The government responded to this shift in public sentiment by convening the Departmental Committee on Homosexual Offences and Prostitution. In 1957, the committee passed down its final report (popularly known as the Wolfenden Report, after the committee chair, Sir John Wolfenden), which recommended that 'homosexual behaviour between consenting adults in private should no longer be a criminal offence'. This was the first piece of progressive policy concerning queer people proposed in Britain for five centuries.

By 1963, as Louise was luring boys back across the dance floor to Tommy, the government had yet to act on the report's advice. Clubs like the Rockingham could still be raided if police took offence at what the patrons were wearing or decided the men were dancing a little too intimately. Stuart Hopps was there for one such invasion. 'We ran for our lives. The one thing my dad said to me when I came out was, "Please promise me you won't get arrested. You'll bring shame on the family." Little did he know I was going to the Rockingham.'

Nevertheless, there is paradoxical power in being part of an oppressed minority. David could sense it, and it would have been clear to anybody who spent time in a space like the basement on Archer Street. A straight club reproduces the accepted social order; it is mainstream society, its mores and relationships, reproduced in miniature. By contrast, a club for queer men exists outside convention, even if it might present a front of being 'respectable'. Historically, the club was a space where these people could go to 'let their hair down', as the saying went – to reveal their true selves before a like-minded crowd. And in this liminal space – like a border town, not quite one thing or another but something in between – many commonplace rules were subordinated beneath an ethos of solidarity, of possibility.

In the Rockingham, Tommy Nutter, son of a seating upholsterer, could brush shoulders with Grenadier Guards and movie stars like Charles Gray. The 'classless spirit' that Mary Quant would say personified the sixties was magnified tenfold here, and along with it the sense that self-invention was a legitimate avenue to freedom.

Indeed, many of the most important, enduring connections Tommy and David would make in their lives originated in, or were strengthened by, the gay underworld. In clubs and parties, a fleeting brush on the dance floor could, like the beat of a butterfly's wings, change everything in time.

The Rockingham gang, with Louise Aron crouched in front alongside Tommy.

Tommy and David never talked about the remarkable serendipity of them both being queer. There was no great revelation, no 'coming out' or anguished heart-to-heart behind a closed bedroom door. Two gay brothers: this was no more remarkable to them than their shared love for Dusty Springfield.

The same could not be said for their parents, however. One evening at Kilburn, Tommy treated an outbreak of acne using a stash of concealer, then said goodbye to Christopher and Dolly and headed out to meet some friends. Christopher noticed the make-up, just as he'd been noticing Tommy's matelot tops and bright hipster jeans. After Tommy left, the door closing behind him, David then overheard his father talking in the living room.

'Do you think he's one of those?' Christopher asked Dolly.

The atmosphere in Kilburn was noxious by now. Christopher's racist tirades and bigoted remarks were more frequent than ever, turning the house into a suffocating trap.

David began spending nights at his friends' houses, shuttling back and forth from Eresby Road like a shift worker. Crashing on couches gave him breathing room, a break from his father; it also allowed him to continue investigating the city's underbelly – the places where 'those' people tended to hang out. David got caught up with drag queens. He developed a preference for black men, whom he liked to pick up in bars around Brixton.

A drag queen performs on London rooftops in 1963.

In 1964, the Alvin Ailey American Dance Theater, from New York, arrived in London to give its debut British performance of Ailey's *Revelations*. ('This three-part, hot-gospelling hymn to Negro faith is a magnificent piece of choreography, moving, deeply felt and exquisitely made,' declared *The Times*.) David caught a show and was floored by the whole thing, which was, he thought, 'so American, so wonderful'. Along with some friends, he gained access to the backstage area, where he met a dancer named Dudley Williams. They quickly became involved.

On subsequent nights, David would then stand in the wings to photograph Williams and afterwards accompany him to post-show dinners, where Ailey taught him black slang, and some of the dancers discussed the American civil-rights movement. For his part, Williams seemed extremely fond of David; he knitted him a sweater while travelling on the Tube. But both knew it couldn't last long. As David recalls, 'It's impossible to have a relationship with somebody who lives on the road.'

Tommy soon began imitating his brother's nomadic living arrangement. His friend Michael Long shared a basement flat with a hairdresser in Kensington, and Tommy was allowed to stay whenever he wanted. But Tommy soon tired of lugging overnight bags to and from Kilburn, so he and Michael found a new flat on Elvaston Place, a short stroll from Hyde Park, that was Victorian, spacious, and private enough that Tommy could have his boyfriend sleep over.

Christopher Tarling – a handsome, extremely tall young man from Essex – had also started work in the tailoring trade, at a shop named Blades. He met Tommy at the Arts and Battledress Club and was immediately smitten. 'The word "charismatic" is really over-used, but I can't think of another for Tommy,' Christopher later told a journalist. 'He had this way of making you feel like you were the centre of the universe when he turned his attention on you . . . He was someone you just wanted to be with, have good times with. He embodied everything you wanted to be. I wanted to live forever with him.'

Once David and Tommy had flown the nest, Dolly was left alone with her husband and mother. She was probably upset, David thinks; her sons had abandoned her to purgatory, failing to turn up even for Christmas. 'We just completely checked out from it all.'

But Dolly did her best to maintain the connection. Squinting at her increasingly unfamiliar sons from afar, she gleaned scraps of information from brief encounters with their friends, fleeting mentions of what they were doing in their private lives. Then she arranged these scraps, puzzle-like, trying to make out a picture she could comprehend using her limited frame of reference.

For example, Dolly noticed Louise Aron was often hanging around Tommy. Louise was pretty and warm-hearted, clearly infatuated – and

'We just completely checked out from it all,' David recalls.

Tommy seemed to like her too. The two of them even shared the same birthday, a few years apart. So why didn't the pieces fit together?

'Why won't you marry Tommy?' Dolly asked Louise. 'Is it because he's not Jewish?'

Tommy often had a female alibi on hand to dispel any suspicions. Louise, for instance, would follow Tommy and Christopher Tarling to Brighton and lie out with them on the nudist beach at Telscombe Cliffs. 'Tommy went tits out, everything out,' recalls Louise. 'People used to look over the top down at us.'

In early 1964, Tommy went to Paris for a weekend with his brother, Michael Long and a girl from the Rockingham named Julie Evans. Julie posed as Tommy's girlfriend (although, how much she realised this was a *pose* is debatable), and they toured the major sites: the Sacré-Cœur, Eiffel Tower and Moulin Rouge. To cut costs, they all shared accommodation at a cheap hotel – a detail that Tommy found disconcerting enough to highlight in a letter to a friend. His friend replied, 'Your weekend at gay Paree with Julie & Co. sounded marvellous, especially the bit about you and Julie being in the same bed(wait for it)room, in single beds of course! Dogs.'

Tommy's relationship with women combined attraction and repulsion, reverence and something bordering on misogyny. To some extent, this fraught medley was born of necessity: confronted with women who seemed intriguing, like potential allies, Tommy and his friends would have to 'drop sequins to find out if they'd pick them up' – drop hints,

Julie Evans, Tommy and Michael Long
outside the Moulin Rouge in Paris.

in other words, to see if the women understood exactly what kind of men they were dealing with here. This could lead to disastrous stand-offs if somebody's intuition was off, as with the ex–child actress who realised the truth about the Nutters and their friends and began to scream, during a dinner party, 'You're all queer. You're all *queer!*'

Yet even when the women were clearly on their side, a great deal of caution insulated the relationships. Carol Drinkwater was perhaps Tommy's closest lady friend. To save herself a long commute home to Essex, she often stayed overnight at Tommy's flat – in Tommy's bed, no less. But Carol recalls that Tommy would always build a wall of 'bloody pillows' between them. 'I'd say, "I'm not going to touch you, for God's sake!"'

'Just in case,' Tommy would reply.

Despite this aversion to the female body, Tommy could also be fiercely loyal to the women he respected. Carol had met her first fiancé, Leonard Wiltshire, when she was just fifteen years old. She knew Len was homosexual, but saw herself as modern; she pretended not to worry about such things. Still, when Len disappeared during her birthday mini-break to Paris, off having a dalliance with an Australian million-aire, she decided to call it quits. Tommy and Michael were holidaying in the south of France; she phoned them up, explained the situation, and they raced up the same day to commiserate over a lunch of celeriac remoulade.

Back in London, one following Sunday, Carol went with her friends to the Rockingham. As usual, everyone was very smartly dressed, Tommy in a tweed suit and Carol with her hair up and a plait exten-sion flowing down her back. Suddenly, Len emerged from the crowd. He was incredulous, despite his sexuality, that Carol might try to leave him after years of codependency. He grabbed her hair and yanked. The plait tore away, taking a false eyelash with it. Everybody froze. But then Tommy and Michael pushed Carol into a Facel Vega and sped her across town to Elvaston Place. Louise Aron was there; she mended Carol's look until it was flawless. Then they returned to the Rocking-ham, strolling in with eyes narrowed down their noses, Tommy icily unperturbed. 'We went back to prove that I didn't care,' Carol says. 'That was a typical night.'

A few years later, a journalist would try to provoke Tommy by opening their interview with a personal question: What kind of women did he like?

'I don't know, really,' Tommy replied sharply.

A pause.

'I don't know,' Tommy said again, though this time with 'obvious enjoyment' at the thought. Then he alighted on a word that seemed to satisfy him. 'Glamorous,' he said. Tommy Nutter liked glamorous women.

It was in pursuit of two glamorous women that Tommy and David had first experienced the miracle of air travel.

Dolly's best friend had two daughters, Valerie and Cheryl Garland, who were, growing up, closer to Tommy and David than their actual cousins. Like a tight posse, the two brothers and two sisters had accompanied their mothers on excursions into the country – to Oxford, say – and lazed around the flat together while their parents went out to drink. It helped that Valerie and Cheryl happened to work in show business, that they had bouffant movie-star hairdos and performed a torch-song and dance routine that was good enough to get them cast in a Palladium pantomime. In 1960, the Garland Sisters (their stage name) performed at a Butlins holiday camp on Jersey, in the Channel Islands. Swallowing their nerves about being in an aeroplane, Tommy and David flew across to cheer them on.

While visiting Jersey, the brothers caught a ferry over to France to see the surreal confection of Le Mont Saint-Michel. This marked, for both of them, the beginning of a passionate obsession with the Continent that would last several years. Throughout the early 1960s, Tommy and David took as many budget holidays as they could possibly afford – to Paris, to Venice, and to Italian resort towns like Rimini and Riccione on the Adriatic Sea.

In the summer of 1964, Tommy and David found themselves on the French Riviera. In Cannes, they ran into the Garland sisters on holiday with their parents. The meeting was unplanned, and unexpected. They laughed about the strange coincidence, then rumbled through neighbouring towns and up into the Alps on a shared coach tour. But by then something had changed between them: an estrangement, though there was nothing hostile about it, just a palpable drift. The brothers and sisters stayed in different hotels and remained, for all intents and purposes, on very different holidays. In the evening, the Nutters would go their own separate way. 'We never knew what they were doing,' recalls Valerie.

What they were doing, David admits, was frequenting a bar 'where all the male prostitutes would hang out. We used to watch them and this German actor – he's in a lot of horror movies now – picking up men. And we were drinking heavily, so I was blacking out a lot.'

At the same time, Tommy was engaged in collecting European admirers, a hobby he'd begun pursuing with the attentive dedication of a lepidopterist.

One of Tommy's 'glamour boys', as David describes them.

Some of these boys wrote Tommy yearning letters after he returned home – letters he hoarded, even though their discovery could have been catastrophic.

> *My dear Tommy I am always thinking of you and remember the happy days we spent together and will live on these memories until the next time we meet.*

In more than a dozen handwritten missives, all dated to 1964, Tommy appears as an attentive, intoxicating lover, the kind who could make three short days feel like the 'best days', as M. wrote; who was more memorable, in the words of D., than Marianne Faithfull; who proved so alluring that it was *essential* he provide 'a light of hope' that he would soon be returning to Paris, or agree to fly to Vienna using an enclosed prepaid plane ticket. 'This is the best connection I could find and leaves us at least two-and-a-half days . . .' Tommy was the kind of person open to clandestine reunions in Hilton Hotel suites. And he enjoyed corresponding about all manner of topics: the best music ('Poison Ivy' by Billy Thorpe & the Aztecs); where to cruise for sex; even sexually transmitted infections. In one letter, written from 'ward Sweet 16' in an Australian hospital, its author celebrates the disappearance of his latest ailment, laments that he's 'only had sex once since I've been here' (in the hospital), and then accepts an invitation from Tommy to join 'the Nutter Girls Club' when he eventually returns to England. 'I hope I will be given the position of "Madam" of the house, what with Diamond Ruby Brown as cashier and Lotte & Pam as hostesses.'

Still, Tommy had few qualms about cutting somebody off once he grew a little weary, which only led to more letters.

> *I don't know what I can say to you, the important things I can't write, but you can be sure that's true, when I say I am ~~very sorry~~ bad feeling without you.*
>   *With my best wishes*
>   *and carefull greetings*

According to Christopher Tarling, Tommy was 'one of life's flitters.

He never really put down roots. He was always the leaver in the relationship, never the left.' He was 'always on to the next one, on to the next one', Christopher says, echoing the thoughts of another boyfriend, Christopher Brown, who would date Tommy several decades later only to reach an identical conclusion: 'There's another nice-looking boy, there's another nice-looking boy . . .'

Once, Brown would ask Tommy to define his masculine ideal. What kind of men did he prefer?

Tommy considered the question for a moment. 'A California surf boy,' he replied.

Tommy's ideal man was blond and sun-kissed, sculpted in the waves of Huntington Beach. Somebody carefree, hedonistic and foreign, beamed in from a more beautiful universe. This Tab Hunter figure was a cinematic fantasy, but perhaps its impossibility was exactly what made it desirable. If you can never really have something, after all, you never have to risk being disillusioned.

Peter Brown at his desk in Apple Corps, 1968.

4

THE NEW ARISTOCRATS

I.

One morning in January 1966, an assertive new cutter turned up in the Burlington Arcade to work at Donaldson, Williams & G. Ward. Mr Donaldson (nobody called him by his first name) had decided to retire in the next few months (or years; it remained vague), and he wanted to groom his replacement for an easy transition. In other words: 'He wanted to look at his stocks and shares in the newspaper,' says Edward Sexton, who jumped at the opportunity to become a junior partner in a well-respected firm.

A few years earlier, when G. Ward amalgamated with Donaldson & Williams, the companies had pooled their resources but kept the client lists separate. They remained two different teams, in effect, contributing to a single bottom line. Edward now began working for Mr Donaldson upstairs; Tommy, meanwhile, worked as a salesman for Michael Hall, who owned G. Ward, down in the shop.

The two young men soon became friendly. Edward was twenty-three years old – just five months older than Tommy. He, too, was working class, from the Elephant and Castle, where he'd lived with his family in a tenement. Though he spoke with a thick cockney accent – an accent that had recently been mocked, much to his resentment, as 'a rasp' – he also carried himself with grace, ramrod-straight, as meticulously dressed as Brummell himself.

Like Tommy downstairs, Edward's attitude towards clothes was born of the trends he'd weathered as a teenager. During adolescence, for example, he'd struggled with a 'restless edginess', a feeling of not being comfortable in his own skin. And one way he'd compensated for this was by stealing away into the school toilets, peeling off his grey flannel trousers, laying them carefully across his lap, and then using an amateur backstitch to narrow each leg until they roughly resembled the drainpipes he'd seen on the Teddy boys. Determined and resourceful, Edward, from a young age, had understood that clothes could be a second skin, manipulated as a way of fitting in – or standing out.

When he was fifteen, Edward had gone to work as a commis waiter at the Waldorf in Covent Garden. Until then, he recalls, 'I don't suppose I'd ever really crossed the bridge to come up to the West End.' At the Waldorf, his parochialism was shattered as he found himself fondling the spectacle of wealth: caviar, smoked salmon, steak au poivre. Serving patrons dressed for the nearby opera came as a shock; it constituted, Edward says, 'my first realisation that there were a lot of people doing different, *nicer* things than either I or my parents were doing'.

It was his desire to ascend the class ladder that first introduced him to bespoke tailoring. At a high street tailor, Edward commissioned a mod suit uncannily like the one Tommy had worn at the Ministry of Works: Italian-style, boxy jacket, with very short side vents. The suit made him feel like a *somebody*, and Edward was just as taken with the process, ordering what he wanted, looking at the fit, getting a feel for different styles. This fascination became a habit, freely indulged until he amassed a wardrobe of 'really nice clothes'.

When he entered the tailoring trade immediately after the Waldorf, Edward marked Savile Row as his ultimate goal. 'I figured if you're going to be a good jockey,' he recalls, 'you better have the best stables.'

Unlike Tommy, who, lacking models, had never really known what he wanted to do – 'In those days it wasn't all that easy to become a designer,' he would later say – Edward was content to follow the traditional route to becoming a good cutter. That meant years as an apprentice coat maker crafting riding wear for Harry Hall. It meant night classes at the Barrett Street Technical College, and then work as an under-cutter at Kilgour, French & Stanbury. Moving across Savile Row to Welsh &

Jefferies, Edward had learned how to make military uniforms with razor-sharp silhouettes. He'd come to appreciate the value of a Sam Browne belt: a leather strap that goes over the right shoulder, around the waist, and then is cinched tight, with all excess fabric tucked away using darts and seams until you're left with a snug, close fit – 'a sculpture'. He'd hoarded techniques and experience, and also practised 'all the hours that God gives you'. For Edward, tailoring became life – his *whole* life. 'You can't do it between nine and five and then go home and start living another,' he says.

By the time Edward finally arrived at the Burlington Arcade, he'd built a private clientele of contractors and car dealers, people who were not afraid of trying something a little less orthodox. This side business allowed him to deploy his abilities in idiosyncratic ways: wrapping a tape measure around a client's waist, say, and cinching it tightly to find the ideal shape. Edward had come to believe that the only way to grow as a tailor was to make your own suits, your own style. And your own mistakes. This was an experimental creed that resonated with his new friend down in the showroom.

Tommy quickly noted Edward's extraordinary technical skill. But he was just as intrigued by Edward's moonlighting, which showed the cutter flouting established rules to create clothes that were, at least by Savile Row standards, aesthetically daring. Edward struck Tommy as the kind of person who might consider new ideas with curiosity rather than scepticism. The idea, for example, that 'the fabric you wore, the way it was cut, the lifestyle you lived: it all went together'.

When it came to their own lifestyles, the two men were wildly mismatched. By 1966, Edward was married with a newborn baby, responsible for providing a stable home. He could barely drink more than a few beers without 'throwing up all over the place'.

Tommy, on the other hand, was a promiscuous gay man who was chronically incapable of maintaining a relationship or a healthy bank account, and who believed that a few glasses of wine would just 'loosen you up'.

But ambition has a way of steamrolling the most acute personal differences, and at this moment Tommy was willing to seize any opportunity that happened to come into his purview. As Edward's wife, Joan, recalls, 'Tommy said Edward was just who he was waiting for.'

Edward and Joan Sexton

Tommy was exasperated with his job. The 'little suits' of Donaldson, Williams & G. Ward, as he would derisively dismiss them, left him feeling cold and uninspired. Recently, he'd tried to inject a little flair into the workroom by offering up some of his original sketches, but it had not gone over well with the traditionalist tailors. 'It was all very well this sparky and, they'd admit, presentable lad was being given his chance to potter about the design department, didn't want to be stuffy and all that, but *really* and oh *dear*, what he was suggesting was not only tasteless but technically impractical,' a wry journalist would later report. 'People did not come here to be measured up for tents, dear.'

An attempt by Tommy to go elsewhere had also ended in humiliation. In the Cork Street premises of Henry Poole & Co., Tommy had petitioned Samuel Cundey for a salesman job. Cundey had taken one glance at Tommy's hair, now growing out in dark, fashionable fronds, and sent him away, horrified.

Many evenings after the gates of the Burlington Arcade were shut to pedestrians, Tommy and Edward would migrate together to a nearby pub. Before long, Edward would have to head for his workshop on Brewer Street, where private clients were invariably demanding his attention; but, for a short spell at least, the young men would talk over pints about their discontent: the 'boring establishment' of Savile Row and the larger London scene in which they found themselves bit players.

By 1967, Tommy knew the city's fashion quarters intimately. He had already conquered Carnaby Street, which by now had settled down into tacky consumerism – mini-kilts, Union Jack soup ladles.

Over in Chelsea, bustling like an elaborate costume party on Saturday afternoons, he'd staked out the boutiques along the King's Road by taking Edward's young wife to buy 'a frock', as he called it, and then commanding her to 'do a twirl' as she stepped out from the changing rooms. He'd admired what he saw there, the spontaneous, avant-garde creativity that allowed an in-house designer to transform the shop on a whim (as John Pearse once did at Granny Takes a Trip. 'I saw *East of Eden* with James Dean, and I remember walking into the shop and saying, "It's going to be a moon-jet jacket! It's going to have a half belt on the back! We're going to clear out all this Victorian dandy shit!"'), though Tommy also thought he could do it better.

Closer to work, just round the corner on Burlington Gardens, Tommy had investigated the tailoring firm where Christopher Tarling worked: Blades, named after the fictional gentlemen's club in Ian Fleming's *Moonraker* and There was no question that the owner of Blades,

Rupert Lycett Green, had done something impressive when he co-founded the firm back in 1962, developing a suit cut that sat somewhere on a spectrum between old and new, Savile Row and Carnaby Street. But Blades also seemed unsatisfying when Tommy and Edward got right down to the details. 'They were quite good with colours,' Edward recalls, 'but there was still an aristocratic schoolboy *feel* about their clothes.'

Indeed, the only place that seemed to push all of Tommy's buttons was a single boutique on Clifford Street. Called Mr Fish, it was run by Michael Fish, a talkative, fearless, bitchy aesthete who would once tell a

The 'peculiar' Michael Fish, photographed by David Nutter.

journalist, 'If I don't get whistled at and jeered when I pass a New York building site, I feel underdressed.'

Mr Fish sold gorgeous, ridiculous things, each item sporting a label that claimed it as 'Peculiar to Mr Fish'. There were silk kipper ties the shape of actual kippers. Puff-sleeved shirts straight from a swashbuckling cinematic fantasy. Chocolate-brown velvet dungarees, long leather coachman's coats and white flowing kaftans 'for a man to wear about the house'. Later, there was also a gender-bending white moiré man-dress that Mick Jagger would wear at a Hyde Park concert, flouncing around before a crowd of thousands. And the luscious silk dress David Bowie reclined in on the cover of *The Man Who Sold the World*. Vanessa Redgrave and Picasso shopped at Mr Fish; for good reason, Michael Fish himself would soon be dubbed 'a phenomenon of our age', and the 'high priest' of 'peacocks' – cashed-up dandies who had begun treating clothes as a personal art form.

What Tommy found intriguing about Michael Fish was that he'd managed to make a splash 'without losing the quality and design'. Fish had got his start at Turnbull & Asser, which meant he understood craftsmanship, how to make something *well*. But he was not afraid to apply that understanding in an offbeat way, to create clothes that fitted his outlandish sensibility. Tommy later said, 'I felt I could do the same thing with Savile Row tailoring.' In fact, Tommy asked Michael Fish for a job: Fish declined, encouraging Tommy to open something up using his own name instead.

In many ways, there had never been a better time to embark on a risky venture. The writer Clement Freud, observing the frenzy of fashion stores suddenly appearing around London, remarked, 'One feels almost a fool if one doesn't own a boutique.' And Tommy knew what it took. He'd done, in a roundabout way, the market research. He had an enthusiastic ally scheming with him in the alehouse. As for the rest of the details, the actual step-by-step requirements of launching a serious business – he'd just watched his own brother stumble through those, haphazardly, the previous year.

David had met his business partner, Carlo Manzi, through the Rockingham Club. More precisely, he met Carlo's girlfriend, Kim Grossman, via Sundays at the Rockingham, and Kim had introduced him to Carlo, a handsome young man of Neapolitan descent with a penchant for Tonik suits and gold jewellery.

Carlo was working in his brothers' record store, Manzi Records, on the Finchley Road at the time. He was hoping to start something of his own, though, using money from his parents, who'd made a small fortune selling coin-operated slot machines. David, for his part, was looking to break away from Robert Horner, whose erratic behaviour was by now abominable. After Kim orchestrated a meeting between them at a local fast-food restaurant, Carlo had decided that photography seemed like a compelling proposition. 'David had developed a fantastic reputation as a world-class black-and-white printer,' he recalls. 'Here was a man at the top of his game, but he needed help, he didn't have any particular business nous.' In Carlo's view, that was exactly what *he* had. 'And I wanted to be involved in something artistic, so it seemed like a good opportunity for both of us.'

Things had started modestly, with the two men processing test film in Carlo's parents' garage. (One day, a spider skittered across the floor, and they'd shrieked in unison and run for their lives – and Carlo's mother.) But then Carlo had signed the lease on an empty railwaymen's club overlooking Primrose Hill Station, an impressive headquarters for any new outfit. They'd transformed the bar area into a dedicated darkroom, and left the large empty ballroom as a studio that could later be rented out independently for extra revenue. They named the business NUTTER. Singular, to sound more commanding, in bold orange capitals across a light-pink letterhead.

NUTTER LABORATORIES & STUDIOS

Then they began making phone calls. David had an extensive contact list: actors and actresses looking for headshots, creative types he'd met out and about with Tommy, and the magazine and fashion people he'd worked with through Horner's. 'I guess they all jumped ship,' David recalls. 'Or maybe I stole them.'

Thus established, virtually overnight, NUTTER fast earned a reputation as one of the best photography production facilities in London. It was both supremely proficient on a technical level (lighting, developing) and endearingly eccentric, which was something that Carlo and David only encouraged further by, for example, sending out Christmas cards to industry contacts showing themselves in the Nativity.

'Amazed I haven't been struck by lightning,' David says.

David and Carlo as Mary and Joseph.

Tommy had many of the same qualities that David had relied on to make NUTTER a reality: raw talent, passion, a flair for self-branding and a generous dose of bravado – or, at least, enough dreamy-eyed vision to overcome any apprehension one might reasonably feel about taking on such a precarious project.

But he lacked money, a financial backer. And where would he find one of those? At least David had a track record of sterling photograph printing work when Carlo had come sniffing. What tangible evidence did Tommy have to show for himself? Who in their right mind might pledge support to 'a comely youth from Edgware', as one writer would condescendingly peg him, 'without influence or capital', and with 'no qualification of any kind, beyond the sweetness of his smile'?

II.

Peter Brown first spied Tommy Nutter in 1967, at a dinner party thrown by Brian Epstein in his Georgian town house on Chapel Street. Before anything else, though, this fact invites another important question: How did Tommy come to be socialising with the manager of the Beatles? What was he doing in Brian Epstein's Belgravia house in the first place?

There are two stories.

In the one told by Tommy to journalists over the years, he 'got into the whole scene mainly by going to the Ad Lib Club'. The Ad Lib was frequented by Julie Christie, Rod Stewart, the Who – and Tommy glided right up to the VIP section. 'It was where everybody went,' he later said. 'Brian Epstein would throw parties and everybody would be there.' It must have been hard to keep up with all the big spenders, but, Tommy said, 'I survived, like you do when you are young . . . It was all slightly calculated but I enjoyed it as well.' In Tommy's narrative, he was an agile social climber, working the Ad Lib dance floor until it 'paid dividends'.

However, in the memory of Peter Brown, somebody simply brought Tommy to dinner as his date. 'That's really how Brian and I met him.'

It was a warm evening, summer, June or July. An intimate sit-down for a handful of people. Peter thought Tommy was remarkably cute, though Tommy, perhaps dazed by his surroundings and the famous host, gave no indication of even noticing Peter.

Afterwards, Brian had a conversation with Peter in which he made some 'approving comments' about their young guest. It was not that Brian Epstein had any interest in Tommy for himself; despite his stiff-collar demeanour, he preferred rough trade to 'gay boys'. But he knew what Peter liked, and was, in that regard, always encouraging.

Peter Brown was Brian Epstein's best friend and personal assistant. By extension, that meant Peter was also personal assistant to the Beatles. At Brian's management agency on Argyle Street, Peter kept their passports locked in a drawer of his desk. On top of his desk was a red telephone that John, Paul, George and Ringo could call whenever they wanted something, like the phone Commissioner Gordon would use to reach Batman. 'I supervised and conducted all of their personal and business affairs,' Peter later wrote, 'from getting their signatures on contracts to getting them out of jail.'

Just thirty years old in 1967, Peter had a dark beard, sparkling eyes, and an accent that sounded more West End than Bebington. ('If you lived in this suburb of Cheshire,' Peter explains, 'your parents made sure that you didn't have a bad accent, because in those days a regional accent would stop you being successful.') He was responsible, direct and extraordinarily self-possessed. From the moment they'd met in Liverpool in the late 1950s, Brian had admired Peter's poise and attitude. Peter, in turn, had looked up to Brian as someone who was 'very special' – although, he later wrote, 'I remember thinking that if one scratched the surface one would find a very unhappy man'.

At least part of Brian's unhappiness had to do with his homosexuality, which had already seen him beaten up, blackmailed, arrested and discharged from the army on 'psychiatric grounds'. By contrast, Peter seemed fairly level-headed about his sexual orientation after he got over the guilt, accepted the truth and let down a girlfriend. When his parents found out, they'd confronted him with an ultimatum: 'give that whole thing up' or get out of their house. Peter's response had been to move in with a Swiss hairdresser. His parents had ignored him for six months, then tried to make amends; Peter had ignored them for a further three to make a point. This difference in temperament between himself and Brian had set the tenor for much of the friendship, which was platonic (after an initial encounter), but loving, in the way of many gay men. Peter and Brian represented a constantly adjusting equation of impulsive, self-destructive recklessness and stubborn sobriety.

When Brian discovered the Beatles playing a lunchtime set in the Cavern Club, in 1961, Peter was already working with him at his family's chain of music stores in Liverpool. By 1965, when Peter moved down to London to help Brian manage the band, he would do almost anything for his friend, from signing the property deed on a country estate to accompanying him on holidays to Cap d'Antibes, Mexico and Spain, where they liked to watch the bullfights together.

In 1966, they both went to Japan – and that is where things began to go wrong, on a tumultuous world tour Peter now blames for Brian's rapid deterioration.

Brian had insisted Peter come along to attend to the band's personal problems. Consequently, Peter was there when right-wing militant students threatened to assassinate the Beatles for 'perverting' Japanese culture. He was there in the Philippines when Brian rejected an invitation for the boys to perform at a party thrown by Imelda Marcos, the president's wife – a rejection that caused, in short order, the entourage to be attacked and spat on at the Manila airport. In New Delhi, Peter was in attendance when Brian became so anxious, blaming himself for these calamities, that he refused to leave his room for four entire days. On the plane back to London, Brian then broke out in hives. 'I was sitting next to him,' Peter says, 'and it became so bad that we had to have the pilots radio ahead for an ambulance to meet us.' Later, in America, they encountered evangelicals burning records (Lennon had made his ill-advised remark that the Beatles were 'more popular than Jesus now'), and there was fear the band might be shot while performing onstage. 'Brian went through extra hell and torture over that.' It was Peter who'd found him slumped next to empty pill bottles and a suicide note, then helped get him to a hospital so his stomach could be pumped.

Indeed, by the summer of 1967 and that sit-down dinner party where they both noticed Tommy, Peter was 'virtually living' at Chapel Street with Brian, who needed constant company.

On 25 August, Peter travelled to Brian's country house of Kingsley Hill, in East Sussex. He and Brian were supposed to spend the entire weekend there with Geoffrey Ellis, another colleague, but Brian became bored when some other expected guests failed to appear. 'It was ten o'clock on Friday night when Brian announced that he was going to take a drive around the countryside,' Peter later wrote. 'This hardly surprised Geoffrey and me; we were by then inured to Brian's moods and disappearances.' What was surprising was that Brian drove all the way back to his house in Belgravia.

The next day, Brian called Peter from Chapel Street and said he was going to drive *back* to Kingsley Hill . . . just as soon as he'd had breakfast and checked his post and watched *Juke Box Jury* on the television.

The day after that – on Sunday, 27 August – Brian had still not materialised at Kingsley Hill. Peter went to lunch at a local pub. When he returned, there were frantic phone calls from Chapel Street saying that Brian was locked in his room and no longer responding to anything. A doctor was summoned. Fifteen minutes passed. And then, Peter wrote, 'I said to break down the doors'.

> I remained on the line in Sussex, listening to the grunts of Antonio [Brian's butler] and Brian Barrett as the double oak doors splintered and caved in under their combined weight . . . The drapes were drawn and the room was dark. In the light from the

hallway they could all see him, lying on his right side, his legs curled up in a fetal position. Saturday's mail was open on the bed next to him.

Much has been written about the impact Brian Epstein's death from an overdose of Carbitral and alcohol had on the Beatles professionally. For Peter, however, the shocking loss of his best friend was agonisingly personal.

The next day, he was standing in Brian's drawing room, looking through a window onto a street that had just been swept through by paparazzi, like a flash flood. He had already shared the news with the Beatles, who were still on their retreat in Wales with the Maharishi Mahesh Yogi. Peter was numb, but starting to realise that *he* would be primary witness at the inevitable inquest. And that the enormous responsibility of running the Beatles' office would now fall squarely on *his* shoulders.

At that moment, the telephone rang. Peter walked across and picked it up.

'How are you?' asked Tommy Nutter, who had somehow acquired Brian's private number.

'Awful,' Peter said. 'Really awful.'

So the young man from the summer dinner party invited himself over for company and comfort.

At the time of Brian's death, Peter was dating Kenny Everett, a comedian and disc jockey famous for his broadcast work on pirate radio stations. Things had become quite serious, but Kenny had never been in a relationship with a man before. He was naive and inexperienced, a little high-maintenance. Suddenly, with all that happened, Peter couldn't cope with it any more. 'I wasn't being nasty,' he recalls. 'I wasn't being difficult. I was just a mess. I thought, "Kenny is too needy. And Tommy is sweet and affectionate: I need *that*."' Having reached this conclusion, Peter told Kenny it was over – an abrupt break that wounded the comedian so deeply he immediately retreated into the closet and remained there for the next seventeen years.

———————————————

For the first few weeks they were together, Tommy acted as an emergency flotation device for Peter. The Beatles were coming off the unpredicted success of *Sgt. Pepper's Lonely Hearts Club Band*. They were also facing a complicated tax situation with the Inland Revenue. Wracked with grief, Peter found himself inundated with work. Tommy was not particularly touchy, not much of a caretaker; but he was a distraction. He had a dry sense of humour – so dry it was almost 'perverse', Peter thought – and he was canny and sharp, not to mention sexy. His sparkling presence buoyed Peter up, so much so that Peter would come to believe Tommy saved his life, 'emotionally speaking'.

Peter's sudden appearance caught Tommy's own friends by surprise. There was no announcement, no explanation. David first spotted the couple strolling down Portobello Road and was left to work things out himself. Eventually, Tommy brought Peter over to the NUTTER studio for a photo shoot with silly hats. He joked with his brother that Peter's posh speaking voice was all an affectation; Peter was really 'common as muck', Tommy said. Whatever Peter's background, though, David soon decided he liked him enough to dub him 'Peggy the Bearded Lady'.

Carol Drinkwater, staying over at Tommy's flat on her side of the pillow wall, also decided she liked Peter Brown – particularly his parties, where pop stars like Mary Hopkin could be found lounging around on the furniture. But some of the other women in Tommy's life were a little more ambivalent. Kim Grossman found him overly 'grand': 'The link with the Beatles and Brian Epstein – he was very pleased with where he'd got in life.' Meanwhile, Louise Aron, besotted with Tommy since the days she'd scavenged the Rockingham for his prey, saw Peter as a kind of invader: 'Peter came on the scene and I got pushed off.'

But perhaps the friend with the keenest insight into this burgeoning romance was Christopher Tarling, Tommy's ex-boyfriend turned confidant. As the weeks became months, and then more than a year,

Christopher found himself accompanying Tommy and Peter to extravagant dinners around London. There would be a small group – two couples, plus Christopher to make five – and plenty of expensive wine. After dinner, Tommy would nudge him, announce to the table that they were heading out, and then leave Peter with his friends to finish off the bottle.

Some nights, the two of them went to the Coleherne Arms, a leather-fetish pub in Earls Court. Christopher tended to linger by the bar, though Tommy strode through the place with unblinking confidence. 'He loved glamour,' another friend recalls, 'but he also felt equally comfortable in these sordid clubs with shady people.' Because a licensing law mandated that pubs like the Coleherne couldn't sell alcohol without also selling food, these 'shady people' sometimes cruised around while clutching paper plates of ham salad.

On warmer nights, Tommy and Christopher might take a post-dinner taxi to Jack Straw's Castle, near Hampstead Heath. Christopher would wait with the driver, paid to keep the engine idling, while Tommy dashed across the road onto the Heath. Prowling through the trees, Tommy would momentarily shed his suit, his second skin. There would be an assignation in the grass with somebody he would probably never see again (and maybe not even then, if the moon was particularly hidden that night). Then Christopher would watch his friend re-emerge from the dark, climb back into the cab, and direct the driver to continue home to Elvaston Place.

―――――

In Peter's memory, his earliest days with Tommy, once the grief had settled down, were defined by dinners and parties, and by weekend mini-breaks out to the country to stay with John Pritchard, a conductor who had recently directed the London Philharmonic Orchestra.

Anything else that Tommy may have been getting up to at the time – the Coleherne, the cruising – Peter lumps together as 'his separate life of the American Express situation'. The 'situation', in this instance, refers to the American Express building in central London, which reportedly featured a public lavatory popular among gay men. Depending on whom you ask, Tommy once slipped on a toilet bowl in flagrante delicto and ended up with either a shoe full of water or a bruise on his thigh that lingered for months, like a cattle brand.

Peter was not one for 'cottaging' – anonymous hook-ups in public lavatories – which he would later describe as seeking 'physical satisfaction in the saddest of ways'. But even if he'd known the full extent of what Tommy was getting up to, it probably wouldn't have bothered him anyway. Peter did not believe in monogamy; neither of them did. Though the government had finally legalised homosexuality in 1967, it did not necessarily follow that homosexual relationships would conform to a heterosexual norm. Peter and Tommy made their own rules. 'He didn't tell me, and I didn't tell him about anything else we were doing,' Peter recalls. They had their time together, they had their time apart, and the pieces fitted together well enough. Which is not to say that there was never drama. 'Tommy was *not* cooperative. He could be very difficult – at times impossible. He gave me a hard time, though he could probably have said the same thing about me.' (Tommy did, in fact, say the same thing in letters to his brother in the 1970s. 'I have had Miss B. here which has proved to be extremely exhausting.') But, Peter adds, 'I do like people who are a challenge.'

One episode illustrates the complicated dynamic that would eventually settle in between them. It was 1968 or 1969, perhaps even 1970: Peter and Tommy went for a few warm weeks to the Greek island of Hydra, in the Aegean Sea. There were almost no motor vehicles on Hydra; only mules and donkeys could traverse the small picturesque port town of stucco, terracotta and marble cobblestone streets dotted with a scattering of Orthodox churches. In a converted manor house, there was also the National Merchant Marine Academy, filled with impressionable cadets.

Peter got into a conversation with one of the white-uniformed men – handsome, charming, relatively fluent in English. Each evening, a trumpet would sound to signal the academy curfew. But if he really wanted to, a cadet could sneak out after dark. 'Which he did,' Peter recalls, 'to see me.'

Peter and Tommy were staying in a beautiful house with two of their close friends, one of whom was a model named Judith Allera. A self-described 'total innocent', Judith had no idea what was going on in the rooms around her. She did, however, witness the fallout one night in a bar overlooking the ocean. 'I don't know why Tommy stood up. Sometimes he'd just go a bit – just decide he wasn't happy. And then he ended up in the water.'

Tommy had jumped out of a window into the ocean.

He was 'flapping about, saying he couldn't swim', Judith recalls. And so, 'like a fool', she threw herself in after him – and landed straight on a sea urchin.

Peter suggests that Tommy was inebriated in the moment, moved to act in a snap fury. But over what, exactly? Peter wasn't doing anything with the cadet that Tommy wouldn't do himself, given the right opportunity. Was Tommy jealous? Or was he irrationally incensed at not being the centre of attention – at being a supporting act instead of the main event?

Tommy would never explain his behaviour to Judith, who spent 'months and months' extracting painful spines from her backside. 'He'd do things like that, and then it was all . . .' Nothing. Like nothing had even happened.

In the early months of 1968, Tommy vacated his room on Elvaston Place and moved with Peter into a gracious one-bedroom flat on Conduit Street, in Mayfair. They decorated the place with art deco furniture and Clarice Cliff ceramics, then bought a cross-eyed cat, which Tommy called Clarence.

A Conduit Street address meant Tommy now lived less than a five-minute walk from the Burlington Arcade, strolling down Savile Row and turning right. Peter, though, had an even shorter commute. The Beatles had just founded their multi-tentacled corporation, Apple Corps Limited, of which Peter was appointed administrative director. In June, the group spent nearly £500,000 on a five-storey town house at No. 3

Savile Row. They installed a private mixing studio in the basement, a press office, a film department, a film library and a lavish kitchen overseen by two cordon bleu chefs. Peter was awarded a stately office on the first floor at the back; to jazz it up a bit, Ringo gave him an enormous set of decorative chrome headlights.

On a Friday in August, Peter was sitting at his desk wrapping up some work when Paul McCartney called him on the telephone. For the previous few days, the Beatles had been working on a new single, an experimental track that had caused tension in the group – McCartney versus Harrison over guitar riffs – and raised the concern of their record producer, George Martin, who'd suggested it might be too long for radio play. Now it was nearly completed, and Paul asked Peter to come round for a first listen.

Peter walked through Soho to Trident Studios, where the boys had chosen to record the track. Inside, Paul and John installed him in an armchair near some high-quality speakers. The song was cued, and then Peter sat still for seven minutes and eleven seconds, from Paul's first plaintive croon to a heaving coda of bass and tambourines, hand-clapping, and choral shrieking of *nah, nah, nah, nah-nah-nah-NAH, nah-nah-nah-NAH* . . .

Stunned, Peter shook his head as the tape ran out. He told them he thought it was 'enormously special'.

This review must have come as a huge relief. 'I was always a bit in limbo with a new single,' Paul would later recall. 'Your heart's in your mouth when you first hear it played on the radio, for instance. I knew it was a lot to expect people to swallow the whole thing.'

Paul and John told Peter they wanted to go out and celebrate. But Peter demurred; he was due to drive out to the country with Tommy for the weekend. Paul told him to call Tommy and bring him along; they had all met him by now, and there was no problem with Peter having a boyfriend.

When Peter called him using the studio payphone, Tommy refused, wilfully non-compliant. He didn't want to go out and celebrate in Soho. It took Paul to snatch the receiver out of Peter's hand and beg him to 'come hear this' before he finally surrendered.

Tommy arrived at Trident and was installed in the armchair, told to prepare himself. The song was cued for a second play. As he then listened for the full seven minutes and eleven seconds, Paul and John watched him closely, trying to gauge his reaction.

After it was finished, Tommy remained impassive, unreadable. There was a long pause.

He told them he didn't like it.

The Beatles were 'crestfallen', Peter recalls, until they were informed this was Tommy's idea of a droll joke. Indeed, Tommy would eventually admit that 'Hey Jude' was 'the most incredible song . . . because we'd never heard anything like that before'. What impressed him was not so much its groundbreaking form, though, as how uncalculated it seemed. In Tommy's view, the Beatles hadn't set out to break the mould; they'd just wanted to express themselves. And expressing themselves – *honestly* expressing themselves – meant making the song in a way that happened, by the by, to be groundbreaking. 'It just came from within them,' he later said admiringly. 'That's what they wanted to do and they did it properly.'

What finally inspired Peter to offer the financial backing for Tommy to launch his own business? Tommy never understood it – or at least pretended not to understand it for the sake of modesty. 'I don't know, I can't say why they did it,' he would murmur when asked for an explanation about his first financiers. 'They trusted me, they thought I might be successful. I suppose they liked me.'

Sometimes Tommy would come home in the evening to the Conduit Street flat in a glum mood, complaining that he had all these ideas, but there was nothing he could do with them, because the only suits made by Donaldson, Williams & G. Ward were 'conventional'. Peter had already noted his wonderful eye for line and colour. He saw that Tommy had a remarkable ability to throw together disparate things, patterns, materials in a way that seemed both exactly right and irresistible.

Peter's investment was no doubt helped along by the fact that he'd been surrounded, since his Liverpool days, by people who'd shown their natural creativity to be the source of immense power. Or that he was now the administrative director of a corporation that was devoted, in no insignificant way, to funding unlikely projects based on intuition and perceived artistic merit, rather than strict financial requirements – 'to not being nasty businessmen', as Peter recalls the ethos motivating Apple Corps. In other words, it was a normal course of events at No. 3 Savile Row that somebody like Tommy Nutter might be given an opportunity to explore their latent potential – be given a little *lift*.

'It wasn't that I was so brilliant,' Peter says. 'I just had a feeling that this kid knew what he was doing.' And that feeling, as Brian Epstein had once famously illustrated, could take you to some interesting places if you just went with it.

Edward Sexton has a vivid memory of sitting at a table opposite Peter in Madame Prunier's fish restaurant, on St James's Street. A formidable establishment – oysters from Brittany, caviar from the Garonne – Edward had been invited to Prunier St James's for, perhaps, a kind of interview: Peter appraising the man Tommy had chosen to be his head cutter. Or perhaps Peter was simply being friendly. Either way, Edward set out to make an impression.

When the waiter came round to collect their menus, Edward ordered for both of them: Dover sole and a nice bottle of Pouilly-Fuissé.

When the waiter came round with the fish, Edward instructed him to leave it on the table, on the bone. Then he set about deboning it himself. He separated the head from the body with a pair of spoons, flaked off the feather bones from the delicate flesh, and lifted out the skeleton whole to set off to the side.

When he was finished, Peter, having watched in amazement, asked, 'Where did you learn that?'

In Edward's memory, this question rang as a moment of triumph – proof he had shown himself as sharp and capable, unintimidated by highfalutin pomp.

Peter, however, has no recollection of any dinner with Edward at Madame Prunier's on St James's Street. 'I don't know *why* I would have been taking him to dinner,' he says – the first of several such moments where his and Edward's narratives diverge around Tommy Nutter, like water around a rock in a turbulent stream. 'But it could possibly be,' he concedes. 'I probably just thought he must have been a waiter at one time.'

III.

After Peter Brown, the person who would become the second financier of Tommy's new enterprise appeared sometime in the middle of 1968. James Vallance White, a tall, thin thirty-year-old with an aristocratic mien, was a junior clerk in the House of Lords. He'd just undergone surgery at a private clinic in Harley Street, and the doctor, noting his restlessness, had recommended he take restorative strolls around Mayfair. Inevitably, these walks led James south towards Piccadilly, through the Burlington Arcade, where he noticed Donaldson, Williams & G. Ward. James needed a new coat, so he decided to step inside and order one.

Tommy greeted him politely, then immediately began asking the usual questions. But James, feeling a little starved of human interaction as he whiled away hours recuperating in the clinic, wanted a chit-chat. He asked Tommy if he liked his job.

Tommy hesitated. He looked around. James noticed he was quite nervous about the other, more senior members of staff overhearing this conversation. Carefully, Tommy admitted that no, not really, he didn't like his job; and actually he was thinking about leaving to open something of his own.

This was a brazen confession, James thought. Tommy had revealed his seditious plans to a perfect stranger, right there in the showroom.

What James didn't know, however, was just how much further Tommy had already gone in subverting his workplace.

Recently, Michael Hall had been away on holiday at the same moment Mr Donaldson happened to be visiting Australia, which effectively left the firm without an overseer. A young man had entered the shop. Tommy had made his overture . . . but the boy didn't want what Donaldson's was peddling. On a usual day, this would have ended with polite apologies: this was what they sold, sir, and there was nothing else on offer. But this was not a usual day. Tommy called Edward down to the showroom. Together, they contemplated the situation. The boy wanted something distinctive. They wanted to make something distinctive. And so they took the hacking jacket style Edward had been working on after hours, tweaked it according to Tommy's fancy, and drafted the earliest iteration of an entirely new look – which the young man commissioned. Then they used the firm's resources to assemble the suit, fit the suit, alter the suit, admire the suit and ship the suit out before either of the bosses had returned from their travels.

James didn't know any of this when he encountered the confident salesman. But he was intrigued nonetheless. He placed his order and went away to wait, mulling their conversation in the meantime.

As James saw it, the city around him was going through a period of peculiar upheaval, when all sorts of things seemed to be happening outside the status quo. *Time* magazine had written about it in 1966: 'In a once sedate world of faded splendor, everything new, uninhibited and kinky is blooming at the top of London life.' Yet James, now seven years out from his studies at Oxford, remained mostly unstimulated by his government position. He was *bored* with routine. So why not get involved with something outré and have a little fun? Perhaps, he reasoned to himself, it would provide 'another aspect to life'.

When James returned to the Burlington Arcade for a fitting, he told Tommy that his idea sounded rather attractive. Not long after, Tommy called James and asked him to meet Peter – who then laid out the whole proposal.

'Tommy didn't have any money,' James recalls, 'but what he did have was a modern slant on tailoring. Instead of being stuffy and traditional, he wanted to make a shop that was going to be a sort of sitting room, where people would drink coffee, look at magazines, talk to their friends, and then go into one of the rooms to be fitted for clothes. The *image* was going to be very different. I do seem to remember, too, that the Beatles, who were by then becoming quite seriously famous – the idea they were under the influence of Peter was not uninfluential in our thinking that the thing might take off and be successful.'

James and Peter discussed money: how much it might cost to stock a business, hire some staff, and secure the lease on a desirable showroom. Coincidentally, a small space had just become available on Savile Row at the base of a new multi-storey garage. *That* multi-storey garage. If Tommy acted quickly, he could open on the very spot where G. Ward had once stood before being razed by the local council.

James was convinced; he added his name to the project. And in the months following, he sent several notes about it to Tommy at the Burlington Arcade. Noticing the return address, Mr Donaldson began to grow curious: Why was a salesman receiving post from the House of Lords? Edward came to suspect the old man was trying to steam open the envelopes before giving up, and begrudgingly handing them over.

The final financial backer – or backers, being a couple – were also the most famous: the singer Cilla Black and her angelic-looking boyfriend, Bobby Willis.

Peter had known Cilla since Liverpool, when he'd routinely thrown her out of the Lewis's department store where he worked; Cilla would listen to records over and over as she tried to learn how to sing them for the local clubs. A tiny, sylph-like redhead with a pronounced overbite, Cilla had been an unlikely candidate for pop superstardom – but that was Brian Epstein's genius. 'I watched her move,' Brian once said, 'and I watched her stand and I half-closed my eyes and imagined her on a vast stage with the right lighting. I was convinced she could become a wonderful artist.' She had a vocal style that ranged from throaty whisper to explosive vibrato, and there was something disarming about her working-class lack of airs and graces. She was relatable; people liked her. Brian had signed her in 1963 – his sole female artist – and by the time of his death, four years later, she'd had two number-one hits on the UK charts, sold millions of records, and cemented her reputation as a national darling. A weekly BBC variety show, arranged by Brian in one of his last acts, was already preparing to go into production.

Brian had respected Cilla more than perhaps any other woman outside of his own family circle. However, he'd also scrupulously excluded her from anything *gay*, which meant freezing her out of much of his personal life. By Cilla's own admission, she was something of an ingénue in the early days. 'When an acquaintance had come up to me in the Blue Angel Club in Liverpool and said: "You do know he's queer?", I just thought he meant that Brian was an oddball.' Brian was intent on keeping her in the dark. Peter, on the other hand, thought the enforced separation of business and personal when it came to Cilla Black was all quite ridiculous; when Brian died, he threw the policy out.

Following the overdose, Peter and Cilla drew together in a shared medium of anguish. This meant that Cilla also inevitably drew closer to Tommy, who was virtually inseparable from Peter, and who soon became inseparable from Cilla, too, because she came to adore him.

In January 1968, Cilla began filming her eponymous variety show at the BBC Television Theatre in Shepherd's Bush. Peter and Tommy would go and watch the recording live, then meet her and Bobby Willis for dinner somewhere around town. Eventually, the foursome were holidaying together in Portugal. Cilla would monopolise Tommy's attention, until Peter was moved to snap, 'Tommy, *come on . . .*'

'Oh, are you jealous?' asked Cilla, mock-serious.

For his part, Tommy thought Cilla was 'a big star'. And he took great pleasure in expanding her mind, in filling in the gaps about queer life that Brian had so fastidiously maintained. One evening in Kensington, for example, Tommy, Cilla, Peter and a small cadre of friends pulled up in a Rolls-Royce outside the Sombrero, an upmarket club that catered to a predominantly gay clientele. Peter skipped the queue – Peter did not do queues – and strolled directly inside. Cilla, though, hung back. 'She wasn't sure at first,' recalls a friend who was part of the group.

'But then Tommy said, "*Yes*, you're coming" . . . and sort of dragged her down there. Of course, she loved it. All the queens were going mad. Cilla Black!'

Years hence, Tommy would credit Cilla with a leading role in getting his fledgling business off the ground, though in reality she came on late, out of love for her friend, to offer a minor financial stake and some priceless publicity for Tommy's new venture.

On 22 December 1968, the *Sunday Express* ran a cartoon of the pop star with a measuring tape draped around her neck. Ms Black, the journalist noted, was taking the 'rather surprising step' of setting up business as a gentlemen's tailor. She was hardly the first musician to associate herself with fashion enterprises, but perhaps she was the first to aim right for the heart of such a traditional niche: Savile Row.

'It's going to be terribly posh,' Cilla told the paper's readers. 'It will be a very snob tailors. There will be none of the common gimmicks of Carnaby Street, and no gaudy décor.' The clothes would be exquisite, 'made on straightforward classical lines', and the demographic would be 'lords, ambassadors and royalty'. This was her first venture into the rag trade, Cilla acknowledged. 'In the past I have always been advised against it. My former manager Brian Epstein didn't believe in my advertising women's clothes.' But, she continued, 'this is something entirely different.' How so? 'The tailoring will be in the hands of Mr Thomas Nutter,' Cilla announced, finally debuting his name in the press. 'I think he is the best tailor in London.'

interlude

CILLA AND BOBBY GET MARRIED

Cilla Black and Bobby Willis fought, as the saying goes, like an old married couple. Or at least Peter thought they did. He'd watched them during a dinner at San Lorenzo, on Beauchamp Place, going back and forth across the table, arguing about nothing. It had given him an idea: If they were going to bicker like an old married couple, then they probably should just get married and be done with it.

This came as news to Cilla and Bobby, who were going about their day at home when Peter rang the intercom and said that he was on his way to the Marylebone Registry Office: Did Bobby want to come along?

'I guess it's on,' Cilla told him.

A few days later, on 25 January 1969, a horde of journalists besieged Priscilla White (they recognised her real name listed in the public notices) outside the registry office. She wore an £8 burgundy dress, hastily shortened the night before, and clutched a bouquet of anemones. Bobby wore a blue suit with a red rose in the buttonhole. Peter (who gave Cilla away) and Tommy (who was Bobby's best man) wore early iterations of the new suit style Tommy was designing with Edward.

David Nutter was recruited as the official wedding photographer. He followed the small party from the registry office to the Ritz, where they had lunch; and then on to Cilla's flat on Portland Place, where there was cake and champagne, and where Cilla pretended to stab her new husband with the serving knife.

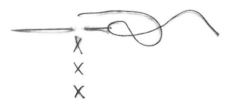

PART II

1969–1976

*First, touching Dandies, let us consider, with some scientific
strictness, what a Dandy specially is. A Dandy is a Clothes-
wearing Man, a Man whose trade, office and existence
consists in the wearing of Clothes. Every faculty of his soul,
spirit, purse and person is heroically consecrated to this one
object, the wearing of Clothes wisely and well: so that as
others dress to live, he lives to dress. The all-importance of
Clothes . . . has sprung up in the intellect of the Dandy
without effort, like an instinct of genius; he is inspired
with Cloth, a Poet of Cloth.*

THOMAS CARLYLE, *Sartor Resartus*

Tommy poses in the showroom of Nutters of Savile Row for the *Evening Standard*.

5

DISCOTHEQUE IN A GRAVEYARD

'Thomas Nutter is opening what he calls a "thoroughly square" tailoring shop . . . in Savile Row next week. Well, that will make a change,' snarked a writer in the *Daily Mirror*. 'I mean there can't be more than a dozen there now. Mr Nutter, who is twenty-six, is weary of "all those Carnaby Street gimmicks" and thinks that clothes, like hair, are settling down to something more sober . . . What then of rumours that Ringo Starr has ordered a pair of scarlet PVC trousers from Nutters, which is being backed by such notables as Cilla Black?'

Tommy replied, curtly, 'They'll be very square scarlet PVC trousers.'

Nutters of Savile Row was located at No. 35a, on the western side of the street. The glass frontage was framed by a waxed pine portico with four Corinthian columns, all topped by acanthus leaves, and an ornate wooden door, salvaged from a house in Isleworth, that began to stick almost from the moment it was installed. Fixed to the door were two heraldic crests – each one sporting an original *H* snapped to the more appropriate *N* – that resembled Napoleon's monogram on the gates at Fontainebleau.

Pushing inside, the showroom was not particularly spacious: just 540 square feet. To best exploit the tight fit, Tommy brought in his friend Michael Long, who brought in a Jaeger shop-fitting expert. Together they conspired to evoke Tommy's desired aesthetic – 'elegant with a touch of the sombre' – through a combination of old and new furnishings: chocolate-coloured carpet, a Greek frieze, chic Wassily chairs, and dark lacquered slat shelving for bolts of British cloth. One entire wall was given over to a twelve-foot mirror, conjuring an illusion of greater depth. Spotlights, suspended from the ceiling behind carved wooden pelmets, illuminated a single rack of finished samples, where each garment was draped from a NUTTERS-branded hanger. Rounding out the decor were two changing rooms with pull-curtains and a small desk with a bottle stashed in the top drawer; Tommy liked to sip sherry from a teacup. He also liked to use an atomiser to scent the showroom with patchouli. 'People seem to think that our shop is going to be all flashing lights and music and we'll all be freaking out all over the place,' he once remarked. 'It is not like that at all.'

Well, maybe just a little.

The front window displays were a masterclass in exhibitionism. While everybody else on Savile Row hid behind frosted glass and modest bronze nameplates, Nutters opted for clear sheet glass, prominent stencilled lettering – N U T T E R S – and a rotating line-up of eye-catching installations beamed straight from the brain of Michael Long: a painted mural of Egyptian ruins; a Punch and Judy puppet show; 'a riot of Royal Purple and Fuchsia-coloured ostrich feathers'. Huntsman may have had royal warrants, and Poole may have had bits and pieces left over from the Great Exhibition of 1851, but Nutters, for a time, had red ribbons dangling champagne bottles that clinked deliciously every time the door was wrenched open.

Tommy liked 'the idea of an "old look,"' he once claimed, the traditional muted understatement of Savile Row. But he also defended his outrageous windows as an opportunity to 'show what we do, so that people will not be frightened to come in'. Compared to its intimidating neighbours, Nutters was intended to be 'a lot more relaxed', the kind of place where a stranger should feel emboldened to walk in uninvited and ask for 'something different'.

In this respect, it turned out to be successful before the official launch date had even arrived. One evening, Tommy and Cilla were sprawled across the carpet laughing and drinking wine, yet another raucous celebration in the two weeks since her surprise wedding. It had recently come to their attention that Tommy was about to be the first new tailor to open on Savile Row in more than a century – and, perhaps, the youngest ever.

Suddenly, a group of Americans knocked on the door. Attracted by the warm glow, they'd peered through the window, spied the party, and decided they wanted to join. The door was thrown open. Space was made on the floor. Another bottle of bubbles was uncorked. Everyone was welcome at Nutters.

Everyone, that is, except Louise Aron, the boisterous girl from the Rockingham.

Jack Aron, Louise's father, had recently died, an awful, cataclysmic change for her family, and she was looking for something to cheer her up. She told Tommy she could barely wait for his launch, that it would be a grand party, glitzy, boozy, to which she was planning to wear something camp – 'big feather boas and all that stuff', just like the old days. But one morning Louise was in the HMV on Oxford Street, where she worked, when some friends came in and told her she'd missed it. The launch had already happened. Without her. Despite their comforting words – 'You don't have to worry, though, because everyone was asking where you were' – Louise was devastated by the news. She started to cry. No invitation when she needed one most. 'It was an awful thing to have done to me,' she recalls. 'I'd been friends with him for *years*.'

Louise immediately blamed Peter ('He didn't like me, that's what it was all about'), but she could never quite work up the courage to confront Tommy directly to confirm her suspicions. And so they drifted apart. It broke the love between them, and they didn't speak 'for a long, long time after that'.

Ironically, the official launch party for Nutters of Savile Row had occurred on Friday, 14 February 1969 – Valentine's Day. Peter delegated party logistics to a public relations woman he'd worked with through the Beatles. The star-studded guest list, though, was largely his doing. Peter had dressed the Apple Corps doorman in a Nutters frock coat, which meant that anybody who visited the building received a personal preview. Tommy was a regular visitor to Peter's office, too – the fans who gathered outside, called Apple Scruffs, got to know him so well they'd wish him goodnight as he'd stroll past – and Peter had introduced his boyfriend to the staff and impresarios. Nutters of Savile Row had garnered some serious advance buzz, in other words, and the glitterati were encouraged to come out and toast Tommy as one of their own.

The final guest list is lost, though Paul McCartney is said to have shown up, along with Twiggy, 'It Girl' of the moment, and her manager/boyfriend Justin de Villeneuve. Several of Tommy's friends did make the cut, as did (according to Cilla) 'a bunch of East End gangsters'. And the financial backers, of course: Peter, Cilla, Bobby Willis and James Vallance White, huddling together as a flashbulb popped in the candlelit showroom.

AN HISTORICAL OCCASION
NUTTER'S OPEN THEIR DOORS and Cilla meets the Row

From *Tailor & Cutter*

Tommy had arranged the purple candles to foster a more intimate atmosphere. 'God,' Cilla told him, 'I've never seen such big candles.' He gave her a few to take home, and it wasn't until the next day, taking a closer look, that she noticed they were penis-shaped. 'I burned them then and there,' Cilla later said. 'Destroyed the evidence.'

Also at the launch was Tony King, a music promotions manager who drew a great deal of attention for what he was wearing. Tony had met Tommy 'at parties, of course', and been entranced by his 'languid nonchalance' – Tommy had a tendency to move slowly, and speak slowly, almost as though he were slightly sedated. 'And he was all angles,' Tony recalls, 'like Fred Astaire. He had all the right angles for the clothes he was wearing.' In fact, everything about him was 'elegant, not only physically but also emotionally'. Tony was fascinated. At one party, he'd walked right up to Tommy and said, wanting to emulate his look, 'I'd love to get a suit made by you at your tailors.' Tommy had smiled shyly and asked Tony if he'd prefer to be a model; he was currently looking for somebody tall and lithe to test out a new experimental silhouette. Tony said yes and accompanied Tommy to meet Edward, who struck him as 'a mischievous man but a brilliant cutter'. The result of that meeting was the first commercial Nutters suit to be produced at No. 35a, a suit Tony was now proudly showing off at the opening launch, like a walking advertisement.

Tony King

On Savile Row in 1969, the standard suit was narrow and staid, designed to deflect attention away from the male form beneath the layers. Suits at Nutters promised a different approach. Edward was an expert at building hacking jackets: long, full-bodied coats originally intended for horseback riding, with wide skirts that could spread out across a saddle. The Nutters silhouette took this template and exaggerated it, adding 'masses of shape and flare' to the skirt, as Tommy once explained, and a tight waist and chest that would emphasise the wearer's body. To this close-fitting creation ('long and leafy', says Edward) they then went totally overboard on the width of lapels, adding double-breasted lapels to a single-breasted coat that were so enormous they grazed the sleeve heads. The coat pockets were straight and flapped, with the outside ticket pocket cut 'deep, deep'. The waistcoat also sported seriously capacious pockets. The trousers, by contrast, were such a snug fit that pockets were impossible, though these were suits for people who liked to *move*, so there was flexibility there too. The full effect, when you stepped back and took it in as a whole, was pleasing to the eye; it displayed a 'gallant Nutter character' that *Punch* would once memorably pin down as 'an eccentric mix of Lord Emsworth, the Great Gatsby and Bozo the Clown'.

Nothing else even remotely like this existed at the time. Tommy, deliberately echoing the language once used to describe Christian Dior's revolutionary women's collection of 1947, would boast that his design represented an entirely ' "New Look" for menswear'.

But what was most remarkable about the Nutters suit was not the design so much as what the design represented. Edward gets to the heart of the matter when he says, 'We weren't two clever guys who wanted to go out and create history; we just wanted to express ourselves through our work.' To express themselves through their work meant, inevitably, to express their collective influences. Teddy boy street fashion. The kind of neo-Edwardian dandyism seen in Rockingham homosexuals. A youthful fantasy of grace and glamour, pop music and movie stars. Even the 'louche-but-sharp flamboyance' of *West Side Story*. The first Nutters look represented a culmination of everything modern about Tommy and his cutter, everything mod, smashing, subversive, Continental, American, queer and camp – combined with a keen fidelity to old-school Savile Row craftsmanship.

Tony King's suit was just the beginning. 'I thought I would play things down a little by making the first suit in Alsport tweed,' Tommy admitted. The more dramatic iterations would come later, when clients were more accustomed to his subversive sensibility. It was like slowly spiking the punch to raise everyone's tolerance for the hard stuff.

Yet even Tony's 'soft' suit caused something of a scene after the launch party.

A few days later, Tony turned up for cocktails at the house of Hardy Amies, dressmaker to Queen Elizabeth. In 1961, Amies had made fashion history by staging the first ready-to-wear catwalk show for men; he'd also published his *ABC of Men's Fashion*, a bible of good masculine taste (underwear, for example, 'should be as brief as wit and as clean as fun'). Not long after, Stanley Kubrick had commissioned him to imagine the costumes for *2001: A Space Odyssey* – to imagine what clothes might look like thirty-plus years hence, when men circled the Earth in centrifugal spaceships. In other words, Hardy Amies was one of the country's foremost authorities on style. When Tony arrived at his house, though, Amies was on the staircase wearing a dressing gown. He was running late.

'Oh, hello,' Amies said, looking Tony up and down before ushering him through to the drawing room. 'Do go in, do go in . . .'

When Amies finally emerged, fully dressed, he strolled up to Tony and introduced himself properly. Then he asked, 'Where did you get that suit?'

Tony said, 'Tommy Nutter, opposite you' – Amies ran Hardy Amies Limited from No. 14 Savile Row.

'The new boy?'

Amies barked across the room for an associate to join him. Then, surrounded by fascinated guests – 'in the middle of the bloody cocktail party', Tony recalls – Amies pulled out a tape measure, unravelled it, and began to measure the Nutters lapel, which he deemed 'extraordinary'.

***

Accuracy can become collateral damage in the polishing of a good anecdote. 'Imagine this,' began a journalist as recently as 2011. 'You're 26, from Barmouth, and a bit of a whiz with a needle and thread. You turn up at work for a day's tailoring, nervous in the knowledge that John Lennon and Yoko Ono are due in soon for a fitting. However, upon turning the corner to your atelier on London's prestigious Savile Row you see they're already there, standing in the window and both absolutely stark naked.'

Really?

Tommy seemed to suggest as much. John and Yoko visited Nutters and stripped naked to browse through the clothes, he once said. 'The customers were complaining, but what could I do? This was John Lennon.'

Edward remembers things a little differently. 'It was on a Saturday,' he says, 'and John was prancing around in his underpants. He was in and out from behind the curtain; we had a big tartan one. And Lady Harlech came in to pick up a check coat. Of course, next thing you know, the curtain comes back and there is John Lennon in his pants.'

Not naked, then?

'Probably got exaggerated slightly,' Edward admits. 'But everyone is dead and buried now, and I wouldn't want to contradict Tommy if he said there was nudity.'

———————

John and Yoko wanted to get married. Not like Cilla or Paul McCartney, though; not with the circus of attention that inevitably resulted from posting the legally required banns notice forty-eight hours in advance. John and Yoko didn't want any publicity. In fact, John didn't even want to tell the other Beatles. 'They are as big-mouthed as anyone,' he said. He and Yoko had tried to tie the knot on a cross-Channel car ferry but were foiled by visa issues and an uncooperative captain. They had also considered travelling to a country like Germany, which turned out to require a three-week residence first before marriage. Eventually, they just got sick of all the roadblocks, flew to Paris, checked into the Plaza Athénée, and asked Peter Brown to sort it out for them.

Peter's response to the couple, hatched with Apple lawyers, is immortalised in 'The Ballad of John and Yoko':

> You can make it O.K.,
> You can get married in Gibraltar, near Spain.

As a British Overseas Territory, Gibraltar recognised John's citizenship, but imposed none of the conditions of home and no residency requirements. Peter chartered an executive jet to collect the couple in Paris and promised to meet them at the Rock with a discreet photographer.

He phoned David. 'I knew he was talented,' Peter recalls – David had, after all, just shot Cilla's wedding at his request – 'and I knew he was honest. I said to him, "David, I want you to go to Gibraltar tomorrow. Don't ask me why. Just get there, and take your camera."'

David was promptly collected at his Primrose Hill studio and driven to the airport. He had no idea what was happening, although when he did find out, en route, he was not particularly moved, almost never getting star-struck. 'I was like, "OK, let's do it."'

On 20 March, John and Yoko arrived in Gibraltar at around 8.40 a.m. after a three-hour flight. Yoko – described by *The Times* as 'an actress, painter and maker of a film on human bottoms' – wore a white floppy hat, a white knitted minidress, white tennis shoes, and the kind of giant black sunglasses people wear to hide from the world while simultaneously drawing attention to themselves. John wore Nutters: a cream corduroy suit he'd been fitted for in Savile Row. He also carried a coat that was made, according to one newspaper report, from human hair. ('John said it was monkey fur,' recalls Peter. 'Black and rather stylish.')

John liked Gibraltar, the symbolism of the Rock, strong and enduring, which reminded him of his relationship with Yoko. But there was little time for sightseeing. Joined by Peter and David, the couple drove to the British Consulate to swear affidavits before a magistrate that there were no impediments to their getting married; then they bought a special licence. The registrar, a man named Cecil Wheeler, had spent a restless night worrying that word of the ceremony would leak, leading fans and media to storm the building. But it was a quiet affair, over in minutes. Acting as witness, Peter stood to the side of the desk, though both 'Peter Brown' and 'David Nutten' [*sic*] would be listed on the marriage certificate. David snapped away, barely pausing for a moment to contemplate the surreal tableau of a superstar musician wearing his brother's new design, his brother's boyfriend, and a small, inscrutable Japanese woman, in what would quickly become known as one of the most infamous weddings of the decade.

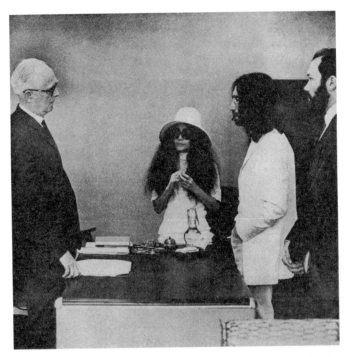

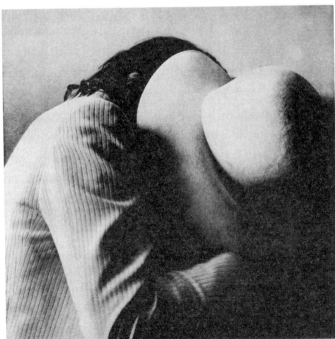

David's photographs were later used to illustrate
John Lennon and Yoko Ono's *Wedding Album* (1969).

Back on the runway, press photographers had somehow received word and materialised at the side of the jet. Perhaps as a taunt, John waved the marriage certificate above his head; then he climbed aboard, having spent all of sixty-five minutes on the ground. David exposed a few more rolls of film during the flight. 'John was being funny and we were all laughing,' he recalls. 'Even Yoko.'

Peter Brown turns the camera back on David.

Once the jet touched down in Paris, John and Yoko jumped into a car and sped off back to the Athénée, where they would hide out for a few days before heading on to Amsterdam to stage their first 'Bed-In for Peace'. (Having successfully executed a low-key wedding, they would now try their hand at a spectacle.)

Meanwhile, David was accosted in the terminal as he prepared to fly home to London. The crowds pressed in, David recalls, 'and this woman from some tabloid came up to me and said, "I've been instructed to take your film."

'I thought, "Wait a minute, you cow. Don't try *anything*."'

Sitting on the plane, downing champagne as they crossed the

English Channel, David realised he hadn't brought any money for taxi or train fare. He had to ask the pilot for a lift into London.

Back at NUTTER in Primrose Hill, he began going through negatives. Outside the darkroom, Carlo, his business partner, attempted to man the telephone. As Carlo recalls, 'We had Camera Press calling every ten minutes' – Peter had made a deal with the agency – 'and the guy was asking, "When can we get this film from you?" I said, "Well, it's in the processing bath and you can't have it until it's dried." He said, "We *need* it! You don't understand. Every paper in the world wants this stuff." I said, "Well, you just have to wait. We've got to do the contact sheets." He said, "We're not fucking waiting for contacts!" And the guy who owned Camera Press got a cab over and virtually beat down our door. "*Where's the film?*" I said, "It's in the drying cabinet." He went to the drying cabinet and just started unclipping it. It was really dramatic. I was quite taken aback.'

One day on Savile Row, Hardy Amies stepped out of his studio and rushed into the street, pursued by a writer who was furiously scribbling in a notebook as if taking dictation. Amies was talking non-stop – 'Marvellous tailor,' he muttered – as he waved away a procession of speeding cars that threatened to knock them both to the ground. 'Absolutely marvellous.' Finally, he reached No. 35a and completed his thought, which the writer obediently recorded: 'Tommy Nutter is the most exciting tailor on Savile Row in decades.'

The morning after admiring Tony King's lapels, Amies had swanned into Nutters and spent several thousand pounds. Later, he would explain what appealed to him about Tommy like this: 'Savile Row is a street of bespoke tailors. They execute the orders of their customers. They help with advice but do not attempt to originate. Tommy Nutter did.'

But what about those other bespoke tailors? Amies loved his young neighbour; what did the rest of the Row make of the new arrival?

Tommy would offer two conflicting accounts, depending on how he wished to present himself at any given moment. In the first version, he was cast as a brave iconoclast overcoming the odds to introduce something new to a hostile land. 'When I opened up in my own right . . . I guess it did alienate me from the traditional Savile Row establishment,' Tommy once claimed. Nutters 'was regarded with suspicion' by some of the more long-standing firms – Huntsman, say, which was made to look 'rather dowdy' by comparison.

However, in the second version, Tommy was embraced by his peers as though he were the next Prince of Wales heralding a return of the golden age. 'It's amazing,' he'd say in 1972, 'but since we set up here in the Row everyone has been most kind to us, although I'm so young.' By 1980, this forced modesty would give way to calmer self-assurance: 'In fact, they were rather nice. I think they needed [Nutters] to lift Savile Row up.'

More objective accounts suggest Tommy was actually welcomed with cautious optimism. Robert 'Bobby' Valentine, who worked next door at No. 9, told *Tailor & Cutter*: 'Nutters is going to be extremely successful because they will continue to bear in mind and maintain the standard and quality expected of tailors in the Row. Tommy has the experience and design ability, and Edward possesses very fine technical qualifications.' He wished them 'all the best of luck'.

Meanwhile, over in Cork Street, Henry Poole & Co. paid respects in its own peculiar way. Though Samuel Cundey saw Tommy as something of an upstart (that long hair!), his son, Angus Cundey, admired Nutters so much that he convinced his father to throw a 'stylish brick' through their own obscured frontage and install a see-through window display just three months after Nutters set its unconventional precedent. Angus was soon telling *Men's Wear*, 'I would like to see this stuffy image removed from the West End, but in doing so we should not forsake our reputation for quality. I want to show that Savile Row keeps up with the times.'

Indeed, the Row turned out to be mostly on Tommy's side. After nine years of apprenticeship he was one of them, after all, and could be trusted to modernise the trade without betraying the basic tenets of bespoke.

Any scepticism he did experience came predominantly from outside – from the media, for instance, which was still pushing (and would continue to push, for decades to come) the idea of an industry in irreversible decline. 'Savile Row today is in a rare state of schizophrenia, and looks it,' declared the *Daily Telegraph* in one characteristic example. 'Among other funny things, the street itself has been described as a discotheque in a graveyard. A new generation knows it simply as the place where the Beatles have their headquarters.' Tommy didn't quite fit into this reductive narrative, so he was condescendingly dismissed, just one of the new 'clothes artists' whose shops stood out mostly as 'bright parodies of the old style – a sort of Space-Age Regency', as though the future had no business mingling with a consecrated past.

Tommy had a curious relationship with the press. He was fond of journalists, actively courting them to offer leads and pronouncements and theories and predictions about next year or next decade or what people would be wearing in the year 2000. Yet at the same time, he couldn't help but subvert them mercilessly, turning interviews upside down with hidden meanings, innuendos, abrupt shifts in tone or direction. Publicity was important to Tommy Nutter, but it was also ridiculous, a parlour game of wits in which the rules of engagement were clear to almost nobody except himself.

On one occasion, a fashion correspondent observed the turn-ups on Tommy's tweed trousers and asked him if this meant turn-ups were 'making a comeback'. Tommy bristled at the line of enquiry. Going 'all formal', he replied, 'That's the sort of question I don't want to answer.' It went 'against the grain', he said. Having thus thrown the correspondent completely off balance, he then answered the question anyway. 'I think people will wear what they like . . . I certainly don't think turn-ups are coming back' – even though, yes, he happened to be wearing them.

Another time, a writer would ask about his clientele. What kind of people shopped at Nutters? 'Don't ask me for a list of names,' Tommy replied, saying this particular line of questioning was 'too naff' to be countenanced. However, he continued, *naff* was actually his 'favourite word', and probably destined to be the Word of the Seventies. Writing it down, the journalist asked him for a definition. Stone-faced, Tommy said it was difficult to explain . . . as though he weren't perfectly aware that *naff* was camp slang for 'boring', or 'straight', or even (though perhaps apocryphally) 'not available for fucking' – that is, NAFF.

Nevertheless, while Tommy enjoyed tying the media in knots, he was also determined to get *good* press. In late July, just five months after Nutters opened, the *Guardian* sent a columnist named Fiona MacCarthy to conduct an interview in the showroom. 'Are you sure the sleeve's not wrinkled?' Tommy fussed as he posed for a picture by the interior front window. The suit he was wearing, he explained to the photographer, looked best when he was standing, not sitting. MacCarthy observed this pantomime from the sidelines. 'He is very, very worried in case the camera catches him not looking quite his best,' she wrote. 'He is careful, oh so careful, about how the jacket's hanging and how the collar's sitting and the sharpness of his creases.' She then asked, 'But can anyone, even a top tailor, really truly always look completely perfect? Does he never once let up?'

'Well, yes,' Tommy admitted sheepishly. There were times 'when nobody's looking' that he might climb out of bed in the morning and pull on a pair of denim jeans.

MacCarthy was amused. This 'vision of reality', she finished drily, must 'restore one's faith in human nature. Even Thomas Nutter can't be bothered all the time.'

The album cover of *Abbey Road* (1969), by Iain Macmillan.

6

A COMPLETE LOOK

It was a clear, humid day in early August when a Scottish photographer named Iain Macmillan climbed a stepladder in the middle of a street in St John's Wood. As he fiddled with his Hasselblad, a policeman directed traffic, and the Beatles stood by the side of the road, impatient to get things over with. Linda McCartney snapped some behind-the-scenes shots. Paul adjusted the collar on Ringo's frock coat. Finally, they began to march, back and forth, over the zebra crossing, while Macmillan snapped a few frames: John out front, dressed in eye-catching white, followed by Ringo, Paul and George in a solemn procession. 'Come on, hurry up now, keep in step,' John barked. Too many people were hanging around for his liking, and he wanted to be back in the studio finishing the album, 'not posing for Beatles pictures'. After a few crossings, they paused to readjust. Paul lit a cigarette and kicked off his sandals. Later, conspiracy theorists would notice he'd gone barefoot, and notice, too, the VW Beetle parked in the background, and somehow deduce that all this was a secret visual code signifying that Paul McCartney was actually dead, and portrayed here by a body double. Really, he was just wilting in the heat and didn't feel like wearing shoes. The navy-blue double-breasted suit was quite enough, thank you.

McCartney would eventually select the fifth of six photographs Macmillan took that day for the album cover of *Abbey Road* – the one with their legs perfectly synchronised, mid-stride. George Harrison looked casual in his jeans and open-neck oxford shirt, but the other three matched in elegant bespoke. This was pure coincidence; nobody had told them to all dress in Nutters. Indeed, they'd just turned up wearing what they wanted to wear, the clothes that best expressed how they felt at that particular moment, when a hopeful decade was taking its final breaths, preparing to give way to a far more ambivalent one.

Within the first six months of opening, Nutters of Savile Row did the business Tommy had expected in a year. Within the first year, they sold more than 1,000 suits, about 470 of them to Americans who seemed to have no qualms about dropping several hundred hard-earned pounds for 'the Nutter line, and the Nutter cut and the Nutter fit and the Nutter style and the Nutter flair and the Nutter feel and the Nutter cloth'. In the cutting room, Edward struggled to keep up with the pace. 'It's been very hard work since we started here,' he told a reporter, a black-and-white tape measure curling around his neck. 'Long hours and everything. Very long hours.' Tommy complained that he no longer had time to do many of his favourite things. When he did find an evening to visit Covent Garden for a performance of *Giselle*, the French ballet in which men are forced to dance until they die from exhaustion, he moaned theatrically, as though he too were being worked straight into the grave: 'I haven't been for ages. I'm out of touch . . .'

By 1970, Tommy was boasting in his promotional literature that Nutters had already been mentioned by Johnny Carson on *The Tonight Show*, Carson having asked more than one of his high-profile guests where they'd bought their unusual suit and been told, 'Tommy Nutter'. The patronage of Cilla Black and the Beatles was invaluable, of course, but there was a longer list that revealed the breadth of his appeal: Eric Clapton, Peter Sellers, Lionel Bart, Kenneth Tynan, Tommy Tune, the Duke of Bedford, Leonore Annenberg, Pattie Boyd, and even Nancy Reagan, First Lady of California – or 'Mrs Ronald Reagan', as a press release referred to her. Robert Stigwood, the Australian entrepreneur and manager of the Bee Gees, had ordered eight summer suits in mohairs, silks and light worsteds. Twiggy had one made in crushed tomato velvet. David Hockney had a tweed check suit made in something like the colour of healthy gums, which he allowed Cecil Beaton to photograph him wearing with an op-art tie and mismatched socks (red and green). Once, a cutter at Nutters asked Hockney how he managed to achieve his rakish, crumpled look. Hockney replied, 'I don't have any hangers in my wardrobe.'

Prince Rajsinh of Rajpipla, son of the Maharaja of Rajpipla, a former princely state in the west of India, first noticed Nutters in a newspaper and stopped in because he wanted something fresh. 'Pippy', as his friends called him, soon commissioned a full range of clothes, including a contemporary twist on Indian formalwear: a modified Nehru-collar tunic that doubled as a dinner jacket. He was particularly taken with Tommy's method of working with his client. 'He would stand there and sketch something in two minutes, every detail,' Pippy recalls. 'You'd never seen anything like it. It was a gift. "Do you like this? You like that?" Tear it up! "Now, what about this?"'

Between trips to the racetrack, where Pippy preferred to spend his days, he became tight friends with Tommy and began accompanying him and Peter to restaurants like Provans, a fashionable eatery that had recently opened in a disused ladder storeroom next to Brompton Cemetery. Hidden up a rickety staircase, pop stars and influencers crowded together on rattan furniture in a narrow, unpretentious dining room, leaning over smoked haddock soufflés and giant platters of fresh vegetables that teetered precariously on bright yellow tablecloths. Thanks to its amiable host, Stewart Grimshaw, Provans soon became another crucial advertisement for Nutters: the slender, long-haired Scotsman would amass more than two hundred suits over the course of a few years, and share the name of his tailor whenever it was requested by one of his guests. As Grimshaw recalls, 'Tommy was prepared to indulge one's *whim*.'

And his own, inevitably. The relative restraint of Tony King's original suit quickly gave way to more ostentatious flights of fancy. For example, a green velvet jacket with brocade lapels. A reversible tweed coat with candy-orange trim. A grey-and-gold shooting suit. A waistcoat made from dozens of coloured patches painstakingly hand-stitched together. An evening jacket with an art deco shawl collar in white, green and burgundy. A biscuit-and-black-checked worsted Norfolk jacket, paired with puffy knickerbockers, for the man about town. Tommy made a signature out of braiding coats with grosgrain or Petersham ribbon, which outlined modern elements like the vast lapels and made them stand out even more brazenly. He also began to experiment with contrasting patterns and materials, so that a coat made from one thing might feature patch pockets and trim made from something entirely different, velvet and tweed, pinstripes offsetting a Tattersall check. Even on suits where the pattern was uniform, Tommy might turn it on the bias for flaps and pockets, making stripes go one way = and then another way // and then another way || to induce a sense of sartorial vertigo. 'A tailor should not be scared of giving his customers styles which may seem a little outrageous,' he claimed, adding that the two essentials for success were 'creativity and courage'.

Tommy combined contrasting patterns and materials on a single coat.

Checks might be turned on the bias to induce a
sense of sartorial vertigo.

By its first anniversary, Nutters was being described without irony in the *Daily Mail* as '*the* place for men's clothes . . . a whizz-bang success'. Meanwhile, Tommy was 'now in the class of actor Terence Stamp, photographer Brian Duffy, and hairdresser Vidal Sassoon, all the stylish young Londoners who have shot themselves out of their backgrounds and into the new aristocracy'. Within just twelve months, Tommy had transformed himself from a frustrated salesman with zero clout into an innovator who was being compared with defining figures of the era: a talented, preternaturally lucky peacock who bridged the gap between classic British tailor (praised by his peers as 'one of the best') and men's fashion designer.

For nearly a decade, Tommy had dreamed about dressing people 'the way I like to see them looking', about a look that 'changes people's personality' into what he thought they *should* be: graceful, liberated and bold. In Tommy's view, the hype and success that greeted Nutters was irrefutable proof that 'what I thought was good everyone else liked'. It vindicated his instincts, only making him more confident. 'What I am doing is what I want to do,' he affirmed. 'It's very nice to be able to live it all for real.'

Nutters of Savile Row may have been an instant hit among the famous and fashionable, but it was not reserved for their exclusive use. Indeed, the early order books were filled with 'a comprehensive cross section of the public', including lawyers, doctors, accountants and bankers. To cater to this demographic, Nutters also offered what Edward called 'Block Two', a somewhat quieter silhouette, less deliberately exaggerated, for professionals who wanted to be seen patronising a fashionable tailor without subverting conventions in the workplace *too* much. These were wealthy men, mostly self-made, who liked the quality of the past but felt no allegiance to its fusty stylings. At least two of them were over seventy years old.

Peter Sprecher, a young investment banker on holiday from Los Angeles, was walking down Savile Row in shorts and a T-shirt when he did a double take outside No. 35a. Framed in the window was, Sprecher recalls, 'this crazy suit': navy blue, pink lapels, with flared trousers in a box plaid. He had never been to a tailor before – 'never even thought about it' – but he was mesmerised by what he was seeing. He marched into the showroom and announced his intention to purchase the window display.

Tommy explained that it wasn't for sale.

Sprecher was confused. 'Well, how much is it?' he asked. 'I want to buy it.'

'No, let me explain,' Tommy said. 'We're *bespoke –* '

'But listen, I just want to buy the suit,' Sprecher said, cutting him off. 'So what do I have to do?'

Tommy said that there had to be several fittings, at least three, and that it would be quite expensive.

Sprecher was undeterred. 'OK, fine, I'll take it,' he said.

'No, let me explain,' Tommy repeated. 'We can't make the pattern just for one suit. You have to buy three suits.'

Three suits? Nobody needed three suits in California.

Tommy shrugged. 'It's a three-suit minimum.'

Sprecher placed the order. It was only later that he realised the 'three-suit minimum' was bogus, that Tommy was probably testing him because of the way he was dressed.

When the suits were finished, any indignation he may have felt at being hoodwinked immediately dissolved. 'They were absolutely the most beautiful suits I've ever seen, before or since,' Sprecher recalls. A little too warm for Los Angeles, but so stunning he would wear them anyway, with mini-platform shoes beneath the flares. As he strutted down the street, people would stare, mouths open. Sprecher didn't care. 'How do I say this? It made me feel that I was really *dressed*. Like I was wearing a piece of art.'

Back in the 1830s, nearly 140 years before any of this happened, Henry George Poole had been a young dilettante less interested in the technicalities of his father's tailoring business than in the hedonistic pleasures of London high society. Henry worked in the back room, assisting the head cutter; his heart, though, was set on the kind of lives enjoyed by the sons of gentlemen – on drawing rooms and fox hunts over sprawling country estates. James Poole was exasperated by his son's dreaminess, but he decided to make the best of a bad situation. He outfitted Henry in elegant bespoke, then sent him off to stalk the society he so craved in a bid to lure new clients back to the family business. Soon, before he was twenty-one years old, Henry was driving through Hyde

Park in his own horse-drawn phaeton. He was attending the Albrighton Hunt, then the Quorn Hunt. One night after dinner, over a game of billiards at the Earl of Stamford's house, he spied a guest wearing a badly made coat and used a piece of cue chalk to mark up corrections, telling the gentleman to take it to his father back in London for improvements. Charming and audacious, Henry Poole had known how to work a room. He understood the *value* in working a room. And he was so successful in his gambit that he would one day find himself at Compiègne, in the court of Napoleon III, with many people, the emperor included, wearing his clothes.

This was the strategy that Tommy now restored to Savile Row. As one onlooker noted, Nutter was 'definitely not the kind of tailor who appears with his chalk and his tape measure as if he has just been chained to a design bench all day'. Instead, like young Henry Poole, Tommy made socialising part of his job description – at restaurants, bars, gallery openings, even the Annual Snow Ball. He set out to know everybody worth knowing, and he became adept at subtly convincing them they needed their own Nutters look. When they would visit him on Savile Row, he would then listen to their requests, politely deferential, before steering them in the direction *he* wanted, because Tommy's guiding principle was to imagine how something would look if he were wearing it himself. Good? Then they could put it into production. Bad? Then nobody on earth could pull it off.

Edward's input usually began during the measurement stage. But here, too, Nutters diverged from the standard practice of other Savile Row firms. When Edward worked collaboratively with Tommy they could be like two lions toying with unsuspecting prey. They were unfailingly proper, of course; every client received impeccable service. But the duo practised decorum during a consultation or fitting while simultaneously satirising the pomposity of it all. 'Tommy and I used to have terribly funny games we'd play with each other,' Edward recalls. A man with prominent shoulder blades might have them traced out with whimsical loops of chalk. Or Tommy might come in 'looking all authoritative', evaluate the man's figuration, and then announce to Edward, in a tone of clinical concern, 'Crook in the elbows' – a mostly meaningless phrase. 'We put on a show for the person, and it would be hilarious,' Edward says. 'We'd fucking die.'

Behind the scenes, Edward would then need to become 'part engineer, part scientist' to surmount the tailoring challenges set by Tommy's imagination. In this he was aided by a staff of nearly two dozen workers, all of them under thirty, including Roy Chittleborough and Joseph Morgan, who both came aboard as his assistant cutters. Some of the workers – the Italians and Greek Cypriot boys – 'wanted to feel special', Joseph recalls, so Edward would have to 'give them a kiss and a cuddle' to get what he wanted in the work. But diva antics were mostly kept to a minimum, because everyone shared a common understanding: they'd all lived within the limitations of a traditional Savile Row firm, and they all appreciated how progressive, how *free*, Nutters was by comparison.

They also respected Tommy and Edward as bosses. Once, Joseph walked into the showroom for the final fitting of a white gaberdine suit. 'At a traditional tailor's, when the suit's finished, that's your suit, sir, off you go . . . But Edward and Tom started putting more pins in it. I thought, "We're remaking this thing!" But that was the integrity of the look and design they wanted to give out to their clients.' At a traditional tailoring firm, most subordinate workers would also never have encountered the clients face-to-face; they would have hid behind closed doors like the kitchen staff at Buckingham Palace. Nutters followed a more egalitarian philosophy, encouraging clients to meet the boys and appreciate the labour involved – or, as Edward puts it, 'the relationship *in* the garment'. A Nutters suit was more than Tommy Nutter; more even than Tommy Nutter and his brilliant head cutter. It embodied the skill and dedication of enough people to make up a football team.

Tommy liked to employ handsome young men. Even if they were straight, even if there was no chance in a million years, 'it always helped' to be good-looking, says Zance Yianni, who walked in off the street with next to no experience, scored a job as a trimmer, found himself promoted to striker, and then ended up running a Nutters workshop on Heddon Street.

To say that Nutters had a queer ambience is probably to state the

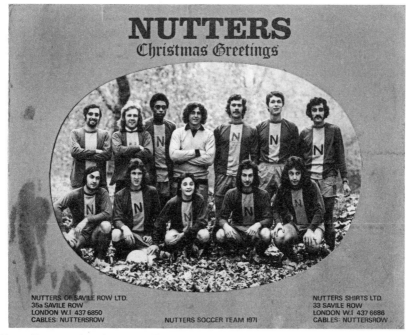

NUTTERS
Christmas Greetings

NUTTERS OF SAVILE ROW LTD.
35a SAVILE ROW
LONDON W.1 437 6850
CABLES: NUTTERSROW

NUTTERS SOCCER TEAM 1971

NUTTERS SHIRTS LTD.
33 SAVILE ROW
LONDON W.1 437 6686
CABLES: NUTTERSROW

Team Nutters played once, at Finsbury Park, against the Initial Towel Company, losing 11–1. 'And that was the end of that,' says Joseph Morgan (bottom row, second from right).

obvious. Because of Tommy, there was a considerable clientele of gay men, and it was not unusual for somebody to step into the showroom and begin describing their latest conquests regardless of who might be in earshot. 'I used to go in there, and Tommy would be holding court with some friends of his in a corner,' remembers James Vallance White. 'One did feel the whole thing was sometimes being run as Tommy's private club, rather than a business.' Frequent drop-ins included a local art dealer who sold voluptuous Rodin sculptures, and Manolo Blahnik, who saw a visit to Nutters as 'great fun, a great hoot, because Tommy always had wonderful stories and gossip'. Blahnik had yet to find his footing as a fashion designer, so Tommy – 'an amusing boy' – cut him a deal until he got ahead in life.

As for the atmosphere created by all this coming and going, Tommy made absolutely no effort to tone down the camp. If anything, he encouraged it by introducing elements of Polari into the workroom, a slang language that once allowed queer people to converse in public without being understood by their (potentially hostile) straight neighbours.

> *Vada the dolly dish with the big thews*
> Look at the handsome man with the big thighs

Tommy also corrupted those covert abbreviations tailors used to note bodily defects by inventing some new ones.

TBH   To be had

Given that most of the staff was heterosexual, this immersive education in a subculture that many of them had barely known existed could be, to put it mildly, disorientating. One day, an assistant cutter went out to conduct a fitting at a client's house, only to walk in on the client in bed with two other men. 'But hey,' says Joseph, slightly breathless at his memories, 'it's just London, and everything was full of energy.'

And once they got used to it, everyone in Tommy's staff seemed to accept the situation with good-natured equanimity. In this regard, perhaps they were following the example of Edward, who took to calling Tommy 'Pamela', or 'Pammie', as though it were an eminently reasonable nickname for his male colleague; he accepted the sobriquet of 'Roxanne' in response. 'Tommy enlarged our world,' Edward explains, speaking for himself and his wife. 'We'd sit there and smoke pot – '

'*Once*,' insists Joan.

' – and experience all that sort of life we would never have learned about otherwise.'

Zance Yianni, fresh-faced and open-minded, loved being pushed outside his comfort zone. Tommy would drag him to the clubs and throw him into the melee to see how he'd react in a frenzy of gay men. 'It was so glamorous, and so *wild*,' Zance recalls. 'It was almost as though they were just out of the closet, making the most of it, so they didn't give a damn. They were out there having fun.'

Sometimes Tommy could have a little *too* much fun. One evening, he attended a dinner party with Peter at a friend's house. When they arrived, walking through the door, it was immediately clear that something was wrong. One of the other guests thought Tommy looked terrible: a sickly shade of mustard yellow. Soon, during dinner, he confirmed her suspicion by announcing that he wasn't feeling particularly well. That he was weak and achy. Could barely move, actually. The host called for a doctor and installed him in a guest bedroom. Tommy would spend more than a week there, housebound in semi-quarantine, weathering the effects of a hepatitis infection.

During the extended period it took for him to make a full recovery, Nutters continued to operate under the stewardship of Edward, who now found himself both cutting *and* selling, an already substantial workload becoming even more formidable.

According to Edward, Peter soon acknowledged his tireless efforts by rewarding him with several appreciative gifts: a bottle of Eau Sauvage, by Christian Dior, which Edward would make his personal fragrance; a small stake in the company in the form of some shares; and promotion to the level of a company director, making Edward now one of six partners. Indeed, he is described as 'a director of Nutters' by Tommy in a newspaper as early as 20 January 1970.

Nevertheless, Peter rejects the details of this account. 'It's very strange that I, as the controlling shareholder, don't remember that,' he says. In Peter's recollection, no shares were redistributed while Tommy was convalescing. 'And there's no way that Edward was a partner while I was in control.'

When it came to his partnership with Tommy, Peter had not really been in control for a while, a fact that was signalled most clearly by a change in their residence. The Conduit Street flat, though beautiful and well positioned, had only a single bedroom. And somewhere along the line both of them had become '*distracted*', as Peter puts it, and ceased sleeping together. They remained companions and confidants, even functional family – but they were no longer lovers. The passion had evaporated, perhaps as early as 1969. Still, except for a fleeting moment when Tommy had declared that he 'couldn't put up with it any longer', there was never any question that the two of them would part. They liked living together; it felt right. They just had to make some minor adjustments.

By now, a two-bedroom flat had been found in Hays Mews, a few streets further west in Mayfair. While nowhere near as lovely as the place in Conduit Street, it afforded them privacy and intimacy in more acceptable proportions. Since the move, life had resumed its regular routine: Peter had begun throwing dinner parties for his famous friends again, while Tommy let his own friends sleep over, like old times, and decorated the sitting-room walls with his original abstract paintings.

For all intents and purposes, Peter and Tommy remained loyally committed to each other. This was put on public display in October, when both men found themselves travelling independently to New York. Peter arrived on a business trip for Apple; Tommy, touching down in America for the very first time, arrived to represent Britain at *Playboy*'s Creative Menswear International Designer Collection, a tweed knickerbocker suit with full-length cape stuffed inside his luggage.

Tommy stayed with Hardy Amies in his penthouse apartment on West Fifty-Eighth Street. Amies threw a cocktail party to introduce Tommy, like a debutante, to the city's fashion and design set: Bill Blass, Vera Maxwell, Valerian Rybar. 'It turned out just the way you'd expect it to when one Englishman gives a party for another Englishman,' a gossip columnist quipped afterwards. 'It was all too much for young Nutter.'

But Peter was there to lend his support. He accompanied Tommy to the *Playboy* gala at the Plaza Hotel, sweeping down a grand staircase as part of an awkward-looking threesome, Amies leading the way with an imperious scowl. 'Hardy never liked me because he fancied Tommy,

Tommy and Peter on Jones Beach, in Nassau County, New York.

and I was Tommy's boyfriend,' Peter recalls. 'He would always call me "Peter Baker", just to annoy me. Which I purposely tried *not* to be annoyed about.'

A month after Tommy returned to London, a photograph of him appeared in *Vogue* under the title 'Checking Out the Men'. Dressed in a white shirt and tie, his hair perfectly coiffed, he bites down on a cigar and projects what the writer describes as 'a cheery, cheeky, insouciant sort of look' – a flirtatious twinkle in his eye, smugness in his square jawline. 'It makes us want to add him to our Christmas list this minute.'

By December, Tommy was feeling very sure of his abilities and prospects. A little too sure, perhaps; the adulation had started to go to his head. 'Many Savile Row tailors have recently been amalgamating or going in with each other in order to streamline the efficiency and economics of their operations,' he told *Men's Wear*, confidently setting himself apart. 'I've wanted to expand for some time now.' Old Savile

Row was spluttering, in other words, while he shot out in front. The rush of success made him feel impervious, and he began to press his foot down even harder on the accelerator.

One of these recent amalgamations had left a showroom empty on Savile Row at No. 33, just two doors down from Nutters. Tommy now convinced the partners to let him lease it for a business extension. He installed the familiar glass frontage with large stencilled letters, then lined the interior with chrome scaffolding. He appointed Christopher Tarling, his ex-boyfriend, to be the store manager, and announced to the media: 'There's no limit to what we'll sell at the shop. It is really a personal thing, and there will be no rules concerning merchandise. If I see something I like, I'll sell it.' Even more clearly than at No. 35a, what this new accessories boutique was peddling was Tommy's particular taste: Liberty-print shirts with cutaway collars; kimono-style dressing gowns; hand-knitted pullovers and hand-knitted argyle socks; over-sized newsboy caps; and dandyish silk scarves with a monogrammed *N*, like Louis Vuitton, or something Quentin Crisp might choose to wear.

Years before Giorgio Armani and Ralph Lauren, Tommy's ambition was nothing less than to create 'full wardrobes with a complete look and style for our patrons'. He hoped Nutters Shirts, following another lavish launch party, with champagne and sprays of flowers, would be the first of many expansions under the Tommy Nutter name – an international franchise, eventually. World domination.

The counterculture would not go down without a fight.

7

BLOW-UP

According to Eleanor Lambert, an influential fashionista and the founder of New York Fashion Week, Thomas Nutter was one of the sharpest dressers in the world by 1971, when he first appeared on her International Best Dressed List alongside names like Hubert de Givenchy and Sophia Loren. 'The common denominator of all the winners is durability,' explained Eugenia Sheppard in the *New York Post*. 'They go everywhere, and their faces and fashions become familiar to all those who watch or read.' This was an auspicious vote of confidence at the start of what *Vogue* was titling 'A Gentleman's Year', the year during which a decade of 'good, healthy fury and change' would finally settle down and allow men to 'revel in the rewards of the male evolution'. Having thoroughly established his bona fides, Tommy seemed poised to reap the benefits.

First, though, a personal upheaval: open boxes were scattered around the Hays Mews flat, half filled with worldly possessions.

Peter was leaving.

On New Year's Eve, Paul McCartney had initiated proceedings in the High Court to legally dissolve the Beatles. Writs had been served to John, George, Ringo, and Apple Corps, as their parent company, formalising the animosity that had swelled and stoppered any meaningful collaboration between the group members since their *Abbey Road* sessions. Paul was suing his way out. At the same time – in fact, the very same day – Peter handed in his resignation, though it had been coming for a while. The arrival of Allen Klein, who became the Beatles' manager in 1969, had transformed Peter's role as 'nurse' following

Brian's death into something more akin to an unwilling executioner. A ruthless, avaricious bully, Klein had forced Peter to purge Apple Corps through mass lay-offs, emptying out the Savile Row headquarters in the name of cost-cutting. Peter hated being forced into complicity, hated the atmosphere it created at Apple ('a mausoleum just waiting for a death'), and hated Klein, above all, who would have pushed him out as well if he thought the Beatles would allow it. And then, suddenly, Paul wasn't speaking to John, Peter recalls, 'and I was in a difficult situation there because I was torn: they were both expecting my loyalty. We'd all worked together over the years very intimately, like a *family*, so it was torturous for me.' Eventually, enough was enough. Peter handed in his notice. Then he told the *Evening News*, 'I have had an experience which has been invaluable. I sometimes think of it as a crash course in survival.'

The boxes in Hays Mews were destined for Manhattan. Peter was taking a job with the Robert Stigwood Organisation, as president of a newly formed US branch that would deal with music and theatre productions. It was an exciting, challenging opportunity, and it promised a fresh start. On 22 January, Cilla threw her friend a farewell party, which Peter thought was a huge success. Ringo came to bid adieu, though the other Beatles failed to make an appearance.

But what about Tommy? In the *Evening News*, the journalist made a careful allusion for readers able to spot the pattern in some judiciously arranged details: '[Peter] is, at 33, unmarried, and plans to leave his cat Clarence with his good friend, Savile Row tailor Tommy Nutter.'

In fact, Peter planned to leave his 'good friend' with something more substantial than the cat. He knew that overseeing Nutters from New York would be impractical, if not downright impossible. He could sell his stake to a new investor, but that could go wrong down the road. And Peter was feeling benevolent; he wanted to give Tommy ownership of the company. True, none of the partners had yet been reimbursed for their initial investment, but they'd done very well in bespoke clothes. Peter pointed this out when he raised his idea with the others: Why didn't they all (Cilla, Bobby, James and himself) surrender their shares as a combined gift? It would be a sweet gesture, and Tommy needed the asset more than they did. 'That was my whole logic,' Peter recalls.

Edward, however, offers an alternative take. 'They were guaranteeing the bank loan, and they didn't want to guarantee the bank loan any more because the company needed money.' Handing over their shares was a way for the backers to absolve themselves of any financial responsibility at a moment when the business seemed to be inflating at a rapid rate. 'Otherwise, can you imagine Peter Brown, Bobby Willis, just giving up on it? They didn't want to finance the business any more. And a part of it was because some rush spending had been done.'

James Vallance White agrees with Edward's recollection – 'I was actually getting rather worried,' he says – but again, Peter dissents. 'As far as I remember, everything was in good shape. Why would I give Tommy a failing situation? It wasn't my style. I would *never* have done that. I gave him my part and persuaded the others to do the same, because now he would have something to live off. And also, I suppose, now that I'm thinking about it: maybe I had a little guilt about walking out and leaving him behind. At least I was leaving him with a business.'

Judging by his actions, Tommy weathered the radical change in his life with stoic acceptance. As Peter prepared to make his transatlantic migration, Tommy moved into a new one-bedroom flat back on Conduit Street. He then decorated it with the reckless abandon of somebody who has never lived alone before, who is excited by the prospect of living alone. He added road lamps, a geisha doll, more Clarice Cliff ceramics and art deco furniture. He co-opted a mannequin's leg for use as a flowerpot. He covered the walls with bright, lacquered collages, and upholstered the couch cushions in leftover suiting cloth. He hired an Irish cleaning lady, Bridie Mullen, who thought his taste in decor was 'unusual', but 'trendy'. By his own admission, Tommy was 'desperately untidy' at home, but Bridie would pick up his clothes without complaint, and she'd make sure he had enough clean socks and wine glasses (the two essentials). She liked him and his friends, who refused to treat her like a servant, even after one of their messy all-night parties. With Bridie watching his back, Tommy continued to function like a somewhat responsible adult. He showed up for work on Savile Row. He became momentarily obsessed with lightweight Bermuda shorts, until he was accused of a patent violation, at which point he dropped them.

Life went on.

And then, one evening in February, a few weeks after Peter had departed for the airport, Tommy went to the Tate Gallery. A new Andy Warhol exhibition was being advertised around London with a poster of Marilyn Monroe's garishly painted face. For a limited six-week run, the galleries would be filled with Campbell's Soup cans, race riots, car crashes, cow wallpaper – a 'world of death and flowers' that constituted a serious solo show for the acclaimed American pop artist. Serious enough, at any rate, to warrant a major celebration for patrons and supporters. Tommy arrived at around 9.30 p.m. with a group of his friends, including Stewart Grimshaw, the owner of Provans.

He did not have a ticket to the party. Everyone else had a ticket, but not Tommy. The group had strategised in advance, though, and come up with a plan of attack. They would hand the Tate staff what looked like an approximately accurate number of tickets, and then, en masse, as an amorphous scrum, shuffle inside with Tommy as a stowaway.

No chance. The Tate staff sorted the tickets and separated Tommy out from his friends.

Faced with the prospect of humiliation, Tommy did not react well. He turned and, without a moment's hesitation, fled back towards the road. Stewart watched in horror as Tommy dodged traffic across busy Millbank. He reached the embankment on the other side, heaved himself up, onto the wall – and then threw himself into the Thames.

'We all gasped,' recalls Stewart.

His friends ran after him. Stewart expected to see Tommy being swept away in the notoriously strong current. Yet he arrived at the embankment and peered over the edge to find Tommy just down below, poking out of the mud in his tweed suit.

Was this another tantrum – an 'almost Shakespearean overreaction' (as his brother recalls it) to being rejected from a society event? Was Tommy drunk? Or did the rash act suggest a more unsettled emotional state?

Like the episode on Hydra several years before, Tommy wriggled his way out of proper explanations. He would refuse to discuss it, except, perhaps, in dark jokes about suicide thwarted by a low tide.

A rope was fetched. Some calls were made. One to Christopher Tarling, who was told that Tommy was being taken to the hospital with something broken – a rib, or maybe an arm. Another went to Peter, who (he recalls) received a frantic message from Edward at the shop: 'He jumped into the Thames!' Peter had lived with Tommy for so long through similar episodes of operatic drama – an arrest in Hyde Park for 'importuning'; a half-arsed drug overdose after Tommy caught him fooling around with another designer – that people assumed Tommy was still his responsibility. Well, not any more.

'What can I do?' Peter replied. 'I'm in New York.'

Rewind to March 1969: John Lennon and Yoko Ono's wedding in Gibraltar. Sitting on the executive jet, laughing as they drifted high above the rolling topography of Europe, David managed to strike up a rapport with the couple. Encouraged by Peter, this rapport had then catapulted him through several months as a semi-official photographer. David trailed the group – Lennon, in particular – like the press corps of a US president. In other words, Tommy was not the only Nutter to be directly affected by the dissolution of the Beatles.

Just four weeks after the Gibraltar wedding, David was standing on the roof at Apple Corps witnessing John change his name before a Commissioner of Oaths to John Winston *Ono* Lennon. Later that day, David accompanied the couple to the studios on Abbey Road, where he watched them work on a track for their upcoming *Wedding Album*, an avant-garde recording of them calling out each other's name over audio of their heartbeats. John and Yoko lay on the floor to apply a hospital microphone so sensitive it picked up the entire moist symphony of their internal organs; as John lifted his shirt, David snapped a picture. Back in the darkroom, David then made his own experimental composition using an enlarger, splicing the image with a second frame showing clouds over a London skyline.

John and Yoko in the clouds over Primrose Hill.

Another day, David returned to the Apple Corps roof to shoot John for the cover of a proposed Penguin book – a sequel to *In His Own Write* and *A Spaniard in the Works*, full of poetry and nonsense. The book was fast abandoned, though David kept the picture anyway: John's face, almost serenely blank, deliberately elongated 'to make him look more like Jesus'. (David had appreciated Lennon's irreverent comment more than the American evangelicals.) The photo proved a nice complement to an X-ray that John soon procured of his own head. He asked David to make a positive print; David complied, but also duplicated the X-ray, and then superimposed John's eyes and wire-frame spectacles from the previous cover shot. In effect, without quite planning it, David created a startling twin portrait of Lennon at a moment of profound transformation, a moment when he was asserting his identity as an artist separate from the Beatles.

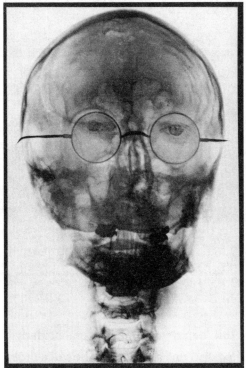

David's twin portrait of John Lennon, 1969.

David would put these two pictures in a drawer, showing almost no-body – not even John and Yoko – for several decades. In his view, they were nothing particularly extraordinary, just something made to pass the time. Like Tommy with his suits, the impulse to create just flowed naturally, the unfiltered expression of some basic instinct. Though his images were unquestionably art, David had no aspirations to be considered an artist. He was just reimagining the world through a Nutter lens, daydreaming in his darkroom.

Over the next few months, David would complete several other assignments either for or around the Beatles. He photographed Pattie Boyd, George Harrison's wife, at the Glyndebourne opera house in East Sussex. He snapped Mary Hopkin, the Welsh folk singer, not long after the release of her first studio album, which was produced by Paul McCartney. When John Lennon crashed his car in the Scottish High-lands, David was part of the entourage that collected his family from the airport. And then, on 20 September, while hanging out in the Apple offices, David was grabbed by Peter, pulled into a room, and directed to document something that would prove momentous.

Happy scene at Apple Records this week—John Lennon, Paul McCart-ney and Ringo Starr are pictured with business manager Allen Klein, and John's wife Yoko Ono, after the signing of the contract giving the Beatles increased royalties from Capitol Records (EMI's U.S. out-let), and other benefits. George Harrison, due to sign soon, was away in Liverpool at the bedside of his sick mother. — Picture by Beatles friend David Nutter.

In truth, this 'happy scene' was not particularly happy, and its most pressing subject was not the renegotiation of a record contract, but the beginning of the end. Lennon announced to the room, 'The group is over, I'm leaving.' Paul McCartney's smile masked his shell shock. 'We paled visibly and our jaws slackened a bit,' he later recalled.

At this point it would still be more than another full year before Paul filed his lawsuit in the High Court (a year during which he, too, would announce his departure from the group, though a little more publicly than John had). But David knew that he'd reached his own stop on the Beatles Express. 'Bad timing,' he says. 'Everything fell apart.'

In 1970, David's business was prosperous enough that he could turn his attention elsewhere. He landed a regular gig photographing musical acts for the BBC. He worked for Rod McKuen, the bestselling poet and songwriter, during McKuen's album collaboration with Rock Hudson (and consoled McKuen when Hudson ignored his romantic advances). David also worked as a printer for *Harper's Bazaar*, which would take him to Paris on incredibly tight deadlines. The magazine would phone, and David would rush across the Channel to a hotel with a makeshift darkroom. Then a fashion house – Yves Saint Laurent, say – would release its season collection to a media queue: first to newsprint, because it was more immediate publicity; and afterwards to the magazines in a variable rank, so *Harper's* might be given a collection after *Queen*, or before *Vogue*. Staff would sit up all night waiting for the clothes to arrive, photograph them quickly but meticulously, then ship them off to the next group awaiting its turn. Meanwhile, David would develop negatives and produce contact sheets, even if it happened to be three o'clock in the morning. This was thrilling work: he found himself collaborating with extraordinary photographers like Hiro, Frank Horvat and a young Bill King. It was also terrifying work, as his partner Carlo Manzi recalls: 'Can you imagine fucking up the film?'

But after the Beatles job fizzled, the thing that brought David the most genuine satisfaction was *Oz* – a 'monument to psychedelia', as Richard Neville, the Australian editor, once described the glossy underground magazine with gorgeous graphic design.

First published in Sydney in 1963, *Oz* had launched in Britain four years later and rapidly became infamous for its uncensored engagement with anything taboo (gay issues) or transgressive (the fierce feminism of Germaine Greer). It was not unusual to find a poem about revolution by D. H. Lawrence; an article on 'the biggest tool in show-biz' (ten inches, belonging to Roddy McDowall); a faux advertisement for a 'yum-yum rubber fun substitute'; a classified ad promising 'Gay Young Men with Style & Pose & Lack of Clothes'; and a real court transcript with 'CONSPIRACY' watermarked across the page – all in a single issue. Indeed, nothing was too extreme for inclusion in *Oz*. Not a 'barechested long-hair' sticking a needle into his arm, not a couple simulating sex as a baby watched on from beside their dirty mattress. When the mainstream media complained about the content, *Oz* simply incorporated the angry headlines into future issues. *People,* for example, once published a notice to parents: 'Your kid may pick up a magazine in a discotheque or a record shop. It will look way out, switched on and hippie.' *Oz* took the warning and turned it into a special lift-out souvenir poster. The magazine seemed immune to criticism, swallowing everything into itself, like the Blob, only growing bigger and more threatening.

David adored all this flagrant insolence. While hardly a hippie himself, he appreciated anything that agitated for a more open-minded conversation by treating alternative lifestyles as legitimate sources of joy. In this regard, *Oz* was '*so* important', David thought. It seemed to embody the radical potential of the entire previous decade. Reading it made him feel like there were other people out there who understood what was possible.

When David met the magazine's art director, Jim Anderson, out in a gay bar, he confessed his admiration for the cause. Anderson liked what he heard, so David soon found himself working with the *Oz* art department as a photographer-at-large.

Anderson and the other editors gave David free rein to create the images he wanted. For one shoot, an Anderson/Nutter co-production, a woman held up an axe and a severed penis (represented by a strap-on dildo) while wearing a sash that proclaimed 'Pussy Power'. For another, a naked woman straddled the shoulders of a man who had somehow misplaced his trousers. The man was Carlo, David's business partner. 'We were set up to do the cover in our studio,' Carlo recalls, 'and the editor said, "The male model has pulled out, so you're going to do it."

'I said, "What do I care? You can sit a naked girl on my shoulders."'

White arrows were then scrawled all over David's final print, diagnosing Carlo with watery eyes (glue sniffing), hand tremors (amphetamines), disorientation (barbiturates) and 'diminution of genital area' (cocaine).

Oz, No. 34

On 22 April 1970, David arrived at Jim Anderson's house to photograph an inside spread for *Oz*, No. 28: 'The Schoolkids Issue'. Recently, the magazine had published a small advertisement: 'Some of us at *Oz* are feeling old and boring. So we invite any of our readers who are under 18 to come and edit the April issue . . .' Now, in an overgrown backyard budding with hollyhocks, a dozen or so teenagers gathered around Richard Neville as he sat in a garden chair waving a stick like a headmaster. The teenagers were all guest editors, and this, Neville later explained, was a parodic class portrait. 'On my left knelt Berti, a fifteen-year-old from Aldershot who was sweet and pretty, and dreamed of living in a commune. Beside her was Vivian Berger, sixteen, the wildest of the bunch, a self-proclaimed anarchist who claimed to have smoked pot at nine and tripped at eleven.' As some Russians played volleyball over the fence, David stood behind his tripod, snapping pictures of the unruly mob. None of the teenagers, smiling and horsing around, had any idea how poorly their work was about to be received. Neither did David.

The gang behind *Oz*, No. 28: 'The Schoolkids Issue'.

'The Schoolkids Issue' came out in May, covered in naked women. Among other things, it featured masturbation, spanking, tips for survival during the apocalypse, 'Jail Bait of the Month', and (most egregiously in the eyes of authorities) a comic strip of Rupert Bear penetrating a virgin.

In early June, police raided the *Oz* offices under the Obscene Publications Act.

In October, Richard Neville, Jim Anderson and Felix Dennis found themselves standing in the Marylebone Magistrates' Court for a preliminary hearing on charges of obscenity. As *The Times* later explained: 'The five charges against the three men and the company, Oz Publications Ink Ltd, were conspiring with certain other young persons to produce a magazine containing obscene, lewd, indecent and sexually perverted articles, cartoons, drawings and illustrations with intent to debauch and corrupt the morals of children and other young persons and to arouse and implant in their minds lustful and perverted desires.'

Refusing to take the charges seriously, the editors turned up dressed as little schoolboys, complete with satchels and caps, and sent *Oz* subscribers gilt-edged invitations to attend the first in a series of 'obscene court room dramas – fancy dress optional – RSVP Scotland Yard'.

The trial of *Oz* properly kicked off the following summer. Just before it did, David invited the three editors to his studio in Primrose Hill to express his contempt for so-called justice through a subversive photo shoot.

David showed his solidarity with the *Oz* editors using his camera.

The trial ran for six weeks. Its circus-like atmosphere – 'a touch of reefer madness in the dock', as Neville would later write – made it an immediate sensation. At one point, Judge Michael Argyle told the jury not to worry unduly if they didn't understand everything: 'Neither do I. We shall get a grip on it as we go along.' Another time, George Melly, the pop critic and jazz musician, was put on the stand and asked to define 'cunnilingus'. Melly offered: 'Gobbling, going down, sucking off. Or as we used to call it in the Navy, "yodelling in the canyon."' Melly was also quizzed about why he thought the magazine was even being prosecuted. 'It couldn't be about the alleged pornography – there's too much of that about elsewhere,' Melly replied. 'So it's really a trial about an attitude to life.'

This liberal attitude to life, fertilised by a decade of remarkable progress in terms of sexual and personal freedoms, was actually on trial in more places than just the Old Bailey. Earlier that year, two Christian missionaries, returned to Britain after a long residency in India, had founded a nationwide 'Festival of Light' to counteract what they saw as an appalling degeneracy in moral standards. Their targets were por-nography, abortion and homosexuality: basically anything *Oz* maga-zine treated as either intriguing or important. Holding a series of rallies in places like Hyde Park, the festival organisers denounced sex and vio-lence in the media while simultaneously promoting a return to biblical teachings – that is, a straight, conservative (and bourgeois) existence with traditional gender roles.

Many people on the left pushed back against this kind of regressive moralising. In what amounted to an overnight culture war, the Festival of Light was attacked by members of the Gay Liberation Front, who organised under the code name 'Operation Rupert' (after the lascivious bear). The GLF swarmed at least one festival rally in drag and released white mice through the righteous crowds. At another rally, a Reverend Father Fuck (of the Church of Aphrodite, in Tooting) set up a sacrificial altar and served out slices of a cannabis cake baked in the shape of a giant phallus; he then joined hands with his friends and danced 'Ring a Ring o' Roses' among the outraged Christians. Meanwhile, at the *Oz* trial, stink bombs were thrown outside the courthouse, and an effigy of

Judge Argyle was set ablaze while the crowd chanted, 'Roast pig, roast pig, roast pig . . .'

As the *Oz* editors were sentenced to prison for up to fifteen months each, David, appalled by the verdict – which was, after all, also a verdict on his *own* work – documented the pandemonium that erupted in response.

Peaceful disobedience outside the Old Bailey.

The counterculture would not go down without a fight. And yet, in David's fatalistic view, it would go down all the same. Indeed, the best of it had already started to fade. 'It was wonderful in the days of Carnaby Street and the hippies, but at the end of the decade I found it all becoming so boring.'

Nor was David the only one to feel that way. John Lennon and Yoko Ono, disgusted with the persecution of *Oz* (and various other things, including the Troubles in Northern Ireland), packed their bags in September. 'It's like 1940 here,' John complained on his way out the door to New York. 'It's really the sticks, you know.' London was over, Britain was over, and the seventies were 'gonna be America's'.

Riding a wave of popular support, the *Oz* editors immediately appealed the verdicts. Finally, in November, the Appeal Court chief justice reversed their convictions and dismissed the prison sentences, even though the three men showed up to his courtroom wearing luxurious Regency hairpieces. It was a huge moment, a stunning reprieve for free speech; *Oz* supporters were ecstatic. David marched in the victory parade behind a giant penis.

Nevertheless, he was not in much of a mood to celebrate himself.

When asked why NUTTER LABORATORIES & STUDIOS collapsed around the exact same time the *Oz* trial was wrapping up, David offers two possibilities. His depression was worse than ever; maybe his drinking, which he'd begun to use as a form of self-medication, damaged one too many business relationships. It is hard to develop quality prints when you can barely focus the enlarger.

Or maybe the business was no longer making enough money because Carlo, instead of helping with the work, 'just sat around languidly smoking cigarettes'.

Carlo remembers things a little differently. 'The issue that made us part company was that David was having arguments with his boyfriend, and one day he came in and said his boyfriend has smashed all the cameras. As I recall, I said, "David, that's the final straw. We're not doing enough business to be able to carry this kind of aggravation, so let's call it a day."' (To which David responds: 'It was an impossible alcoholic relationship with an African Muslim named Ismaila. Only one camera was broken, and it was seldom used anyway.')

Whatever the true cause of the break-up, it meant that David, marching along behind that giant penis, was now unattached, disillusioned and suddenly floundering in his career, with no sense of direction at the tail end of 1971.

Perhaps it was inevitable that his thoughts would turn westward. He had dreamed of New York since the 1950s, swooning over *West Side Story* with Tommy at the matinees. In 1965, on his first American holiday, he had passed through the city and been electrified by its 'erotic' charge. New York's clandestine gay scene, concealed behind curtains to dissuade the police from raids, had seemed particularly attractive to a rebellious twenty-six-year-old. On a more recent visit, David had encountered the *new* New York, renegotiating its social boundaries after the Stonewall riots, which had only made him desire it even more for its atmosphere of defiant queerness. New York was the dream place – 'the Rome of today', as Lennon called it – while London seemed to be drifting backwards towards its old grey conservatism. It was time to go.

Just before Christmas, David worked up the courage to tell his parents; Dolly and Christopher were more remote than ever from the lives of their two sons. He said goodbye to Tommy, who took the surprising news well, considering it was only ten months since Peter's exodus to Manhattan. David then packed up everything he could carry, including so many photography samples that he exceeded the maximum weight allowance at Heathrow. Thankfully, a sympathetic stewardess let him board the plane anyway. Perhaps she recognised wild-eyed desperation when she saw it.

It was only after David arrived in New York, stepping out of the terminal into a frigid chill, a million new plans racing through his mind, that he realised he'd forgotten to bring a coat.

Tomcat at Piccadilly Circus.

8

PICCADILLY TOM

'It seems that at the moment we are in a transitional stage as far as the fashion business is concerned, something of a pause.'

Six industry hotshots – tailors, designers, consultants – were gathered around a table with cups of tea to discuss the future of menswear for *Tailor & Cutter* magazine, which would publish a full, unedited transcript of their lengthy talk, as though it were a groundbreaking inquest.

'I do think that we are now in an age of a non-suit,' said one of the gentlemen. 'I rather like it, because I am a bit bored with the ordinary jacket and trousers.'

'You're bored,' said a fashion consultant, 'but is the customer?'

'Well, they obviously have to be educated,' replied the gentleman.

'How does one do that?'

'Bags of publicity, I would suppose, and offering it to them in a way to make it attractive.'

Finally, Tommy interjected. 'I don't find that fashionable people are bored with the suit,' he said. Take his hugely successful silhouette at Nutters, for example: 'We try to change the look of it, but it is still a sort of classical suit, with wider lapels, more shaped.' When the Nutters look first appeared, people were 'horrified', sure, 'but now lapels are getting much wider', he said.

'Can they get any wider?' asked the fashion consultant.

'Well, they can overlap,' Tommy said, 'but I think it would look rather hideous.'

Seated near him was a cutter named Eric Joy, who ran his own business from Old Burlington Street. An irascible, brilliant craftsman, Joy had worked at Blades before an epic argument with the other directors caused him to walk out. He liked to be contrarian, and now he began challenging the basic premise of the discussion, that fashion and tailoring were interlinked. 'This whole fashion concept is not valid when you are talking about the classical suit,' he declared grandly to the table. 'Somebody claims that they are designing a fashionable suit – it's just a different suit from what is being sold at the time. Forget about these highfalutin words like fashion, etc.'

Then he started to needle his neighbour. 'One particular shop develops a sort of a look and gets noted for it,' Joy said, 'and in its time the fashion writers and journalists will adopt it as their sort of scene. They will say this is what we like, and they will zoom somebody to the top of the tree as being fashionable. Two years later, you think whatever happened to so-and-so?'

Everyone knew who Joy was talking about. 'That's an interesting point,' said the fashion consultant. 'How important is this sort of publicity? Tommy, you've had quite a bit of it of late.'

'It helps a lot,' Tommy said. He was proud of his press, both at home and in America, and he was not about to shrug it off as valueless.

'The bespoke industry is getting smaller and smaller,' Joy mused.

'Yes,' agreed Barry Grigg, a cloth designer who was friends with Tommy and presently wearing one of his suits, 'because tailors have done very little about being with it . . .'

Joy was having none of that. 'The reason the tailor is part of a dying breed has nothing to do with his fashion sense at all,' he snapped. 'It is the fact that he is an incompetent and incapable man. Time has passed him by.'

But what about Tommy? He started with a look 'which was probably ahead of its time', Grigg noted.

'Hopefully it was,' Tommy added, though he preferred to think of his look as transcending time – certainly the trends of bespoke tailoring.

But all this talk seemed to bore him. Tommy fell silent for a moment. Then he became defensive. 'I just do what I like. I am creating clothes in a look I like.' He designed his look with Edward several years ago, 'and we are still doing it. We put some braids on now to outline the shape, and it has become our most popular seller. I don't care what anyone else does . . . I will stick with what I am doing because I like the look of it.'

'That is the most dangerous thing in the world for a designer to do: to like something he has designed,' said Joy. 'You must be absolutely indifferent.'

But indifference was not part of Tommy's nature. He had poured his soul into his work to produce something that combined the person he was with the person he wished to be: why wouldn't he be attached to that?

'You don't mind being copied?' asked the fashion consultant.

'It's a compliment,' Tommy said. 'When Saint Laurent and another designer in Paris came out with a collection in which most things were braided, I was very flattered.'

But what about the lost income that comes with being copied? Tommy didn't care; making money was almost an afterthought. He was 'the originator of a certain style', he said, 'which is built upon my name.'

Joy dismissed this idea with a patronising swipe. 'Tommy, you're labouring under illusions of youth, that you create a look and think you will be known for that look. If somebody knocks it off, they take it and say thank you very much.'

'Even if we have our styles and looks pinched,' Tommy argued, 'at least we have created something for which we will be known. I am known for the look I have designed, and obviously I hope to benefit from the publicity.'

'You're labouring under a tremendous illusion,' said Joy.

⎯⎯⎯⎯⎯⎯

At the beginning of 1972, Britain found itself experiencing a curious crisis. On 9 January, the country's coal miners went on strike because of a pay dispute with the Conservative government, led by Prime Minister

Edward Heath. The National Union of Mineworkers wanted a substantial pay rise, but Heath was resistant. There was frustration, a stand-off, stalled negotiations; by the middle of February, there was a state of emergency. The miners had picketed power stations and other sources of fuel. Trains were suspended, bank trading hours reduced, and milk deliveries cut back. The weather was icy, and rolling blackouts began plaguing London and the rest of the country: the Central Electricity Generating Board was trying to ration its dwindling resources. As elsewhere, Savile Row was plunged into darkness, sometimes for up to nine hours at a stretch. At No. 35a, Tommy lit gas lamps around the show-room, trying to fill the space with a cosy glow; with work all but impossible under such circumstances, he then sat down at his desk, and began to write a 'little notette'.

> *Dear David*
> *Thanks for letter. Glad everything is going all right for you!*
> *We are still very busy but are being hit by power cuts*

From the moment David moved to New York, Tommy began a correspondence with his brother that is remarkable for its breadth and candour. Over the previous few years they had drifted apart, dwelling in separate circles that occasionally overlapped like a Venn diagram. But now that David was gone, physically, Tommy set about restoring the relationship to its former intimacy.

> *Went over to Eresby Road last Sund with Jimmy in the Central*
> *Heating Van*

His early letters have the quality of two brothers back in their childhood bedroom, sharing banal talk of holidays, another trip to Europe, the blazing Mediterranean sun ('She became very tanned!' Tommy writes of himself). There is tender concern for David's debilitating moods ('Hope you are working hard and not having too many UPS and DOWNS'), as well as regular suggestions to check in with 'Miss B' – Peter Brown, who was used to dealing with manic characters. There are also frank discussions of sex: 'Not much trade but a few members hovering. Had a big black beauty that you would have liked called Marion? He is a model from New York . . .' And appreciative nods to the other thing uniting them, that Nutter sensibility: 'If you have any ideas photo-wise, writing-wise, or art-wise, let me know. Perhaps we could get something published together.'

On this occasion, though, Tommy began by writing about their parents, whom he'd recently visited with his friend Jimmy Clark, who worked for British Gas (thus the van).

> *They were thrilled & Gran came down & Jim looked at her bits of old glass. Some of them are worth something. Took away a lovely old sepia photo of Mum which I will frame and put next to Twiggy's in the flat. The flat is great now – very respectable. Wall to wall curtains etc.*

But Tommy was stalling. This is not what he wanted to say. Suddenly, he turned to Monty Python for help, borrowing the title of their latest film.

> *And now for something completely different*

The shirt shop had closed.

> *it just did not work & we were losing money*

This was a shock. The original shop 'could not be busier so that's all O.K.', but Nutters Shirts was a debacle, deeply embarrassing. Later, when a journalist would bring up the failure during an interview, Tommy would wince. 'Do we have to mention that? I hoped no one would notice.'

The truth was that neither Tommy nor Edward had any idea what they were doing when it came to accessories. The boutique had chugged along on idealism rather than any sound business sense. Of course, its closure meant that Christopher Tarling, whom Tommy called 'Belle', randomly sliding between gender pronouns, was now out of a job as the store manager.

Belle will unfortunately leave us – he was marvellous about the whole thing but a bit upset. So please drop him a little note soon as he is coming to N.Y. at Easter & I am persuading him to stay there. I think he'll love it – so anything you can do to help will keep him going – of course Miss B will keep an eye on her also.

And with that, Tommy couldn't write any more. He told David to get back to him soon. Signed his love. Then, trying to look on the bright side of things, where he was more comfortable dwelling, he scrawled a final thought up the side of the page.

Monday was our 3rd anniversary of Nutters – very established

Tommy never had much of a grasp on the accounting ledgers. But there is no reason to doubt his assurances to David that things were still 'all O.K.' in the early months of 1972. His public profile, for one thing, had never been higher. Once again, he was named in the annual World's Best Dressed List in New York. His 'label' (a relatively novel concept) was now being mentioned in terms of a 'status symbol'. And two more major rock stars had recently turned up on Savile Row asking to add their names to the Nutters order book.

Elton Hercules John first walked through the door in 1971. Though just twenty-four years old, he had already released three studio albums and was presently preparing a fourth: *Madman Across the Water*, which would feature 'Tiny Dancer'. Elton was wealthy and famous, including in America, where he had just been nominated for a Grammy Award. Not that Tommy was all that impressed. In his opinion, Elton's stage-wear was 'far too flashy' (all those rhinestones), and his regular clothes were not much better: waterproof anoraks ('very nasty'), and hats that made him 'look like Andy Capp', a working-class comic-strip character known for his slovenliness. Elton actually bought much of his wardrobe from Mr Freedom, a 'pop art' London boutique, but Tommy snubbed his nose anyway – or at least feigned horror, the better to cast himself in the role of sartorial saviour.

'It was a big job changing him,' Tommy later said. Like Professor Henry Higgins, lifting a cockney flower girl out of the street to turn her into a fair lady, Tommy focused his energy on making over the piano player from Pinner, Middlesex. 'Fittings would go on for hours, sometimes days. It would get edgy, so I used to send out for a bottle of sherry to smooth things along.' As John Reid, Elton's manager for twenty-eight years, recalls, 'There was a little bit more than sherry. It was quite an event going in to Nutters. You'd write the whole day off. Maybe you'd have lunch, a couple of bottles of champagne . . .' Everyone would become hopelessly drunk.

The process was more collaborative than Tommy suggested too. He would parade samples and conceptual sketches before Elton and his manager, and Elton, with his predilection for eye-catching extravagance, would push Tommy to go even more extreme: add a little bit of this; make this wider, louder, brighter; make sure you can see it from the other end of the street.

Tommy was only too happy to oblige. He soon came to see himself and Elton as good friends, a relationship that John Reid, who also began to wear Nutters suits ('I would buy four and Elton would buy twenty'), attributes to a shared sense of humour.

But there was also an important creative synergy between the tailor and the performer. Elton encouraged Tommy to cut his imagination loose, presenting himself as a muse and willing clothes horse with a seemingly inexhaustible budget. Tommy, for his part, improved Elton's style off the stage (and occasionally on), thus helping curate the superstar's image, about which Tommy would remain wryly protective for years. Eventually, for example, Tommy would make Elton a line of Henley Royal Regatta-style striped jackets for one of his North American tours, then open the newspaper to a photograph of Elton dressed as Donald Duck in Central Park. 'I was rather upset he wasn't wearing these lovely blazers,' Tommy would complain on BBC Radio, only half joking.

The other major rock star to turn up on the doorstep was Mick

Jagger. Tommy claimed to have first met Jagger back in 1969, at a party thrown by the Beatles. 'All of a sudden Jagger just walked up to me and said, "I'll have a suit like the one you're wearing."' This is entirely possible, although it was not until 1971 that Jagger became seriously associated with Nutters.

On 12 May, in Saint-Tropez, Jagger elbowed his way through a mosh

Mick and Bianca Jagger on their honeymoon in Venice, June 1971.

pit of popping flashbulbs, punches flying as he clutched the arm of the Nicaraguan-born Bianca Pérez-Mora Macias. Wincing in the crush, Bianca wore white Yves Saint Laurent: a wide-brimmed hat with diaphanous veil; a long, narrow skirt and tuxedo jacket; and no shirt. Jagger wore a three-piece eau-de-nil Nutters suit with a small star pinned to the acres of lapel. Their wedding was supposed to be a low-key affair, just lords, ladies and music luminaries flown in from London. Instead, it was chaos. Fans swarmed. Pressmen gate-crashed. Photographs of the beleaguered Jaggers – Bianca and Mick in the back of a Bentley, an uncorked bottle of champagne clenched between his well-tailored thighs – were quickly circulated around the globe. As were pictures of their subsequent honeymoon in Venice, where the couple looked very snug. Or Mick did, at least, in another Nutters suit.

If Elton John accentuated the camp quirkiness in Tommy's style, Jagger revealed the sex. Of course, Jagger revealed the sex in everything; he seemed incapable of wearing the most quotidian outfit without charging it with explosive potential. But here the effect was notably subversive, even queer. The tightness, the softness, the lissome curves and loose lower legs, the strong, armour-like shoulder line – here was a suit that was neither masculine nor feminine, but both, combined in a single androgynous assemblage. Mick Jagger in Nutters emphasised the fluid potential of the suit, and not for nothing would Tommy once describe it as his 'Jagger look'. Nobody would ever inhabit it better.

Nobody, that is, except Jagger's new wife.

'When I first said I wanted to go to Tommy,' Bianca told the *Sunday Times* in 1972, 'Mick didn't like it at all. He said that a man's tailor was very special. It was a personal thing that a woman shouldn't intrude on. But I went anyway. Mick would much prefer it if I dressed in old jeans and a tee-shirt. I take ages to get ready when we go out and when I come down he says: "Oh, no! You're too dressed up again. Can't you take the hat off, or leave the cane behind at least?" But I just say, "Why?" and go out dressed as I am. Afterwards, of course, he's proud and pleased, he says: "I was choked, you looked so beautiful. I only said no before we went because I hadn't anything to match up with you." '

Bianca Jagger strolled into Nutters not long after her wedding. A meticulous customer, she demanded numerous fittings – four, sometimes five. If a trouser leg was an eighth of an inch shorter than the other, she would ask for a do-over, coming back into the shop or receiving Tommy's tailors in her mansion ballroom for further adjustments. She was not looking for a suit, exactly; she was looking for a statement. And that statement had to be perfect.

The preceding few years had seen the publication of Kate Millett's *Sexual Politics*, Germaine Greer's *The Female Eunuch*. Feminists had thrown flour bombs at a Miss World beauty pageant at the Royal Albert Hall, and the Women's Liberation Movement had held its first national conference in Oxford. 'It was part of my liberation to be able to wear trouser suits because it makes life so easy,' Bianca later wrote. (She would also wear suits by Saint Laurent and Dior.) However, when Tommy first presented her with a finished jacket on Savile Row – black gaberdine, with bust darts to

Bianca at Heathrow Airport.

highlight her svelte figure – she rejected it. She asked for the suit to be recut 'just like a man's', which meant *no* bust darts, and buttons on the right side. She took Tommy's own jacket and wore it out of the shop to use while she waited.

'We've been making some lovely clothes for Bianca Jagger,' Tommy wrote to David in the summer of 1972. One day, she stepped off a plane at Heathrow dressed in a black bowler hat and white three-piece Nutters suit, clutching cigarettes and an antique Malacca cane as she strode through the terminal.

Another day, she was at the Oval watching a cricket match next to Mick, both of them dressed in Nutters suits that competed to outdo one another in boldness. Then, in New York, she was in the restaurant La Grenouille – in a pistachio-coloured Nutters suit this time – seated at a central table with Fred Hughes, 'discussing life'. But not before she'd made an appearance at Leo Castelli's SoHo gallery for the opening of Warhol's Mao Zedong silkscreen collection: Nutters black velvet, crocheted gloves, art deco jewellery and a veiled hat with a stuffed white bird on the brim. 'I can't stand by her,' complained one of the guests. 'She's so beautiful she makes me feel ugly and old.'

In his 1974 biography of Mick Jagger, the writer Anthony Scaduto would document yet another occasion.

> Bianca arrives at a *Vogue* studio, very, very late, of course, but photographer Norman Eales doesn't mind because he is so anxious to photograph her. When the lift reaches the studio floor, where a dozen people wait so expectantly and nervously for her, out steps a chauffeur carrying a coffin-sized suitcase and a leather box full of hats. Then shoemaker Manolo, of Zapata, with two dozen pairs of shoes with four-inch heels. Followed by hairdresser Ricci Burns, carrying an assortment of wigs and feathers. He is followed by Jay Johnson, one of Warhol's superstars . . . Finally, behind the Warhol superstar, Bianca herself, stepping out of the lift in a $250 green Tommy Nutter suit and carrying her collections of walking sticks, which have become as famous a trademark in some circles as Dietrich's legs.

Tommy was hardly new to dressing women. While many Savile Row firms shied away from making anything much beyond women's riding wear, Nutters had already dressed Cilla, Twiggy, Yoko, and would soon accept the challenges of Joan Collins and Diana Ross. Tommy was all too willing to position himself as a peer to Saint Laurent, who first gave women his iconic Le Smoking in 1966.

Yet unlike Saint Laurent, Tommy was an ambivalent accomplice when it came to women's liberation. About 5 per cent of his business came from them, and while he hoped for more, 'I certainly don't want too many,' he said, taking care to affirm that 'we are still very much men's tailors'. Gentlemen paid an average of £130 for a suit at Nutters; women were charged £160. Tommy claimed that this was because women were 'harder to please', and 'it's much more difficult to get the trousers to hang properly'. But it was also because some of his male clients had begun to complain that there were too many women 'around the place'; the extra £30 acted as a kind of congestion charge. Furthermore, though he would never admit this publicly, Tommy had never quite got over the physical aversion that had once caused him to build a wall of pillows between himself and Carol Drinkwater. He was uncomfortable with the physical closeness involved in designing for women, in conducting their fittings. He told friends, 'I don't know how to deal with women's tits.'

Bianca seemed to override most of these reservations, though, for one simple reason: Tommy was bewitched by her glamour. He would tell a magazine that one of the best days of his life was the day Bianca phoned him up and asked if he'd escort her to a premiere. 'Every young boy's dream.' And he liked that she had her own ideas. Some people took a wonderful suit and screwed up on the accessories, but not Bianca. 'She's so magical, so beautiful,' he said. 'She's quite terrific. She has great style. She looks marvelous any way.'

In fact, Bianca's charismatic power seemed so capable of reducing Tommy to babbling adoration that she could get away with virtually anything. Once, in a letter to his brother, Tommy would write: 'Bianca has been around this week and has been driving us all mad. She is very grumpy, but extremely beautiful.' As though her beauty cancelled out everything else.

———

In April 1973, Tommy turned thirty. Peter was back in London for a visit and took care of the details. The party was held at Club Louise, an upmarket establishment that catered to a clientele of lesbians and gays. The proprietor (after whom the club was named) was an elderly French dame, and her club was dim, with a black banquette and a long wall of flattering mirrors that soon reflected many of Tommy's friends and admirers. The Lord and Lady Harlech came to celebrate. Jean Muir, the dressmaker. Michael Fish, of Mr Fish fame. Yvonne Elliman, who'd played Mary Magdalene in *Jesus Christ Superstar* on Broadway, and Lionel Bart, who'd written *Oliver!*. Edward brought Joan, while Dolly brought Lily, Tommy's grandmother, both of them dressed to the nines with big, bouffant hairdos and costume jewellery. Tommy floated in circles around everyone, Bianca Jagger dangling off his arm for much of the evening.

Years later, Tommy would recall this party with great fondness, telling a friend that 'everyone' had been there. He would say the presents were 'fantastic' but that he'd become so out of it by the end – on alcohol and cocaine – that all of them were stolen. Carol Drinkwater, though, is not entirely convinced. 'Knowing Tommy, he put them somewhere, and then he forgot all about them,' she says. 'That's what Tommy did.'

Tommy with Bianca Jagger and Ingrid Boulting, the ballerina and model.

9

LIBERTINES

Nutters of Savile Row Ltd.
35a Savile Row, London W.1
Tele: 01-437 6850 Cables: Nuttersrow

[c. April 1973]

Dear David,

Will be arriving in N.Y. on or around Friday June 1 with Jimmy.

Thanks for Birthday card, everyone loved it. Will be in N.Y. that weekend & will have masses of new clothes with me & I wondered if you could borrow a camera & take a few snaps as the ones [Justin de Villeneuve] took leave a lot to be desired. Possibly that weekend as I have a large P.R. campaign the third week in June when I return from a little hol in Puerto Rico. Then I will spend the last week of June cruising N.Y., the baths, Fire Island & anywhere new!

It would be lovely to have the pics ready for that 3rd week so I can hand them out to various periodicals (excuse the word).

Missed you at my 30th which was sensational. 500 people, 499 queens. It was great. Bianca came . . .

Belle might be there & I think she hopes to stay with you as I do not think there will be sufficient room at Miss B's pad. This of course is up to you. Belle is not quite sure if I am coming as I feel it is much easier to travel with one person rather than two. Jim is no trouble.

We are desperately busy & I am trying to get things cleaned
up here before I leave. Have a pretty minette stepping into my
shoes for a while. She's good with the queens.

Will see you when I arrive

Keep in touch

Love Tommy X

When David arrived in New York at Christmas time 1971, he dropped his bags at a friend's apartment on East Tenth Street, just down the block from Tompkins Square Park, and wandered off past junkies and homeless camps looking for a place to dance.

Before February, he found himself near Astor Place, in the ex-manufacturing district of NoHo, now mostly occupied by struggling artists. It was after midnight and the streets were unlit. He shivered violently as he approached a nondescript entrance at 647 Broadway. Someone had told him about an after-hours party here – *the* party, really, that was defining what 'party' meant in this city at the moment. It was invitation-only, but David could talk his way through any locked door, his tongue like a skeleton key. He'd told a friend of a friend that he was visiting temporarily (a white lie), and received an invitation with Our Gang printed on the front. Now he entered the warehouse. He located David Mancuso's spacious loft. At the door, he paid a $2 'contribution'. And that was it: everything else was free: the coat check, candy and fruit punch that may or may not have been spiked with LSD. This was more house party than commercial club, though the sound system rivalled anything a club could offer. Under a canopy of multi-coloured balloons, two sets of Klipschorn speakers were arranged to create a sonic swimming pool that David slid into with stunned bewilderment. 'Black Skin Blue Eyed Boys' by the Equals, say, followed by James Brown, or maybe 'Rain' by Dorothy Morrison. It was impossible to predict in what direction the rhythm might flow, but each track resonated with a clarity that seemed to dissolve effortlessly, perfectly, into the next, which was a way of mixing disparate styles to generate mood that David had never heard before. Also unfamiliar was the crowd, gyrating against him in an intimate mosh: gay and straight, black and white, rich and indifferently poor (indifferent, that is, because they had better things to do than pursue money). Mancuso's private discotheque was like an alternative reality, which Mancuso would later explain was precisely his intention: 'Once you walked into the Loft you were cut off from the outside world. You got into a timeless, mindless state. There was actually a clock in the back room, but it only had one hand. It was made out of wood and after a short while it stopped working.'

This was David's first proper introduction to New York City. He quickly decided he would never move back to London.

By the time Tommy's letter arrived in 1973, life had taken some unexpected turns. These were largely due to David's employer, the fashion photographer Bill King.

Bill King had grown up in Cliffside Park, New Jersey, and studied painting at the Pratt Institute. He made his name in London, though, producing fashion spreads during the sixties for *Queen* and *Harper's Bazaar*, eye-popping editorial work that featured, in one memorable example, male models posing with a transgender Puerto Rican dancer, Playboy Bunnies and a Ugandan princess. If King was not quite Richard Avedon (his idol/nemesis), he was highly regarded in the industry, a boundary-pushing star in his own right. David had met him through the printing business and admired his discipline; on a personal level, he found King introverted but friendly. The two men were also roughly the same age, both gay, and maintained an easy rapport – not insignificant in the high-tension environment of a fashion shoot. By the time King returned permanently to New York, their connection was such that David, arriving about a year or so afterwards, could walk straight into a job at his studio.

But something had happened to King in the interim. As Erica

Crome, an editor with *Queen*, later told the journalist Michael Gross: '[King] became a different, much less nice person in America. He developed a destructive streak.'

King's studio was located at 100 Fifth Avenue, near Union Square. The interior struck David as 'very antiseptic'. At King's insistence, many of the staff wore white coats, like scientists in a laboratory. King stuck coloured tape to the floor to restrict where certain people could and could not move. He compiled detailed files dictating how staff should deal with the famous guests: 'You must not make eye contact,' and so forth. Some female models were forced to wear shoes that were purposely too small, 'so they'd be in pain', David recalls, just because King liked it that way. David also recalls standing in the studio during winter, watching a hose spray water up into the air and down over a young girl's head as faux rain. 'Bill kept saying, "Get her in the face! *Get her in the face!*"' These shoots were executed in a cone of silence and could stretch on for hours.

Officially, David was hired as King's darkroom technician. This banal title, however, disguised the true dimensions of their arrangement. More accurately, David became a kind of uncredited executive assistant – and one with considerable latitude to challenge his boss's eccentricities. David refused to stay within the coloured boundaries marked on the floor. He laughed off King's petulant rampages and openly accused him of 'jeopardising shoots by making things go wrong just for the drama'.

Why would King permit such impertinence from a new employee? Well, he didn't – not exactly. King lashed out, belittled David, destroyed prints, and demanded he do things over and over again. But then, David recalls, 'he also seemed to need me'. King was socially awkward; David could loosen up the likes of Elizabeth Taylor before a photo shoot with ease, which was an invaluable asset given King's clientele and contacts. King also got in the habit of using David as a confidant and therapist. Each Monday, he would slink into the studio and summarily dump a weekend's worth of dysfunction onto his darkroom technician. 'Oh, I was walking down Christopher Street with my dick hanging out . . .'

In David's view, King's demons could be traced back to an oppressive upbringing in a conservative military family. King was a classic 'closet queen', according to David, and the strain of maintaining a facade of straightness had produced twin side effects of self-loathing and cruelty. David could sense the shape of King's neurosis: he found it sad, felt sorry for the man. Yet he also liked him – or, as David puts it, 'I didn't *dislike* him.' Bill King clearly needed help; maybe, on some level, David needed to be needed. 'It was an unhealthy and strange relationship, to be sure,' David admits, though he stops short of using another word for it: abusive.

This was the situation that David walked into in New York. He considered leaving to look for another job, but King was dangling a green card in front of his nose, dangling and withholding, dangling and

Bill King and David

withholding, in a torturous game that was still being played out by early 1973. David needed that green card; it made him dependent on King. So instead of leaving, he adopted a coping strategy that saw him focus all his remaining energy on places where he could lose himself – like Mancuso's Loft.

The Loft was open only once a week, but there was always the Sanctuary, a dance club in a converted German Baptist church with a DJ booth where the altar once stood. And the Planetarium, a dingy dive where water pooled on the floor and the music from *Shaft* blared over the heads of drunk drag queens. And Buttermilk Bottom, which also may or may not have put LSD in the fruit punch. And the Tenth Floor, a minimalist, members-only club with elitist attitudes about class and race, as well as unreliable lifts (ten flights of stairs in an ex–sewing machine factory). And Fire Island, of course: Cherry Grove, the Pines, the Sandpiper disco with its Christmas lights blinking on hot summer nights. 'It was like a nun getting out of a convent and just going berserk,' David says.

His swings between mania and depression, still undiagnosed, made him prone to going too hard, to drinking immoderately. David was already a high-risk candidate for addiction. With the added desire of an escape from work, pleasure now merged inexorably into compulsion, and the gay underworld became a kind of fix. In fact, David got so caught in an obsessive loop – bars, alcohol, men; bars, alcohol, men – that eighteen months after arriving in Manhattan he had yet to open a bank account.

Throughout all this, Tommy, despite being nearly 3,500 miles away, remained an important point of navigation. In 1973, David began keeping a day journal; he also recorded his lucid dreams, which often featured his younger brother in a starring role. In one example, David returns to their childhood home in Edgware 'totally shattered' after Tommy has drowned in an accident and then been mysteriously resurrected. 'Nobody seemed as depressed as I was when he drowned,' David wrote. 'It was as if half my life had been taken away.' Everything may have been edging towards chaos in New York – David caught in a savage waltz with Bill King, unable to lasso his emotions – but at least he still had Tommy.

Tommy arrived for a month-long visit at the beginning of June, his first trip to New York since he'd stayed with Hardy Amies on West Fifty-Eighth Street. Peter had secured a stunning apartment on Central Park West, so Tommy went there and took up residence in his ex-boyfriend's guest room. He was joined by Jimmy Clark (of the British

Gas van), which meant it was something of a reunion: Peter had previously employed Jimmy as the doorman at Apple Corps. Rounding out the household was a young American named Gary Lajeski, Peter's new boyfriend. Tommy took a shine to Gary immediately, and the two of them began to 'make trouble', Peter recalls, by ganging up together to terrorise their host.

Tommy was deeply tanned from Puerto Rico and ready to make the most of his extended stay in the metropolis. Peter set the tone by proceeding to throw a series of buzzing parties. 'Lots of people there,' David noted in his diary after the first of these. 'Tommy was in his glory . . . superstar types à la Warhol . . .'

On so-called quieter nights, Tommy would slip away to catch a musical on Broadway (he still adored Sondheim), or meet David and Jimmy for drinks somewhere like Le Jardin, a brand-new 'discotheque pour monsieur' that was packed with beautiful people 'in their whitest T-shirts and tightest jeans'. One afternoon, Jimmy noticed an advertisement in the *Village Voice* for John Waters's *Pink Flamingos*, a critic's quote printed across the top dismissing it as vile trash. Jimmy and the Nutters rushed to the cinema and howled with laughter ('Oh, Babs!').

Things took on a more civilised tenor for the film premiere of *Jesus Christ Superstar*. Dinner, first, with Andrew Lloyd Webber and his wife at Peter's apartment (Peter was working with Lloyd Webber and Tim Rice through the Robert Stigwood Organisation); then a screening of the film itself; then a star-studded celebratory bash at the top of a skyscraper with views across Manhattan.

Occasionally, Tommy paused all the frolicking about to do some work, reminding himself that this wasn't entirely a holiday. 'I'm here promoting my name, getting a bit more famous,' he told a journalist. The news hook, if one could call it that, was the first major new style to come out of Nutters in nearly four years. Tommy and Edward had watched old movie stars for inspiration (Fred Astaire, Rudolph Valentino), and now Tommy was describing the final product as 'a mix of everything. Joan Crawford shoulders. Oxford bags from the Twenties. It doesn't really resemble any suit from the past but it's bits and pieces from different periods. And, then, a bit of me.'

'And, then, a bit of me,' Tommy said.

Sometime in the middle of June, Tommy pulled on an arresting waistcoat (vertical black-and-white stripes on the right side; horizontal black-and-white stripes on the left side) and paid a visit to Andy Warhol's Factory, which was now located at 860 Broadway. After passing surveillance cameras and through a bulletproof door – Warhol had become paranoid since being shot – Tommy sat down on an art deco needlepoint sofa. Seated opposite him was Bob Colacello, the twenty-six-year-old editor of Andy Warhol's *Interview*. Given the stature of the magazine, its fashionable, in-crowd readership, this was a big opportunity for Nutters, so Tommy planned to select his words carefully for maximum charm.

Tommy had recently been named in the Best Dressed List for the third time in a row, Colacello noted.

'I suppose they'll shove me into the Hall of Fame next year,' Tommy said with a sly smile.

What did he predict for the future of fashion?

'The only thing that may die off is the tie,' Tommy said, declining to predict anything much at all. 'There seems to be a revival of glamour with designers like Zandra Rhodes, [Bill Gibb] and Ossie Clark. They all make such marvelous clothes for women. And I'm the only one who makes men's suits that complement these clothes . . .'

Indeed, Tommy was happier making predictions about his own future. He wanted to design for theatre and films, he said. He saw Nutters as a 'couture house', and he was preparing to turn his focus to other things: toiletries, cosmetics, a ready-to-wear line, 'like Dior'. He'd already been approached for licensing deals in America by 'masses of people', he boasted, 'but they're not really good enough. I want it to be done well.'

Eventually, Tommy dropped the posturing for a moment. He was feeling comfortable with Colacello, who now watched him slump back on the sofa and mop his brow of summer sweat. 'You know, it would be so nice to get into some jeans and walk around,' Tommy said. 'Ever since I've been here I've had to make myself look like Tommy Nutter. People expect one to turn up looking like a chic Bozo the Clown. Next week I'm going to do everything wrong and have fun.'

Which is exactly what he did. By the end of his stay, Tommy had sampled all the clubs that David liked to frequent, though he was not content to stop there. While his older brother avoided the bathhouses (except once, to photograph Patti LaBelle performing at the Continental Baths), Tommy spent hours cruising them in a state of dishabille, even renting a cubicle to stay overnight. He also tried 'the trucks' – freight trucks left empty and unlocked near the West Village after dark that were popular among gay men as a place for anonymous hook-ups. In a sign of the times, these kinds of hedonistic hot spots were proliferating across the city. David was aware of them, even valued them as a symbol of freedom, but he had personal limits when it came to sex. 'I remember Bill King taking me to a place called the Toilet. He showed me all these bathtubs. I just didn't get it. Not very romantic.'

Tommy did not have limits. He had a good time.

Return for a moment to that needlepoint sofa in the Factory: 'Ever since I've been here I've had to make myself look like Tommy Nutter . . .'

myself look *like*

To a remarkable extent, 'Tommy Nutter' had become like a good Savile Row suit: less a true and faithful representation of the person than an idealised projection of who that person wished to be, with all flaws and shortcomings artfully concealed. Just as sloping shoulders can vanish beneath the nimble fingers of a master tailor, so Thomas Albert, working to make himself look like 'Tommy Nutter', had tucked his shyness and working-class background beneath the shell of a confident, sophisticated, elegant rogue.

This shell was so flawlessly executed that people would sometimes stop and stare as he walked down the street. Back in London, Simon Doonan was a shop assistant working on Burlington Gardens, just round the corner from Savile Row. 'Tommy would go out for a cup of tea, he'd go out for his cheese sandwich or whatever he had at lunchtime,' Doonan recalls. 'And he usually had this younger, very good-looking boy with him. I don't know if he was Tommy's boyfriend, but he was definitely an acolyte. The two of them strolled down the street looking like an old illustration of art deco glamour, with these wide lapels and very wide trousers with pleats at the front.' Doonan would 'literally wait' for Tommy to pass by his window so he could marvel at the spectacle. 'He was so gorgeous. So glamorous.'

Yet Tommy sometimes needed a break from this heightened performance. At Nutters, he'd come to prefer hiding in his small office, making sketches or gossiping with the accounting lady, to working the showroom; now he'd only emerge if somebody specifically requested to see him and was famous or rich enough to warrant the attention. In the evenings, he often stayed home with a bottle of wine, watching soap operas on the television or jotting down notes for a short story. On weekends, he liked to swap the bespoke waistcoats for sweaters purchased at the Chelsea Antiques Fair.

At the same time, Tommy remained fiercely committed to the continuity of 'Tommy Nutter', and if anything imperilled the quality of this image, either directly or through association, he was not above lashing out.

The 'acolyte' Doonan noticed walking down the street was David Grigg, a young aspiring actor who'd begun working for Tommy as an assistant and occasional surrogate ('Have a pretty minette stepping into my shoes for a while'). One night, Grigg went with a raucous group of his peers to La Popote, a restaurant on Walton Street, where he ran into Tommy. 'He was quite offhand with me,' Grigg recalls. 'I said, "Why are you being so offhand with me? We're good friends!" And he pretended he didn't want to speak to me.'

On Monday morning, Grigg went into Savile Row to open the showroom. Unusually, he found Tommy waiting for him there. 'And he just – *pow!* Punched me right in the nose.'

Stunned, David asked, 'Why the hell did you do that?'

'You mixing with those dreadful people,' Tommy said.

Tommy with David Grigg, the 'pretty minette'.

By the close of 1973, Nutters remained a darling of the London glitterati, worn most recently by Ian McKellen in the pages of *Vogue* and by Cilla Black during her eight-week stage spectacular at the Palladium.

But the reality of business was a little more fragile than Tommy liked to admit. Despite his professed faith that there was still a demand for style 'in a world being overtaken by blue denim', the world was, indeed, being overtaken by blue denim. There was no getting around the decline in sartorial standards across Britain. European imports had swamped the high streets, while an American influence had tipped the scales definitively towards leisurewear. Ready-to-wear clothes had also improved in quality while remaining appealingly affordable; you could now buy an off-the-peg suit that was passably wearable in a firm of solicitors. None of this was new, exactly. Savile Row tailors had been amalgamating for years as they struggled to weather the unpredictable climate of fast, disposable fashions. But Nutters had seemed impervious to the storm, finding success by engaging fashion and applying the workmanship (and cost) of high-end tailoring – it had seemed, in other words, to *embrace* the change. Of course, this worked only so long as people had the money to pay their bills and the confidence to rack up new ones. 'I know people can't believe it but I'm not making much money on a £200 suit,' Tommy once said. Nutters needed to sell a great many every month to turn a healthy profit.

Throughout 1973, inflation and debt continued to climb in Britain. This affected what people were choosing to wear, as the *Financial Post* observed: 'Perhaps, if clothing is an indicator of national spirit (and why not?), today's relative quietness throughout the whole gamut of men's clothing has something to do with the uncertainties over Britain's future in the Common Market.' The country's future became even more uncertain in October, when an oil embargo in the Middle East sent prices skyrocketing on goods and services across the board. In November, the National Union of Mineworkers, resisting the government's anti-inflation policies, began agitating for more industrial action, turning a difficult situation into something almost catastrophic. By December, there was, once more, a state of emergency. To conserve coal stock, television stations ceased nightly transmission at 10.30 p.m., people were encouraged to share hot baths, and Tommy readied the gas lamps again.

Beginning on 1 January 1974, all non-essential businesses were restricted by government order to three consecutive days of electrical use per week. (The rest of the time, they would have to make do like people did before the Industrial Revolution.) This Three-Day Week, as Edward Heath's order came to be called, put tremendous pressure on small companies, which suddenly found themselves running at three-fifths the usual capacity. The misery remained until 7 March – after a full miners' strike, a snap election and the humiliating loss of power by Heath's Conservative government.

It is impossible to say exactly when Nutters began to feel the pinch. As Edward tells it, a day arrived when the business came to rely on an overdraft, to keep things moving smoothly. The bank agreed to extend the overdraft but demanded collateral. Tommy owned nothing with any real equity, so Edward and Joan agreed to step in and list their own house. (It is possible that several other staff members also contributed collateral.) According to Edward, there was simply no other choice. 'The bank insisted on it.'

What is certain is that the Three-Day Week coincided with significant change at No. 35a. If Edward had once been content to toil away in the back room, engineering Tommy's ideas into spectacular suits, he now decided it was time to take on a more prominent role. Nutters was stumbling in the downturn; people were spending less money as the economy convulsed into recession. His house was listed on the dotted line. By securing the bank credit, Edward also raised the stakes of his own involvement in Nutters of Savile Row.

He suggested to Tommy that they needed to become more rigorous as a business. Tommy, it seems, did not disagree with this assessment. In late January, Edward sat down to write his own letter to David in New York that laid out the shift in strategy. 'I felt it only right to compose a few lines and thank you in advance for your very kind offer to show me some of the sights during my stay in N.Y. As you know, this is a new venture for N.S.R. and we anticipate this trip being very successful (with the help of MRS. B), and possibly the first of many.'

Tommy had approached his trip to America as a chance to build his public profile ('getting a bit more famous'). Edward, by contrast, would be going over to make some actual sales.

He arrived in New York on 22 February, checking into the Bilt-more Hotel near Grand Central Terminal. A nice suite, fabric swatches fanned across a table: this was a time-honoured practice for Savile Row tailors seeking customers beyond the British Isles. Yet Edward was mostly making it up as he went along. He had a few names and tele-phone numbers scribbled on a piece of paper; that was about it. 'I didn't even realise New York was divided into four boroughs,' he recalls.

Five.

'Five boroughs! I had no idea.'

Undeterred, Edward reached out to the Americans who already pa-tronised the shop in London: people like Bill Blass, William Haines, 'real aristocratic queens, the crème de la crème'. These men, in turn, connected Edward with more prospective clients, who then came to the Biltmore for consultations. Nutters had always maintained a signifi-cant number of Americans on the books; now the figure climbed even higher. Just as Tommy and Edward had hoped, the trip would prove productive enough to suggest a viable way forward for the company. Edward would take his pile of orders back to London and return later in the year with suitcases filled with clothes for fittings. The finished suits would then be posted direct.

Although Edward came to New York with a serious mission, he was not entirely immune to the city's seductive diversions. David soon ar-rived to welcome his brother's colleague, and they stayed up until five in the morning drinking gin, dishing gossip, and making plans to go out while Edward was in town. A few days into his stay, they even staged a photo shoot on the Biltmore roof, Edward trying out the role of glam-our model for the first time in his life.

Edward probably didn't notice at the time, but David was in the middle of an extended manic episode when all this was happening. During the photo shoot, he tripped and injured his knee. 'Took speed and just kept going,' David wrote a few days later, after a night out with Edward at the notorious Club 82, an East Village haunt known for its drag revue. 'I was so "up."'

Edward on the roof of the New York Biltmore Hotel.

Just before the start of financial turbulence at Nutters, Tommy had secured a mortgage on a small flat four streets east of Brighton Pier. 'It overlooks the sea and has a minute roof garden at the back,' he wrote to David in a letter, thrilled with his purchase of a weekend escape. The roof garden was lined with terracotta tiles, which made it a suntrap, perfect for tanning. Tommy threw down some cushions and a rug to create a Moroccan daybed, and he would lie out with a piece of tinfoil propped under his chin for hours at a stretch.

Like his own Royal Pavilion, Tommy filled the interior of the flat with an exotic melange of pink mirrors, porcelain masks and more of his beloved Clarice Cliff china – 'Mind you, it is all rather expensive,' he wrote. The only downside to the whole set-up was that 'everyone wants to come and stay'. Tommy was besieged by his friends, including Carol Drinkwater. 'We used to get in the back of Jimmy's British

Gas van and drive down to Tommy's flat every weekend,' she recalls. 'I know this sounds daft, but I had a green bikini. I've got a photograph of me and Jimmy on Tommy's bed: he's wearing the top, and I'm wearing the bottom. He was quite a big guy, Jimmy, with my tiny bikini top on. Brighton was outrageous like that.'

When Tommy was not playing the role of reluctant host, he stayed in Brighton alone throughout much of the summer. 'I love it,' he later said. 'I've always loved the sea.' A Friday-afternoon train down from London, and then one back on Monday morning – or Tuesday, perhaps, if the weather was particularly sublime (or Wednesday, if it was transcendental). For those few days between arrival and departure, nothing could bother him there, not expectations or cash-flow concerns or a threatened rent increase by Westminster City Council that was suddenly putting extra pressure on his already fragile business. Brighton was his 'refuge', he told one of his colleagues. In fact, Brighton had been a refuge for queer people to go and be themselves since before the 1920s. Tommy just embraced the tradition and made it his own.

It was not until summer began to graduate to autumn – late August, early September – that something sufficiently extraordinary happened to shake him out of his Brighton daydream and draw his attention back to Savile Row. It involved the 3rd Baron Montagu of Beaulieu – the man who, through the Montagu Case, had inadvertently helped earn people like Tommy the legal freedom to live as they wished and love whom they chose. Tommy and David had been children when the scandal unfolded in 1954, though their entire adult lives had been inflected by the fallout.

Lord Montagu was getting married (for the second time), and now came into Nutters hunting for a wedding suit. His fiancée, the free-spirited Fiona Margaret Herbert, who could not have cared less about the trial even after he gave her a book about it, also came in looking for something original to wear. The two of them had decided to have a *Great Gatsby* theme for their reception. However, Ms Herbert objected to women's clothes from the jazz age – 'all those dropped waists'. She told Lord Montagu, 'I'm going to come as Jay Gatsby.' Indeed, they would *both* be coming to the party as Jay Gatsby. Tommy Nutter seemed like the obvious man for the job.

The future Lady Montagu of Beaulieu was born in Zimbabwe (formerly Southern Rhodesia), 'so I'd never had a smart suit', she recalls. The fittings at Nutters stretched on for ages, though she found the process thrilling and was happy to go with the flow. Lord Montagu, on the other hand, was determined to squeeze out a deal with the tailor. He announced, 'You make us lovely suits and you can come to the party.' ('He was so bad!' recalls Lady Montagu.) 'Lord M', as his friends called him, was famous for the parties he threw at his Gothic country house, and this one promised to be, like F. Scott Fitzgerald had written, a night where 'men and girls came and went like moths among the whisperings and the champagne and the stars'.

Tommy agreed to the proposal.

On 19 October, taking Carol Drinkwater along as his date, he caught a train south-west from Waterloo. Also in the carriage was Stirling Moss, the Formula One racing driver. When the train finally arrived at Brockenhurst, in Hampshire, Lord Montagu was waiting in a Jaguar. As Carol recalls, 'I think Stirling Moss thought, "Ah! He's come to pick me up." But no. It was for me and Tommy.' Lord Montagu had a habit of flouting social hierarchies in a way that endeared him to some and left others fuming with resentment.

Montagu drove Tommy and Carol past open fields and scattered oak trees onto the Beaulieu Estate, which had been in the family since 1538 and contained, among other points of interest, the crumbling ruins of a Cistercian abbey. He dropped them off at his sister's home, where they were both given rooms. They were picked up again, dressed and ready, several hours after dinner, and ferried in yet another vintage car on towards the grand old pile of Palace House.

The Great Gatsby Ball – 'On the Occasion of Edward and Fiona's Marriage (And the Anniversary of Edward's Birth)' – kicked off at 10.30 p.m. Jay Gatsby and Jay Gatsby stood at the entrance of the house, welcoming their guests. All hundreds of them. Lady Montagu was in a daze. 'I'd just married this man,' she recalls, 'and between three parties and various other things going on at Beaulieu, I'd met 1,600 people, because that's how he was.' Their matching Nutters suits were impeccable and much admired: three pieces, white worsted, white satin braiding, paired with ties and silk taffeta shirts by Mr Fish.

The Lord and Lady Montagu . . .

. . . as Jay Gatsby and Jay Gatsby.

As Tommy and Carol swanned into the party, they carried over-sized black matchbooks about the length of a good cigar. On the front of the matchbooks was a drawing of Palace House surrounded by stars and fireworks. Inside, opposite several dozen tear-off matches, was a schedule of the night's festivities.

Dancing in the Lower Drawing Room to
the Orchestra of Christopher Allen.

Further dancing and musical enjoyment
in the Upper Drawing Room, with
phonograph recordings.

A competition (voluntary) for the
dancing of the 'Charleston' – in the
Lower Drawing Room at midnight.

Late supper will be served in the
Upstairs Dining Room at 12.30 a.m.

Newsreel and movies of the 'Twenties'
will be shown in the Upstairs Library.

A pianist will play for your enjoyment
throughout the evening.

An assessment of sartorial elegance
(costume judging) will take place at
1.15 a.m. (Entry optional)

Breakfast will be served in the
early hours.

Well before breakfast, some guests would burn themselves out and fall asleep in odd corners of the estate. At least one man would be disqualified from the Charleston competition for attempting a version on all fours. The Montagus would dance for hours, challenging everyone else to keep up with their indefatigable tempo. Carol would dance with Earl Mountbatten (who would one day be assassinated by the IRA) and the bombshell actress Diana Dors, who came dressed as a flapper. 'The three of us!' remembers Carol. 'Who would believe me? It doesn't sound normal, does it?'

But there was also a moment when eyes turned sharply to Tommy. The orchestra was swinging, alcohol was flowing, and he decided it was his turn to waltz through the spotlight. Taking the hand of the Marquess of Dufferin and Ava, an angularly handsome thirty-six-year-old with foppish hair and heavy horn-rimmed glasses, Tommy began to spin intimate circles around the dance floor, in full view of everyone.

A gossip columnist watched gleefully from the sidelines. 'A lasting memory for all of us,' he reported a few days later in the *Daily Mail*. 'But I could not fathom who was leading. It was never like that, surely, in the Roaring Twenties?'

Tony King and David in Elton John's suite at the Sherry-Netherland.

10

MUSCLE QUEENS AND
MOZART RECORDS

It was on Wooster Street, in run-down SoHo, that David finally signed the lease on a loft of his own. Large and draughty, with a concrete floor and rough fittings that made it barely habitable as a residential address, it cost around $200 a month. David split the rent with an artist – or a man 'who *thought* he was an artist' – who liked to drop acid and then stay up late spray-painting his masterpieces in the common space while David became increasingly irate in his bedroom, trying and failing to sleep.

It quickly became clear that David and the artist were not particularly well suited as roommates. In his diary, David would variously diagnose the artist as 'evil', 'very nasty' and 'a maniac'; he ultimately fled after a troubled eight months of sharing. Before it got to that point, though, when there was still only the occasional screaming confrontation, rather than hot-headed altercations on a near-daily basis, he decided to take advantage of the cavernous loft by throwing a single Mancuso-style dance party.

The guests of honour would be Tommy and Edward, who were back in New York (together this time) to follow up with clients and forage the social scene for new ones.

It was early November, and David set about preparing for his party with all the diligence of Mrs Dalloway. He wrote and distributed dozens of invitations himself, each one falsely announcing the arrival of a new baby. ('I thought they would spark some interest,' David recalls.) He borrowed an excellent sound system and hand-picked disco records from a friend's collection. He assembled a large, freshly scrubbed aquarium in the middle of the apartment, then filled it to the brim with lethal rum punch. Just before the guests began to arrive, he added a dose of dry ice so fog bubbled up and spilled over the sides, cascading down the glass to the loft floor. 'Very excited about party,' he wrote in his diary.

Tommy and Edward turned up first, accompanied by Gary Lajeski, Peter's boyfriend. The rest of the city (or so it seemed) followed afterwards in a heady rush. Bill King and the artist Richard Bernstein, who made the covers for *Interview*. The playwright Tom Eyen and the cast of *Women Behind Bars*, which was in early workshops. A crowd from La MaMa Experimental Theatre Club, which David had begun photographing through his friend Bernard Roth. Then Nona Hendryx, of the rock trio Labelle; Jackie Rogers, the Chanel model turned designer; John Vaccaro, director of the anarchic Playhouse of the Ridiculous; and 'the whole world – everyone', David later wrote, bemused that he had somehow managed to assemble such a stunningly diverse crowd of people in his own apartment. 'The whole thing escalated into the party of the year.' And Tommy and Edward 'seemed overwhelmed by it all', which pleased him immensely.

Another guest at the party was Tony King, the young Englishman who, in 1969, had worn the first Nutters suit as Hardy Amies bent over his lapels with a tape measure. Back then, in London, Tony had caused a minor shift in Tommy's fortunes; now, here in New York, he would trigger a more substantial change in David's life.

David and Tony had two significant things in common. First, they both had a peculiar ability to ingratiate themselves with temperamental rock stars. (Tony, after a stint at Apple Corps, had worked for John Lennon and then migrated to Elton John's recently founded Rocket Record Company.) Second, they were both enamoured with nightlife, and could go longer – and *harder* – than almost anybody else around them. Tony had already crossed paths with David out in the clubs; the loft party only deepened his impression of David's good spirit.

A few days later, Tony called David up and invited him out for dinner. Over Italian food on Hudson Street, Tony mentioned, casually, that he was 'moving in' tomorrow with Elton John at the Sherry-Netherland. (With its sweeping views of Central Park and ample cupboard space, the classic hotel was one of Elton's favourites when he visited New York.) This throwaway comment was not a boast, or not entirely, and it would not have impressed David much if it had been. Rather, Tony had a notion in his head, and he was testing to see if David might be a willing accomplice. 'Elton was going through a rather depressed period at the time,' Tony recalls. 'And I said to him, "Oh, I've got this friend who you're going to love because he's really *funny*. I'll introduce you – it's Tommy Nutter's brother." ' Perhaps David could come cheer Elton up a little.

The next day, David travelled uptown to visit Tony at the Sherry-Netherland. Also in the hotel suite was Mike Hewitson, Elton's loyal valet, whom everyone called 'Brenda'; and Elton John himself, perhaps the biggest glam-rock star in the world at that moment. David greeted him with exactly the same amount of fawning adoration that he offered every cultural luminary he happened to encounter – which is to say none at all. Elton was impressed. 'Hit it off like a house on fire,' David later wrote.

That evening, Elton's bodyguard, 'a huge black Mr Universe' (in David's description), escorted the group to an 'awful party full of muscle queens and Mozart records'. Still energised by his own recent success as the perfect hostess, David began to satirise everyone in sight, which sent Elton into hysterics. Afterwards, they all climbed into Elton's sleek limousine and wound their way through Manhattan to Buttermilk Bottom – 'but Elton saw a policeman and we hot-footed it back to Le Jardin'. The next day, David discovered that Elton's skittishness was actually good intuition: Buttermilk Bottom was raided not long after they fled. But David was too distracted to reflect on the implications of this fact, the barely averted international scandal of Elton John arrested in a gay bar, because Tony King had just called . . .

'Elton really liked me,' David wrote.

On 27 November, less than two weeks after his loft party, David returned to the Sherry-Netherland to collect a pair of tickets left in his name: one for him, and one for his new (fleeting) boyfriend, Maurice. Thursday was Thanksgiving; Elton was scheduled to perform at Madison Square Garden before an audience of some 20,000 people. David and Maurice were granted VIP access.

'The crowd screamed – deafening,' David later noted. 'Never seen the likes of.' Elton was 'unbelievable', peacocking across the stage, and at one point John Lennon walked out (having just thrown up into a bucket because he was so nervous) and performed a duet on three songs. Lennon told the frenzied crowd, 'We thought we'd do a number by an old, estranged fiancé of mine called Paul' – and then launched into a stunning rendition of 'I Saw Her Standing There'. The applause seemed to reverberate into eternity.

The after-party, held at the Pierre, was 'all very gala in the ball-room', David thought. With Maurice by his side, he worked the room as though it were his own, floating past guests like Uri Geller, who was sitting on a couch bending spoons for Elton's sound man. Nona Hendryx invited David over for dinner that Sunday; John Lennon invited him over for dinner 'sometime'. David was 'outrageous again', he wrote, a nimble court jester hovering near Elton, who (like David himself) was wearing a Nutters bespoke suit (Elton's with a '#1' pin fixed to the lapel, in case anyone forgot the hierarchy).

David later wrote that he had 'never felt so good' as he did that

RJS, EJ, EVL & BT

At the not-so-recent Thanksgiving gala held in honor of Elton John's Madison Square Garden appearances the sensational Mr. J took time out for a giggle and a photo. Pictured above, from left, are RW's Roberta (Joyce) Skopp, Elton, Eric Van Lustbader and Bernie Taupin.

Photobombing, far left: David Nutter

Thanksgiving. It had been an entire month of unusually heartening validation, of people showering him with compliments, laughing at his jokes, inviting him out to parties and dinners and musical premieres, of affirming that he was funny, appreciated, loved. An impression emerges through his diary that David had encountered something precious for a moment, something that had long eluded him, and that he was desperate to maintain now he had finally felt it: a strong sense of belonging.

Notably, Tommy was present to witness this rare starburst of unadulterated joy. Though Edward had flown home a few days earlier, Tommy had lingered to wrap up some other business, cruise around the baths a bit longer, and attend Elton's concert. At the after-party, Tommy now watched his brother be the social butterfly, and David watched Tommy watching him from across the room. As a final note on the evening, David wrote to himself, proudly, that 'Tommy was astounded at how bold I was'.

Before heading back to London in early December, Tommy invited his brother on a last-minute reconnaissance mission to Madison Avenue. They were joined by Gary Lajeski – were, in fact, going to the Lajeski Gallery, where Gary exhibited art on the first three floors of a converted town house that had once been occupied by Valentino. There was much to discuss, a great deal of work to do before Tommy would be ready for an opening reception here on 22 January.

It was a difficult time to be a fashionable dandy. The *Evening News* was warning readers that the 'Peacock Revolution' was about to turn into 'a remnant sale'. At Blades, near Savile Row, Rupert Lycett Green was predicting that all the talk of fiscal austerity meant 'moderation will return to men's fashion'. Indeed, even Michael Fish, that stubborn grand dame of British aesthetes, who represented the culmination of 1960s extravagance, was now shutting up shop on Clifford Street. 'Fashion doesn't exist any more,' Fish declared in his dramatic final bow. 'Only clothes.'

Yet it was at this very moment that Tommy decided to publicly exhibit a range of his experimental designs in an art gallery. It is almost as though he were openly defying the grave prognoses, projecting an image of rude health while everyone around him was giving up hope. Whether this was optimism or denial – or both, two sides of the same coin – is a matter of interpretation. For Tommy, as always, it involved no small amount of magical thinking.

Tommy returned to London to finalise fifteen pieces, which he then carted back to New York in mid-January. His intention was for the suits – various checks and tweeds, mixed together in unusual combinations; wide lapels or three-tone shawl collars; trousers so capacious they swallowed up the wearer's shoes – to be displayed on mannequins in small groups. But Tommy also wanted to show what they looked like when worn by actual *people*, so he handed a few off to David in advance. Braving the chill, David gathered some friends for an impromptu shoot in Central Park and other striking locales around the city. Afterwards, he developed the film at Bill King's studio, decided the prints 'looked great', and handed them back to Tommy for installation on the walls of the gallery.

Traditionally, to be a tailor means to follow, to offer suggestions and guidance to clients but ultimately defer to their judgement, because *they* are positioned as the final authority. To be a fashion designer, on the other hand, is to take the lead, to direct style according to a cultivated eye that can tell what is best for clients better than they can tell for themselves. In fashion, the designer is the final authority; the client either buys the clothes or not, but never directs the design process in any meaningful sense. From the moment Nutters opened in 1969, Tommy existed somewhat ambiguously between these two poles; over time, though, he gravitated increasingly towards the latter. As his reputation grew, the standards of tailoring – measuring clients to create bespoke suits in the styles they wanted – interested him less than producing what *he* wanted, building 'Nutters' into a name known for specific styles that belonged to him as the creative director. His comparing Nutters to a couture house, 'like Dior', as he did in *Interview*, was not a throwaway comment; it was a statement of intent. To now have an exhibition in an art gallery, in New York, on Madison Avenue, was to stake

David recruited some friends for an impromptu photo shoot around New York.

a claim even more forthrightly as something different from the usual Savile Row craftsman.

The opening reception augured good things. It was part of a trio of shows premiering simultaneously for a two-week run at the Lajeski Gallery: on the ground floor was 'Paintings', by Gisela Beker; on the third floor was 'Frescos', by Franco Ciarlo; and sandwiched in between was Tommy, with his 'Clothing Concepts'. A large, sympathetic crowd drifted past the displays and photographs, praising Tommy, who wore a brown suit with beige rolled lapels.

Nevertheless, back in London, Prudence Glynn, a fashion columnist for *The Times*, could not help but raise a sceptical eyebrow at the whole affair unfolding across the Atlantic. 'Were Tommy not such a sensible person I should have reservations about his being involved with displays of clothes "as an art form",' she wrote, 'because it seems to me that one of the problems of being a fashionable fashion designer, in an era when fashion is a pop cult, is that you can lose the perspective on your talent. When all is said and done, fashion is one of *les arts mineurs*.' However, Glynn continued, 'Tommy Nutter is not about to believe he is Rembrandt; indeed, as Sir George Clark wrote of Wren, so far as is known he never gives himself airs as an imaginative artist and is a fundamentally practical man, whose buildings (in the case of Mr Nutter, creations) excel "like Vauban's fortresses, in their adaptations to their sites".'

For Prudence Glynn, the idea that a Savile Row tailor might also be 'an imaginative artist' – or even aspire to be considered as such – was just too much novelty to swallow. In 1975, she was not alone in this critical assessment.

David's new-found optimism warmed him through the grim New York winter. He maintained the momentum by staying busy, working hard at King's studio during the day and then partying even harder after the sun went down. Elton John may have left the city after his concert at Madison Square Garden (saying goodbye, David presented him with a funny poem in a card), but there were plenty of other distractions to take the performer's place.

One evening, Tony King took David out for drinks with John Lennon and May Pang. At this point, John and Yoko had been separated for more than a year; Lennon was deep in what he would later describe as his 'Lost Weekend' phase, consuming copious amounts of drugs. May Pang, once the couple's personal assistant and production coordinator, was now John's steady girlfriend – approved of and encouraged by Yoko herself. ('I needed a break,' Yoko later told a journalist. 'We were so close John didn't even want me to go to the bathroom by myself.') Sipping champagne, David and May hit it off immediately, even if he found the whole arrangement between her and the couple mystifying. 'Marvellous time chatting,' he wrote in his diary. 'Cosy.'

Six days later, David went with Tony to visit Yoko at her giant apartment in the Dakota, on Central Park West. They were supposed to be fetching her for a party at Peter Brown's house, just a few doors up, but they ended up staying for hours to gossip instead. David found Yoko surprisingly 'wonderful' on this occasion – an opinion that was only reinforced the following evening, when he found himself sitting between her and Peter at dinner. David cracked jokes, making wry observations. Peter told him he was in 'top form', and Yoko, attempting to offer her own brand of compliment, told him he should be committed to a psychiatric ward.

In early February, David was out and about with May Pang again, accompanying her to a party where they spoke to 'Roman Polanski, Andy Warhol, David Bowie, Divine, etc'. Despite their eleven-year age difference, David felt that he was destined to be 'good friends' with the woman.

Three days later, however, John made things considerably more complicated by abandoning May to reunite with Yoko. The swap back, after some eighteen months of separation, was probably inevitable. But it wedged David in an awkward position. Pang called up her new 'good friend' to vent confusion about what had just happened. Where did it leave *her*? David then spoke to John and Yoko, though he resisted becoming an intermediary. In his diary, he took everything he was told by the three parties concerned and distilled it down into two neutral words: 'Strange dramas'.

On 19 February, Yoko asked David to come to the Dakota for a private conversation. When he arrived, unsure of what he was getting himself into, Yoko was still sleeping, so he had to wait around in the lobby for a while. Eventually, he was welcomed inside. David thought Yoko, who had not bothered to change for her guest, 'looked funny in her nightdress walking through that huge place'.

The two of them sat down to talk – not, David discovered, about May and John, but about a job, the details of which were (and remain) a little vague.

Yoko had acquired a female mannequin with long, wavy black hair. There was to be a catalogue of sorts, or maybe one of her idiosyncratic art pieces. She wanted David to photograph the mannequin doing . . . things, she said. Just regular people things around the Dakota. And as far as David can remember, that was about the extent of direction.

David returned to the Dakota in early March with a camera and several rolls of black-and-white Ilford film. He had selected a low ISO so he could do longer exposures to maximise image quality. It was a bright day, sunlight streaming through the picture windows that framed Central Park across the street. David investigated the apartment, to which he'd been granted unimpeded access. He then examined Yoko's plastic woman: life-size, thin, with a pretty, expressionless face. David noticed that the limbs were remarkably supple.

Over the next few hours, he experimented with a series of surreal compositions. In one sequence, David photographed the mannequin outside from below, so that she seemed to be descending from the overexposed sky, a naked angel bathed in heavenly light. For another few shots, he extended her arms out and upward in a gesture of either rapture or supplication, then placed a telephone in her lap and the receiver in her hand, as though she had just received a particularly transformative phone call. Other poses were more comical: the mannequin dressing up in a hat and feather boa; the mannequin crouched above a toilet bowl preparing to vomit, her hair tucked considerately over her right shoulder.

But perhaps the most mesmerising shot involves Lennon's famous white piano. Were it not for the giveaway joints at her waist, shoulders, and wrists, the mannequin could almost pass for a real woman (Yoko Ono, perhaps?) picking out notes from the open composition.

Yoko's mannequin playing John's grand piano.

In David's memory, he was alone in the apartment when he took his shots, arranging the plastic woman to rummage through a filing cabinet or recline meditatively on the couple's enormous bed. In some ways, the photos represent a continuation of the ones he'd taken back in the Apple Corps days, the next in a series of uncanny portraits inspired by his interactions with John and Yoko.

For days and then weeks afterwards, David waited for Yoko to call him with her thoughts. Did she like the photographs? Were they what she was after for her catalogue, or art project, or whatever it was?

Yoko never rang. The mannequin shots seemed to slip from her mind as she declared an intention to re-stage her Gibraltar wedding 'psychically' for the upcoming sixth anniversary. David was not one to push for an answer. Nor was he one to chase payment for a job well done – a problematic trait he shared with his brother. Instead, David placed the negatives, prints and contact sheets in a manila envelope, just in case Yoko ever did happen to recall their unique collaboration and come calling.

He would leave the envelope in a safe place, untouched, for the next forty-one years.

Back in England, Tommy was stirring up a fuss in Bath, where an exhibition at the Museum of Costume was charting the evolution of wedding attire since 1822. The show was arranged to culminate with two 'contemporary' examples, handpicked by a magazine editor named Anna Harvey. Harvey had selected Gina Fratini to contribute the bridal gown: cream shadow-printed silk organza with satin ribbon streamers and a matching half bonnet ('rather reminiscent of Little Bo Peep', observed one local journalist). But people were more immediately struck by her selection for the groom, an outfit that caused 'a few subdued gasps followed by an initial silence' when it was unveiled by the lord mayor. The slim-fitting frock coat was made from eau-de-nil gaberdine, with a long, flared skirt and cream lapels, finished by a pearl pin stabbed through a silk polka-dot cravat. Explaining her bold choice, Harvey described Tommy Nutter as 'today's best young designer of men's clothes. He is not gimmicky, but imaginative and prepared to be adventurous.' Nobody in Bath could argue with that. The *Chronicle* nicknamed his entry the 'Teddy Boy bridegroom' and declared it had stolen the whole show.

Tommy took David Grigg as his escort to the launch, which was held in the Assembly Rooms, a series of beautiful Georgian chambers that once hosted the kinds of society balls that Jane Austen liked to satirize.

At lunch, Tommy sat next to the lord mayor's wife, who, he later wrote to his brother, 'played with my knee'. He also participated in two interviews for local television news, then retired for the afternoon to a nearby hotel, where he and 'Miss Grigg' drank tea until the spots aired and Tommy could evaluate his on-camera performance. 'I was great!' he wrote to David, in a freewheeling, excitable letter that showed him as non-stop since his successful exhibition at the Lajeski Gallery.

Easter, for example, had been spent in Brighton: Tommy had hosted his friends Michael Long and Michael's Japanese boyfriend, Hatchi, who was somewhat temperamental ('Ms Nakatsu stormed out'). And Elton John had recently paid him a visit on Savile Row, which Tommy knew David would want to hear about. 'P'haps I told you?' Tommy took

Elton to dinner at Morton's and 'got so pissed I fell off my chair onto the floor'. But these things happened, as David could well understand, and the point was that spirits were flying high. Indeed, the shop was busy – 'quite a few lady clients this season' – and everything seemed, in Tommy's telling, to be going on more or less exactly as one might hope.

And so, when it came time for the next business trip to America, Tommy decided to sit this one out. It was the third trip since the trauma of the Three-Day Week, and by now the process of measuring clients in a New York hotel room was basically routine. Edward would take care of it with his assistant cutter, Joseph Morgan, who would also accompany him on a Los Angeles leg (they were expanding their reach). Then Joan Sexton would join them back in New York for 'a little holidayette', as Tommy called it. Indeed, Tommy's main contribution to the effort was to ask David to 'look after them and take them to all the wrong places' when they passed through Manhattan. In the meantime, Tommy, like a creative director who has delegated responsibilities to his underlings, would stay behind and ponder some new design concepts.

Ringo Starr wearing Nutters, photographed by Bob Gothard.

He pondered through much of the summer. Often, he retreated to Brighton, and when the weather cleared up he browned like a roast chicken and became, in his own words, 'quite chubby, really'. Yet the thought of design was never far from his mind. After an extraordinary few months of exhibitions and press attention, what would Tommy Nutter do next? The question gnawed away at him. In another letter to David, he outlined his anxiety with characteristic humour: 'Trying hard to think of a new look, but the problem is you end up with the old look which is really the new look.' He continued, in a rambling, stream-of-consciousness style, 'The saddest thing of all is an in-between look. Like the woman who plays safe all the time with handbag and shoes to match. It's all so easy for her. I think it is terribly sad when a woman gives in like this and instead of setting the trend, follows it. But I suppose this is what it's all about. If there was no one to follow it, what's the use of creating the new look?'

Not everyone at Nutters agreed with this assessment. After returning from America, Edward found himself becoming increasingly annoyed by Tommy's choice of focus – or lack thereof. 'He'd vanish for days, gone down to Brighton,' Edward recalls. 'Then it became half a week.' And when Tommy did reappear on Savile Row, he would glide through to his office at the rear of the shop, close the door and resume work on his sketches. Eventually, Edward says, it got to a stage 'where he just didn't see people' – a situation also noted by David Grigg and the assistant cutters.

In a sign of how much control Edward had assumed in the business since staking his house as collateral for the bank, he took steps in late July, or early August, to rein in Tommy's haphazard behaviour. One day, when Tommy was away, 'we took out this little room where he used to go and hide', Edward says – meaning he ripped open the space that Tommy was using as his studio. When Tommy returned, he was stunned by the renovation. 'He said, "Well, where's my office?"'

'I said, "In the showroom."'

From Edward's perspective, Tommy's role in the business was

supposed to be front-of-house salesman, just as it would be at a more traditional tailoring firm. In which case, he was currently shirking his duties.

After his initial shock, Tommy's response to Edward's remodelling was remarkably muted. If he was angry about the loss of his private workspace, the anger quickly dissipated into resigned acceptance of the new shop set-up. By mid-August, Tommy was writing to David that 'we have gone open plan in the shop here and I am on stage more. Having to flog the suits myself. Still, it's better.'

Why was it 'better'? Because money was tight, Tommy could hardly deny it; and because David Grigg, the proxy who had worked the show-room on his behalf for the past two years, was suddenly no longer there. 'I was told they were making cutbacks, and I think they saw me as an unnecessary expense,' Grigg remembers. Here, too, Tommy was remarkably blasé in his account of the staff reduction. 'Young David with the voice is going but we are still all good friends,' he wrote to his brother. (Grigg spoke with a plummy accent that Tommy found highly amusing.)

Tommy's choice of language in the letter was subtle but deliberate. Grigg was not sacked for financial reasons; he was simply 'going'. Nutters had not been physically rearranged because of a disagreement between himself and his head cutter; it had just 'gone open plan', as though the change had happened naturally, almost by itself. Even to David, the person who'd known him longer than anyone, Tommy preferred to project an image of the steady ship, cloaking any bad news in a tone of reassuring nonchalance. Then, as usual, he simply changed the subject completely.

> No special friends around at the mo but lots of tricks. Rod's is the new bar on King's Rd and it is like Flamingos. Can you believe it in London? Shirts off. Lots of dinge and a few stars . . . Any trips lately? How's Fire Island? Is it all going on?

===

It was, indeed, all going on in New York, though not quite in the way Tommy intended. But such is bipolar disorder: soaring periods of 'never felt so good' can be followed by a rapid freefall to 'rock bottom', as David was describing his life by August.

What triggered this dramatic swing?

Where to begin?

In May, David had moved to the Upper West Side after relations with the artist in his SoHo loft had eroded past a point of no return. Then horrendous eczema had broken out across his body, seemingly impervious to treatment. John Lennon had floated the idea of David taking some photos – a new album cover – but it fizzled out, yet another disappointment from the Dakota. And Bill King was being even more obnoxious than usual, with the cocaine situation at his studio spiralling out of hand.

The cocaine situation: as David recalls, the whole thing began back in November 1974, when King had asked him to collect a package from 'this nice little man' at the Chelsea Hotel. This nice little man was Billy Maynard, a rock photographer of drag bands like the Cockettes who also happened to be a drug dealer, though David failed to make that connection until Maynard was beaten to death a short time later in Room 803. Reading about the murder in a newspaper, David experienced a moment of horrifying clarity. 'And then, of course, when I was "in,"' he recalls – meaning complicit with King's cocaine habit, as though that followed naturally – 'we used to have to test the coke when it came into the studio to see what it was cut with.'

Recently, David and the staff had been testing the cocaine a *lot*. Photo shoots needed the stuff like an engine needs oil, and all income seemed to be outgoing to dealers to keep the supply flowing steadily. David recalls being threatened, more than once, by dealers who were paid late for their services. He also remembers King encouraging an atmosphere of paranoia by, for example, installing bulletproof glass in the studio windows.

David began having trouble sleeping that summer – sleeping too much, not sleeping at all, feeling alternately wired and strung-out, restless and catatonic. He went to the hospital for a prescription of Valium, but the doctors refused to give it to him. He complained to Tommy about how he was feeling (and complained to his diary, meanwhile, that Tommy had 'got so far in life', while he had barely got anywhere). Tommy replied, 'Sorry to hear about all your predicaments. But I am sure they will sort themselves out. They always do.'

In the middle of September, David received a phone call from Tony King that made him race to the Pierre: Elton John was back in town. It was like the moon vaulted suddenly into the sky over Manhattan; the tide of David's mood swelled immediately.

What followed was 'one of the [most] hysterical days of all time', David later wrote. A horse and buggy through Central Park to a restaurant on Lexington. A drama in Chelsea Cobbler that made the whole group walk out in a collective strop. At Maxwell's Plum, Elton threw chocolate cake in his own face, and everyone inhaled helium balloons. Then there was a party for Andy Warhol at Halston's house (David

Society photographer Robin Platzer catches Elton's entourage (including David) leaving Halston's house.

decided that Warhol 'seemed nice') and a concert at the Uris Theatre for Frank Sinatra, Count Basie and Ella Fitzgerald, which David thought was 'magical', with 'wonderful vibes'.

A few days later, Elton told David that he had something for him: a Pioneer Stereo System. And this was only the start; the singer could be breathtakingly generous with people he liked.

At that time, David happened to be searching for work. Not to replace his printing job with Bill King, whom he seemed tied to like a marriage, but something on the side that would utilise his own talents as a photographer. An approach had been made to Jann Wenner, publisher of *Rolling Stone*, on his behalf; David had also taken his portfolio to Howard Bloom, head of public relations at ABC Records (though he was less than enthused about the musicians Bloom represented).

A few days after the stereo arrived, David received another gift from Elton in the form of an invitation. It came via Linda Stein, the band manager, and then through Tony King directly: Would David like to come to Los Angeles to watch Elton perform at Dodger Stadium, the first rock concert to be held there since the Beatles played in 1966?

This was not a job offer as such; there was already an official photographer, Terry O'Neill, who had worked with Elton for years. David would just be part of the entourage, though they wanted him to stay on for a couple of weeks. Money was not discussed – everything was done informally around Elton, who just paid your rent, picked up tabs, gave you gifts or sums of cash from time to time – but David didn't care about those kinds of details anyway. He wanted to get away. *Needed* to get away from New York. 'Can't believe it,' he wrote in his diary after accepting the offer.

Having announced to Bill King that he would be gone for a while, David then flew to the West Coast. It was 24 October. Tony collected him at the airport and drove them to the Holiday Inn in Westwood, which John Reid had rented out for friends and family flown in from London on a private Pan Am jet. David, however, would be staying elsewhere, in Tony's luxurious apartment. And Elton John was staying in Beverly Hills at a mansion that had once been owned by Greta Garbo.

At Dodger Stadium, over the following two days, Elton played for

110,000 people. David watched both concerts from the press box. He also watched Terry O'Neill snapping photographs of Elton, capturing 'what it must have looked like from Elton's perspective', as O'Neill later wrote, 'looking out at Dodger Stadium in front of tens of thousands of fans, screaming fans, people who were singing along with him, songs he and Bernie Taupin wrote . . .'

David had brought his own camera to Los Angeles, and he used it liberally to shoot the action backstage. These images of Elton John – and Billie Jean King and Cary Grant, among others – would turn out to be the first of thousands he would take over the next decade, a kind of dress rehearsal for a position he had no idea was even on the table.

Elton John at Dodger Stadium with Billie Jean King and Cary Grant.

After the second concert, on 26 October, John Reid threw a big din-ner to celebrate Elton's record-breaking achievement. Everyone was drunk and emotional, and David cosied close to Elton, who had already burst into tears during the performance. Suddenly, Elton turned and invited him to Paris. David, without a moment's hesitation, said yes. 'Will join him there,' he wrote in his diary. 'Love him.'

Tommy and Edward arrived in Los Angeles on 7 November, which meant an overlap with David of three days. Plenty of time, it turned out, for Tommy to infuriate his brother by failing to call for the first twenty-four hours; and then, when they did finally connect, by asking him if he was 'getting enough out of Elton' – a question that thoroughly appalled David.

The official purpose of Tommy and Edward's trip was to follow up on Edward's previous visit in April, fitting orders and taking new ones from an elegant suite in the Beverly Wilshire. However, it soon transpired that Tommy had an ulterior motive too. 'It seems so old-fashioned today to look like a hippie and act bizarre,' he told the *Los Angeles Times*. 'What I'm doing is bringing younger men back to suits, glamor, tailoring – things that haven't been in for years.' In other words, he was scheming to open his first American boutique. 'I am going to create a store that is similar in design to a fine tailor's shop in London. And I'm doing my first ready-to-wear line for Los Angeles.' He had been reading about Chanel, he added, and hoped 'to create the first really expensive men's cologne'. He felt that Hollywood was going to be 'very lucky' for him.

Tommy had an accomplice for these plans in the form of Peter Brown, who was also in Los Angeles. Recently, Peter had left the Robert Stigwood Organisation ('I was bored with the music business'), raised some capital on Wall Street, and migrated over to California to develop movies. As far as Peter knew, Nutters was still going strong in London, so he'd arranged some meetings for Tommy on Rodeo Drive, where a space had recently become available to rent.

Edward went along to listen, though he was flummoxed by this whole scenario. 'I was a realist,' he recalls. 'I was thinking, "This is all a pipe dream! We can't even pay our bills where we are, let alone open a shop on Rodeo Drive."'

Hadn't Tommy just moved into a tiny bedsit above the Savile Row store in order to save some money? Edward couldn't understand his reasoning here. But then, Edward understood increasingly less about his partner these days. Edward did not (does not) see himself in terms of an artist. 'I think there's a lot of art in what we do,' he says, but he prefers the label 'craftsman'. He had come to Los Angeles to collect the business they needed to sustain a strong, vibrant *craftsman's* firm on Savile Row, one that could provide them with comfortable incomes while also allowing them to express their taste and ideas through excellent work. From Edward's perspective, that is what Nutters had started out as in 1969, and it was what he'd signed up for as head cutter. 'No one wanted to be a designer. No one wanted to be a legend. It was just two young fellas working hard, believing in what they did.' Only now Tommy was pulling things in a different direction, an 'exasperating' one that seemed foreign to Edward, not to mention financially parlous.

In truth, Tommy didn't like Los Angeles very much. Peter spent a few days driving him around the spaghetti-like freeways, past gated mansions, lonely canyons, endless suburban sprawl, the blue Pacific shimmering perpetually away in the distance. One afternoon, they returned to Peter's new house in West Hollywood, just off Melrose Avenue. Tommy decided he had seen enough. 'So,' he demanded, 'where is the *glamour*?' As though Peter were deliberately withholding it.

'Tommy, I don't think there is any,' Peter replied.

This was not an acceptable answer.

Here is what Tommy told the *Los Angeles Times* about his first impressions of the city (impressions that were based in reality, but then embellished by his rococo imagination): 'I expected to see people dancing down the street doing the conga around palm trees. Fred Astaire has been a big influence on me. But I suppose I'm luckier than most tourists. The first person I saw when I got off the plane was Paul Newman. And the very first time I went to a Hollywood party Mae West walked up to me and said, "Come up and do a suit for me sometime."'

David's diary, 1976

11

THAT WONDERFUL SUMMER

To recuperate in the sunshine after a hectic year of non-stop touring and recording, Elton John rented a mansion in St James, a wealthy enclave on the west side of Barbados. For the 'Christmas season' – that is, from early December until the middle of January – he would retreat from the spotlight and concentrate on his health, both physical and mental. Elton was joined in this convalescence by a rotating line-up of band members, promotions staff, Bernie Taupin, Kiki Dee and David, who was stunned to be included on the list. From Los Angeles, he'd flown home to New York for all of seven days, then rejoined Elton in Toronto ('E. J. took the plunge and came to Manatee with us . . . The kids in the disco couldn't believe their eyes'). Now he found himself in a lavish palace with its own retinue of waiting staff, adjacent to a Caribbean beach that was filled with roving Barbadians. 'Beauties all around,' David wrote in his diary. 'Am going mad.'

Each morning, the first person to wake up had to throw open the windows, initiate prep for a communal breakfast of Bloody Marys, put a record on the stereo, and play their theme song at maximum volume: that was the rule. For Elton, it was 'Babyface', by Wing and a Prayer Fife and Drum Corps. For Tony King, it was 'Jump for Joy', by Biddu Orchestra. For Mike Hewitson, Elton's valet, it was 'All By Myself', by Eric Carmen. And for David, it was 'That Old Black Magic', sung by Frank Sinatra – though it was never David who woke up first.

For six weeks, life passed in a hot blur of sunbathing, swimming, jet-skiing, charades, alcohol binges, hangovers, photography sessions and at least one mock-voodoo ritual. David sat on a towel and wrote cards to Tommy and Dolly back home in London. He went shopping with Elton in the boutiques of Holetown – Elton shopped, David watched – and took a 'native-type bus' to catch *Jaws* at the cinema. Elton and Bernie Taupin drafted some new tracks at the house piano, including 'Snow Queen', which would end up as the B-side for 'Don't Go Breaking My Heart'; David was awarded a song credit after suggesting some dirty lyrics (sanitised before release). At night, the whole group would migrate over to Oliver Messel's house for cocktails – the stage designer was more pleasant than David expected – or hit the local disco so hard that David, next morning, would not be entirely sure how he'd even got home. His propensity to party until the sun came up soon earned him a nickname, as did his preference for darker men.

Dawn Black.

(This particularly entertained Elton, who was already well known as 'Sharon', and Tony King, who was 'Joy' and largely responsible for the monikers.)

Within a matter of days, David watched as his skin began to spontaneously clear from the salt water and fresh air. In fact, everyone was 'looking much healthier', he noticed, including Elton, who had also never seemed so calm or reasonable. Sure, there were still those legendary tantrums – at one point, Elton lost it and announced that Christmas was 'cancelled' – but the outbursts in Barbados were balanced out by self-reflective humility, genuine regret.

One day, Elton left David a letter in which he apologised for his unreasonable behaviour, saying that he was ashamed at how his actions were affecting others. He told David that he was doing his best to improve, to be a better person, and that David's ongoing support was hugely appreciated.

When David found the letter waiting for him in the house, he read it and nearly burst into tears. (He would hold it in safe keeping for decades afterwards.) His relationship with Elton existed in a peculiar liminal state between friend and employee, but it had become vital to his own enduring happiness. The two men shared emotional temperaments, an appreciation of surrealism. More important, though, they reassured each other. David made Elton feel better about himself ('I get depressed easily,' he would soon tell *Rolling Stone*. 'Very bad moods. I don't think anyone knows the real me. I don't even think I do'); and Elton, for his part, made David feel valued. Some nights they would sit together on the sand in St James, rating crashing waves from 1 to 10 while David did some knitting. For months afterwards, David would smell the seawater in his woollies and vividly recall their intimate conversations.

In early January, people began to fly back to America or England, back to their lives and adult responsibilities. David stole glances towards his own return date with a sense of impending doom. 'Only about a week to go,' he wrote in his diary. 'Feel awful about leaving dear Barbados.' But then everyone did, apparently: 'Elton had a good cry after stripping twice.' As the hourglass emptied further, David struggled to control his saturnine moods, until they finally overcame him: 'These last few days are really sad – got depression in morning.'

As David recalls, 'I was thinking that I have to go back to my dismal life after this. Nothing's getting any better. I haven't got any money. I'm either *up*, with no sense of anything, or *down*, and not wanting to even leave my apartment. This is all so unreal, this life, these millionaires ...'

Barbados was manifest escapism, a superior 'unreal' life that he was desperate to prolong. And, in fact, he would prolong it – for several more months. David touched down in New York on 15 January; a little more than four weeks later, he lifted off again for Los Angeles, to do some work for Elton with Tony King. Then, after a blink, he was back in Barbados toiling with Bernie Taupin and Alan Aldridge over the unproduced film script of *Captain Fantastic and the Brown Dirt Cowboy*. Then, another blink, he was up in Toronto, where Elton was laying down *Blue Moves*, for which David would take photographs for the inside album cover.

During this adrenaline rush, intoxicating and propulsive, David made a hurried note in his diary that stands out as jarring and, given all that happened afterwards, particularly important.

2 February: ... Peter Brown has been calling every day to see about Tommy's business, etc. – boring.

Ten weeks later, he then recorded a piece of news that could no longer be shrugged off as 'boring':

20 April: Spoke to Peter Brown. Apparently Edward has taken over the Nutter business from under Tommy's nose.

What really happened at Nutters of Savile Row in the spring of 1976? Was Tommy the victim of an internal coup, Edward and his assistants seizing control above their stations? Or was it more complicated than that, the case of an inattentive owner and his unhappy workers who tried to rescue the ship before it capsized?

In January or February, Tommy had flown to Johannesburg to visit his friend Jimmy Clark, who had recently moved there from London. He'd also met up with a journalist and mentioned his Beverly Hills plan, suggesting, for the record, 'that he might open a Nutters branch here' – in South Africa. That fantasy, recalls Jimmy Clark, 'was undoubtedly the catalyst which caused the total break-up between Edward and himself. Edward was absolutely furious that Tommy came down, because in reality the prospect of any business from such a visit was virtually zero.'

A definitive explanation of what occurred after that Johannesburg visit has eluded curious onlookers for decades. And in the absence of any surviving financial documentation, an objective narrative of 'the total break-up' remains all but impossible. But what does survive is perhaps more fitting for a story about unreliable storytellers anyway: opinion, rumour, hearsay, conjecture, and heated, contradictory accounts from the people involved. A chorus of inharmonious voices, in other words, which may nevertheless offer some echo of the true story.

EDWARD SEXTON This is a whole life story. I've been very much part of this person's life, and the creation of all this clothing. I've got a big investment of *my* life here, haven't I? So I want this to be very open and honest.

CHRISTOPHER TARLING I hope you get the truth from Edward. Didn't they go to America, and then Tommy went AWOL or something? You know, being the front man on a business like that, you have to deal with a lot of shit. Not every customer is easy. And Tommy was still being the front man. He'd got there, not making much money, I don't think, by working his arse off. Then something must have happened that made him think, 'Fuck, what's all this about?'

EDWARD SEXTON We made chic, elegant clothing. That's what I've been doing all my life. Tommy was fantastic at it, nobody could touch him, socialising and bringing in the right type of clients. There's never been another Tommy and there never will be, and as a team we were dynamic. I had some great times with Tommy, believe you me. I've got nothing but love and affection for him as a person and a creative figure.

But as a businessman, he was fucking useless. I'm telling you from the inside that there was a lot of extravagance going on. Tommy was very, very extravagant. He just didn't want to perform his daily duties, like keeping control of the accounts. There were many, many things – quite a few years when he used to just drive me nuts. You're making the most beautiful suits, and then he'd be out with his trick: the next thing you see, the trick is wearing the suits I'd made for him. And I remember that Tommy came on selling trips with me to America, but what did he do there? Fucked off to Central Park West, where Peter was at. He didn't stay in the hotel with me; he stayed with Peter Brown. And he'd go off early instead of staying and working with the clients. He didn't have his finger on the pulse.

DAVID GRIGG You wouldn't have known things weren't going well. They were making so many suits. It's really bizarre. They had such an incredible clientele, all the tailors were working, they were charging decent prices. I don't understand what went wrong, unless Tommy was spending a fortune. But I don't think he was. It wasn't like he was buying large houses. He rented his flat. He didn't have a car. He struggled to buy that flat down in Brighton.

CHRISTOPHER TARLING None of these people were businesspeople. None of us have been good with money. Tommy would spend his last twenty quid on a round of drinks. He was incredibly generous.

ROY CHITTLEBOROUGH Tommy was a designer, basically. He used to come in at ten o'clock, ten thirty, whenever he felt like it. He was his own man. He would just walk in and go into his little office, doodle away there with different designs. In lots of instances he didn't want to see people. He was one of those shy guys. So the three of us cutters – Edward, Joe and myself – sort of got on with the work, saw the clients.

EDWARD SEXTON I'd hired all the tailors, run the workshop, run the diaries – everything. I just saw that the thing flowed and we produced beautiful clothing.

ZANCE YIANNI Edward was an amazing cutter. He basically was the tailoring side. Tommy was, for want of a better word, the salesman, but much more than that too. He was always doing something, getting the name out to people. And the two of them worked together *because* they were completely different. Unfortunately, things did come to a head when I was there for a variety of reasons. I thought there was an element of – maybe Edward didn't feel that he was getting the credit he deserved. Tommy always made sure that he sang his praises; it wasn't like Tommy was trying to slight him in any way. But Tommy was getting most of the limelight, there's no two ways about it.

DAVID GRIGG Tommy was the creative force. That may be disputed by Edward, and obviously there must have been some crossover. Tommy did these funny, very stylised sketches. Edward can say, 'I interpreted them,' and it's certainly a talent to be able to do that.

JOSEPH MORGAN I think Edward wanted to be Tom. I'd say this in front of Edward, because it's only fair. I was there, and that's my interpretation of things. Edward had great skill – *still* has great skill, is a great technician. But he's not Tom.

ZANCE YIANNI Having looked back on it now, Tommy probably felt that he was being ganged up upon. Because Edward was the one who started doing all the business side of things. And Roy and Joe were cutters as well; they were working very closely with Edward. I don't know where their sympathies were. I think they probably, naturally, aligned themselves with Edward . . . I got the impression the business was in a bit of a state, financially. What came across is that they felt Tommy was almost a luxury. Which was quite ironic, because *he* was the business. It was his name. He was the one who attracted the people in. As good as Edward, Joe and Roy were as cutters, none of them had the personality or the contacts that Tommy did.

STEWART GRIMSHAW What I think happened was that Tommy didn't really know the difference, or notice the difference, between a 51 per cent and 49 per cent stake in the company. And he was persuaded to give away 5 per cent of his own shares – not much [but enough to lose his position as controlling shareholder]. By that time, Edward thought he wasn't as serious as he might have been. I think Tommy lost focus on the business side of things, and Edward said, 'Somebody's joining us, why don't we give 5 per cent each . . .' and then instantly turned against him.

JOSEPH MORGAN I think it was when Edward came back with Tom [in 1971] and said, 'We've got rid of Peter Brown and the other investors, and we're going to take the company forward.' And, I think, 'We're going to give you some shares.' I got three shares. I think Roy got about five. And Tommy and Edward had the rest.

PETER BROWN When I left London, Tommy was the sole owner. And then he gives shares to Edward and the staff and didn't do his maths. Then Edward starts bossing him around . . . I'm sure he could make a case that Tommy was a terrible businessman, and he was much better, but that doesn't mean you remove him as the leading shareholder.

EDWARD SEXTON We never had a formal shareholding structure, we just didn't know about doing things like that.

JOSEPH MORGAN I recall that there was talk. Edward said, 'I think it's time that I was made managing director so I can run the company as it ought to be run.'

EDWARD SEXTON I said, 'Look, I'm going to take control of the finances and everything, you can go and have your lunches, bring your receipts in, and you'll get your money back.'

JOSEPH MORGAN Whoa, hold on! And then it was put to Tom, and I think Tom said, 'How can I let you be managing director when my name's above the door? Can't do that.'

EDWARD SEXTON Joe went upstairs and knocked on the door [of Tommy's new flat], and I think Tommy turned round to Joe and said, 'You can't change managing directors because my name is on the window.' Well, his name was not. *Nutters* was on the window. And *Nutters* was owned by the company.

JOSEPH MORGAN So that was that. Then Edward and I went off to America. Roy stayed with Tom, and when we came back, he'd gone.

EDWARD SEXTON Where has he gone? What's happening?

DAVID GRIGG Sometimes Tommy could go off the blink. Like, you couldn't get hold of him.

ZANCE YIANNI I was working there the day Tommy left, but they were quite discreet about it. It wasn't really happening in front of the staff.

ROY CHITTLEBOROUGH I don't recall any big upheaval. I don't know what led up to it. I know at times Edward sort of wanted to do his own thing. I think Tommy sort of didn't like what he was doing at times . . . and he just walked out on us. There was basically no discussion at all. He just left, went to his flat, and I never saw him again.

DAVID GRIGG I think Edward and Tommy must have had some huge argument. I can hear Tommy saying, 'Oh, fuck you all! If you think you can do it on your own, then do it' – and stomping off. I can imagine that. Because they were putting so much pressure on him: 'We're the people who are making this happen . . .'

ZANCE YIANNI I suspect Tommy felt let down by the others. A bit betrayed. Which was horrible, because they were friends.

JOSEPH MORGAN If only he'd come to us and said, 'Look, I think I'm going to have to leave.' We'd have said, 'Hold on, let's try to work this out.' But no, nothing at all. It's very upsetting to think he felt he couldn't talk. Why didn't Tom fight for it? I'm really surprised that he didn't.

PETER BROWN The big picture, really, is that Tommy was this brilliant person with a great eye, meticulous about things when he was *creating*. And then the rest of Tommy was irresponsible, more or less, which is maybe not fair, but is to some degree. And Edward was a brilliant cutter, period, who did see this as a wonderful way of making a living. Which was true. And if Tommy had been more responsible and *stronger*, then they would have made a good partnership. If Tommy had behaved better, maybe Edward wouldn't have felt the need to be so hard. It's a great shame. Joe's right that Tommy should have fought for it. Most people would have. But that was Tommy.

EDWARD SEXTON I don't know what other people are going to tell you, and I'm not interested. I'm just telling you the way it was. We were a great, great team, and it was a tragedy that Tommy was such a big girl, and couldn't sit down and say, 'Fuck it, we're going to get this by the scruff of the neck and we're going to make it work.' He could have been one of the greats.

ZANCE YIANNI I don't think anybody comes out with glory from this whole thing. There must be a few regrets on all sides that it reached the point it did. It's just sad, because it was such a unique situation. Anyway, I don't know that it could have lasted much longer. Things had reached a point where bespoke tailoring felt almost old-fashioned in Britain, like a dying trade. All of a sudden you've got these business-people coming into fashion with a completely different mentality. So Nutters was almost fated to fail eventually. There was something about it that was too innocent.

Like jumping into the Thames or the Aegean Sea, Tommy's jump from Nutters of Savile Row was swift, impulsive and mostly inexplicable. 'I'm definitely leaving,' he told the *Daily Express* in early May, making it public and official, 'but I can't tell you yet whether Edward Sexton will replace me as Managing Director. He's away in America. It's very difficult for me to comment at the moment.' And beyond that he didn't comment, in any consistent way, for the rest of his life. Instead, Tommy preferred hints and allusions, grumbles and sighs, suggesting, depending on how he felt at any given moment, three wildly different versions of events.

1.

In the first version, Tommy walked away because he was bored. At what seemed like the height of his popularity, he simply 'took a year off' to reset and refresh. There was no real argument in the cutting room, no showdown with Edward Sexton. On a radio programme in 1980, Tommy would say, 'I felt that I'd achieved everything I wanted to in the Savile Row area, as far as bespoke tailoring is concerned . . . and I took that wonderful year, that wonderful summer of 1976, and sort of wore jeans and a T-shirt and enjoyed St James's Park.' This was a glamorised version of the past, obviously, but there was at least one germ of truth: Tommy had achieved everything he wanted to as a Savile Row tailor. His ambitions were bigger. That had been part of the problem.

2.

'There was jiggery-pokery going on,' Tommy once told Richard Walker, a Savile Row historian, 'and I felt I didn't want any part of it.' This second version, which could be called his 'down and out' narrative (as Tommy once described his ensuing months of joblessness), was slightly closer to the probable facts. 'I had reporters chasing me down the street, but I kept quiet about it because it was so messy,' he said.

The following year, Tommy would sit down with David Taylor from *Punch* magazine and offer an annoyed explanation that Taylor would then translate into a tour-de-force of breathless monologuing:

> Cutters can turn squabblesome at the drop of a stitch, there'd been an ill-advised attempt to diversify into shirts and talk of toiletries, some felt this was too *loud* or that was too *passé* and what with one thing and another Tommy thought, well, chuck this for a game of soldiers, I'm off. And off he stomped, clean out of the shop into which he had sunk his savings and look at the thanks he gets and, well, he'd just retire to his Curzon Street apartment and week-ending Brighton pied-à-terre and cultivate only the loyal company of Clarence, his cat. He did nothing much for twelve months except slop around in denims and sweaters looking dreadful and feeling if anything worse, wondering whether to abandon the trade, started a noveletta about this girl who makes good from an ordinary background and, it so happens, isn't Twiggy either, and dined out and went to the theatre, and though anybody might think he was rich enough not to mind, is *not*, and is still today a bit pressed, because quality clothes *cost* to have hand-made, you know, and it isn't just profit from tailors' dummies, not by a long chalk-stripe.

Despite its conflations and errors (he never lived on Curzon Street), this stands as Tommy's most comprehensive public testimony of what, in his opinion, actually happened at No. 35a.

3.

There was another version, though, confided to friends after he'd had time to lick his wounds and reflect. It involved a man with whom Tommy had been briefly but intensely involved sometime around 1975: Antony Hamilton, a blond, Adonis-like former dancer with the Australian Ballet. Tommy had been smitten with Hamilton – even, perhaps, seriously in love, more seriously than he ever had been with anyone before. Tommy's friends noticed that when Hamilton was around, Tommy became unavailable, out socialising with his boyfriend, though their relationship could not have lasted more than a few months before falling apart. It soon became clear that Tommy was being exploited; Hamilton, a 'top model' aspiring to Hollywood, was using the famous tailor to get a leg up in his own career.

Years later, Tommy would tell a close friend that his overwhelming feelings during this period had caused his attention to drift from the business. While he was with Antony Hamilton, he could think of nothing else. He was infatuated, obsessed, and it was this that Tommy eventually pointed to as a reason for his downfall. In the 1980s, he would tell his assistant Wendy Samimi that he'd never make the same mistake again: it was either a career or his personal life, one or the other. Tommy could not focus on both, he came to believe, without risking everything.

At the exact moment Tommy began to tumble towards his personal nadir, David, over in New York, received an offer for the job of a lifetime: official photographer for Elton John's upcoming three-month transatlantic concert tour. 'It's a wonderful opportunity, but a shock,' David wrote after Elton phoned him up to ask personally.

Within five days of Tommy walking away from Savile Row, David flew to London. He needed to be in Leeds for the first performance on 29 April. Before driving up the country in a Land Rover, though, he wanted to see his brother to find out what had happened.

They caught up face-to-face, then went to a pub to talk things over. Tommy seemed 'in good shape', David wrote. 'Coping well with the Edward drama.' Still, it was strange how fortunes had suddenly turned, Tommy now a penniless mess, and David (though still a mess, in many ways) preparing for a huge adventure.

Reunited in their old stomping grounds, the Nutters finished their drinks and decided to do something they'd once done together nearly every week of their formative years. The Rockingham was long gone, of course, but now there was Bang!, on Charing Cross Road: strobe lights and a cinema screen showing Busby Berkeley dance routines, DJs Tallulah or Gary London spinning imported tracks for a thousand sweaty men. Times had changed dramatically, but that night Tommy and David got 'très drunk', David later wrote in his diary, and danced to forget about all of it.

LOUDER THAN CONCORDE

Beginning on 29 April 1976, Elton John's British tour lasted for thirty-six days, with an exhausting schedule of twenty-nine performances. Intended as a thank-you to the people who first vaulted him to superstardom, it skipped larger venues in favour of small towns and 3,000-seater halls, the kind of places usually ignored by titans of rock 'n' roll. Inevitably, that also meant modest hotel suites, a lack of twenty-four-hour service, diminutive dressing rooms, and, as Bernie Taupin later put it, 'brown ale and cheese sandwiches'. Not that Elton seemed to mind too much. On opening night, he danced across the stage of the Leeds Grand Theatre with a giant gold banana dangling around his neck, 'really sincere', in the eyes of one local critic, with 'not a trace of arrogance'.

Beginning on 29 June, Elton's US tour then lasted for fifty-one days, with a slightly less exhausting schedule of thirty-one performances. Offering considerably more elevated comfort was *Starship 1*, a private Boeing 720 jet that would be used to ferry Elton and his band between venues across the country. The tour got off to a rocky start, though, after an awful scene in New York, which David carefully recorded: 'The guy said, "What's this, Halloween?" Elton overreacted and threw a glass ashtray at him. Reid hit him in the face. All totally unnecessary, really. Big down for me: Elton told me to shove New York up my arse.'

Indeed, things would struggle to gain positive momentum (in Philadelphia, security was lax, and Elton walked off the stage threatening to cancel the show; at a hotel pool in Charlotte, somebody flashed him and caused another nuclear meltdown) until late July, when Elton phoned David's room to say that 'Don't Go Breaking My Heart' was number one on the UK charts – a morale booster.

Back in New York, the Louder Than Concorde (But Not Quite as Pretty!) tour ended on 17 August, after a week of sell-out concerts at Madison Square Garden in which Elton played for 137,000 people. 'Never seen Sharon so sublimely happy,' David wrote in his diary. 'We all got very emotional about each other.'

At the very last party, Elton sat back down at his piano and dedicated a performance of 'Island Girl' to his photographer, who had documented almost every show from Birmingham to Chicago, and every side-trip from Coventry to the Playboy Mansion, and every single one of Elton's bespoke suits that had been designed by his own brother. Before a roomful of people, Elton anointed David – or Dawn, as everyone was calling him now – the 'International Dinge Queen', and he gave him the queenly gift of a Cartier diamond.

David and
Elton between
performances

Performing
with Bonnie
Raitt; nap-
time; in bed
with Divine.

Foosball with Hugh Hefner and Barbi Benton.

CLOCKWISE: On *Starship 1*; a Playboy Bunny; in the dressing room.

With John Reid (in a Groucho Marx sweater).

With Queen.

With decadent eyewear.

With Elizabeth Taylor.

PART III

1977–1992

Imagine a pleasure in which the moment of satisfaction is simultaneous with the moment of destruction: to kiss is to poison; lifting to your lips this face after which you have ached, dreamed, longed for, the face shatters, every time.

ANDREW HOLLERAN, *Dancer from the Dance*

Freddie Mercury

12

THE VELVET ROPE

The most terrifying episode of David's life began on 4 February 1977 in San Francisco, when he boarded a flight bound for New York with an enormous quantity of Quaaludes hidden in his carry-on luggage. The prescription sedatives, all illegally procured – 'thousands of them', David recalls – belonged to Bill King, who had called in a favour. David had agreed to transport the pills without so much as a second thought, as though it were just another part of his day job. Yesterday he was a darkroom technician; today he would be a drug mule.

Touching down in New York, David managed to clear the airport without being questioned. He returned to his apartment on the Upper West Side, then emptied out his bags. As a kind of carrier's fee, he pocketed a few of the Quaaludes – or 'disco biscuits', as he and his friends preferred to call them.

That evening, David trudged into a deep February freeze, so cold that at least thirty-six people had already died in the north-east, and made his way down to the Meatpacking District. At Fifteenth Street and Tenth Avenue he came to Crisco Disco, a club where the DJ booth was modelled after a giant tub of vegetable shortening, and where everybody bought tickets and then exchanged them for drinks to circumvent the lack of an alcohol licence. David swallowed his biscuits and went inside. He began to cruise the dance floor beneath a cluster of mirror balls. Recently, he'd surprised himself with new-found boldness, noting in his diary: 'Look what's happened to Dawn – rampant woman.' Now he pressed against the men, dancing and pressing until finally somebody pressed back.

And then everything went dark.

David woke up back in his apartment on the Upper West Side. The ludes had triggered a blackout. He had no memory of exiting the club. No memory of travelling home with the stranger. No memory, either, of having his hands bound together behind his back 'like a Perdue chicken'.

As David struggled to regain consciousness, the stranger was standing over him. He punched David in the face and told him he was going to die.

David slumped to the floor, stunned. The man – a shadowy outline, in David's recollection – walked away and began to search the apartment for objects of value: a stereo, a camera, things he could carry. David was terrified; but once the man found enough loot, he just exited through the front door, which slammed shut – and locked tight – behind him.

David tried to calm his nerves. He knew he would never get out with his hands bound together.

First, he crawled into the kitchen. He had, he recalls, a vague, improbable notion of burning through the rope using the flame from his gas stove. But when that didn't work (because of course it didn't work) he shuffled back into the living room. He looked around. On the floor was a rotary dial telephone. This gave him another idea. 'What I did – I dialled my neighbour, Chris, using my tongue.' One number after the other. Round and round.

'He was frantic,' remembers Chris Albertson, a journalist and jazz critic, who hung up the call and rushed over. 'Of course, David couldn't come to the door, so I went around to the fire escape. I don't know how I pulled the ladder down and got up there. But desperate times call for desperate measures. The window to his apartment was half open, so I climbed through. And there he was, all tied up, looking very relieved.'

The next day, 5 February, David had the lock changed on his front door. His face was a battlefield of bruises and cuts, though he didn't bother consulting a doctor to check for more serious damage. When he did finally leave his apartment later that evening, it was to go to the Oh-Ho-So restaurant on West Broadway. Queen had just finished its first-ever performance at Madison Square Garden – singing, among other songs, 'Tie Your Mother Down' – and the after-party by Elektra Records was not to be missed.

At the restaurant, David pushed his way past Eric Idle, John Belushi, the members of Thin Lizzy . . . all the way up to Freddie Mercury, who was holding court. David had met Freddie through Elton John two years before, and since then they'd partied together at bars like Hollywood and the Barefoot Boy, becoming firm friends. Freddie had taken a shine to David, who he thought was hilarious; for one of David's birthdays, he would give him a male stripper and a custom-made maroon jumpsuit with DAWN BLACK emblazoned on the front. Now Freddie took one look at David's face and turned very grave. Why did he have a black eye? What the hell was going on here? Who was responsible? David confessed the truth about his larcenous trick and Freddie became incensed. 'He read me the riot act,' David recalls. 'He said, "Don't you *ever* do anything like that again".'

A few days later, David composed a letter laying out the whole sorry tale for his brother. Tommy, horrified, dashed off his own reproach from London.

> *My dear – what a calamity. No scars, I hope. You really must be more careful . . . I must say it is the ruination of a girl . . . I hope you were insured but I suppose you were not. Must have been an awful shock. I would have gone completely to pieces. I don't think it's ever happened to me – but there's always a first time.*

If there is a strong whiff of fatalism in Tommy's reply, then perhaps that's because he was still living through his own nightmare. Walking out of Nutters had cost Tommy more than just his place on Savile Row. Because he refused to speak to Edward, let alone negotiate with him, he failed to secure any compensation for his share in the company (though Edward maintains there was no real equity anyway). He also lost his home, because 'rent and all out-goings' from the small flat he was using as a residence were paid for directly through the shop (meaning it technically belonged to Nutters). Indeed, Tommy was left with virtually nothing, awkwardly dependent on the generosity of his close friends.

In the immediate aftermath, David Grigg stepped forward to offer a place for him to stay. David lived with his father, Barry Grigg, an older gay man who also happened to work in the tailoring trade and therefore had a great deal in common with his son's former employer. ('My father was incredibly extravagant,' David recalls. 'He and Tommy got on really well, actually.') David and Barry lived on Bayswater Road, in a house facing the north side of Hyde Park. With Barry's consent, Tommy moved into the spare room, like a member of the family who had suddenly returned after a long absence. Tommy was extremely grateful for the gracious welcome, though he was also dazed by his diminished circumstances. He passed solitary hours drinking in the local pubs, reclining on deckchairs near the Serpentine, looking for sex in all the familiar places. 'I was working,' David recalls, 'so I didn't see him during the day. At night we often went out to Bang! or Napoleons.'

After living in limbo with the Griggs for a while, Tommy migrated over to Chelsea, where Stewart Grimshaw (of Provans) and his partner, Simon Sainsbury, maintained an empty flat for their guests on the Vale. Tommy, again, was extremely appreciative of his friends' hospitality, writing to his brother: 'They are very kind and have really helped the old girl out through this tricky period.' This second address gave him greater privacy, even a small degree of luxury. But he knew that it was only a temporary solution.

Once Tommy was settled in Chelsea, he began to sketch out various schemes for a solo comeback. His first idea was for an exclusive bespoke service, a kind of designer-for-hire. He told his brother (in the rush of confidence that comes with a new idea before its requirements are properly considered): 'Madame Pam is back in business. I feel that I will be able to make more bread by keeping the whole thing much smaller – no overheads – and just keep the best clients – i.e., EJ [Elton John], JR [John Reid], and not keep them waiting so long.'

This idea was quickly discarded as impractical, however, and

Tommy turned his sights to America instead. There was a 'marvellous offer' from a man to 'revamp' his fashion business in Los Angeles; a new start in Beverly Hills seemed alluring. But then Peter 'checked him out' by investigating his bona fides and found him to be 'very shady'.

So Tommy looked closer to home: a new Mayfair shop, backed by the Jean Junction, was being managed by Justin de Villeneuve, the ex-manager of Twiggy. Perhaps he could become an in-house designer? 'This might come off but it all takes so long,' he complained.

He also began to eye an empty showroom on the corner of Bond and Grosvenor streets, imagining elegant suits styled in the picture windows of a modern gentlemen's boutique – a kind of Nutters redux. Trying to retread the pathway to his previous success, he put the idea to a potential celebrity backer: Elton John. Elton was intrigued, though John Reid, as his moneyman, questioned the practicalities. Reid thought the rent was exorbitant, the location was awkward for a menswear boutique, and Tommy's vision was far too unfocused. 'He wasn't able to translate anything onto paper. I kept saying, "Give me a plan." He'd say, "But it will be *fabulous*, everyone will flock there . . ."' This vague dreaminess may have persuaded people back in the 1960s, but these were more cynical times. David Grigg was sitting with Tommy when Reid finally called him to say that it would never work, that Elton had to pass on the project. 'It was like popping a balloon,' Grigg recalls.

After that, Tommy crumpled into uncharacteristic anxiety. 'The JR thing really fucked me up,' he wrote to his brother. 'So much time was lost.' He brooded about the Bond Street shop, worked himself into a state, and blamed Reid as personally responsible for his dashed hopes, though he remained cautiously 'friendly' to Reid's face. 'No point in doing a number as I might need him one day.' This was not particularly fair to Reid, but Tommy was so furious at having been given so much contradictory advice on how to get back into business that he was 'almost going crazy'.

His most pressing concern was cash flow. Tommy had meagre savings, which he quickly burned through; he also had a mortgage for the Brighton flat to consider. 'When I bought Brighton I had a loan from the bank,' he explained in a letter to David, 'which they are now wanting me to re-pay and of course until I am back in business this is absolutely impossible.'

The thought of losing Brighton made Tommy morose. Not only was it his sanctuary, it was also a tangible symbol of everything he'd worked to achieve over the past seven years. He'd *earned* it, and now it was imperilled. One day, he swallowed his pride and asked David Grigg to take it off his hands, hoping he could then lease it back to maintain an illusion of continuity. But Grigg, who was still in his early twenties, had to decline. ('I didn't have any money either,' he recalls.) Eventually, the bank increased its pressure to the point where Tommy turned frantic. 'I am being threatened with bankruptcy – if this happens I am completely finished,' he wrote to his brother.

> *I have put Brighton on the market, and the profit I get from this will re-pay the bank. They are quite happy with the arrangement, but in the meantime, to stop me going bankrupt, I need a guarantor to keep the bank happy. This means a deposit with the bank that will not be touched but will keep them happy until Brighton is sold.*
>
> *I have no idea the extent to which you have earned with Elton, but if there is any way you could help me out with this deposit it would guarantee me getting back into business the right way. No-one wants to know about a bankrupt. The ghastly sum would be around $6000. I know it is a hell of a lot but I can assure you that it would not be touched. This would only have to be lodged with the National Westminster in Wall St.*
>
> *David, if this is an absolute impossibility I fully understand. There are other people I can ask, but I do not want everyone to know my business.*

David received this letter – and did nothing, because there was nothing he could do. Even a fraction of that sum was an absolute impossibility in 1976.

One week after the Louder Than Concorde tour had ended that August, David flew to Los Angeles at Elton's request. In part this was for a well-deserved holiday, the wind-down after months of living on the road. But it was also for a meeting to discuss financial compensation. There had been no contract in advance of the tour laying out the terms of David's employment – nothing, it seems, beyond a verbal agreement that he would step in as official photographer for both the UK and America dates. Despite Tommy having prodded him to make sure he was 'getting enough out of Elton', David had been content to coast along on sporadic gifts and rent payments. On 24 August, in Los Angeles, he now wrote in his diary: 'Meeting with Connie and EJ. They want to give me a lot of money. About $30,000. I couldn't believe it.' Like winning the lottery, this lump-sum payment would transform David's life completely.

It never arrived. By October, the offer was revised into a salary, to be paid weekly 'from now on'. Five weeks later (during which time one of David's portraits of Elton appeared on the cover of *Rolling Stone*), this salary, it seems, had also yet to materialise. In November, Tony King called David to express concern about his 'money situation'. Then one of Elton's reps called to offer an explanation, which apparently reassured David. 'They are paying me a wage. Obviously Reid's decision.' But did this wage ever actually come through? David's diary falls silent on the subject (though he does move into a larger Upper West Side apartment around the same period). His memory, too, turns to fog whenever it comes to financial matters. 'The whole thing with money got very complicated,' David says. 'It was the same as with the Beatles: nobody really knew what they were doing.'

Still, what is certain is that David's lack of business acumen meant there was little chance he could have acted as a guarantor for his drowning brother even if he had been receiving a decent wage. David could barely keep his own head above water.

By the time of the incident at Crisco Disco, David had resumed his role as Bill King's darkroom technician to make ends meet. This was a deeply frustrating professional regression. King was still doing interesting work in 1977 – covers for the *New York Times Magazine*; the

Blackglama 'What Becomes a Legend Most?' campaign, with Diana Vreeland posing in luscious mink – but it was *his* work, not David's. King's studio was in disarray, with new 'useless' assistants whom David held in contempt. And King also seemed unwell, showing signs of serious addiction. ('Is he still mainlining?' Tommy asked David in a letter.) One day, the studio was preparing for a major magazine shoot when King called David from a bathhouse to say that he'd taken so many drugs he couldn't get his clothes on. 'You go and take the pictures,' King mumbled. 'They won't know.' Suggesting they probably *would* know, David talked him into his clothes and then into a taxi back to the studio, where King managed to pull himself together just long enough to get the job done.

Another day, King called David at home and summoned him to his apartment on Horatio Street. When David refused, King threatened suicide, saying that if he didn't come David would read about it in the newspapers tomorrow and feel responsible. So David made his way down to the West Village, just in case, and found that King was flying high on pills. Far from contemplating death, however, he appeared to be aroused. King demanded David photograph him performing solo sex acts that were 'obscene and bizarre', as David described them in his diary. David was repulsed – although, as King's boyfriend banged on the door demanding to be let inside, he took the pictures anyway.

These kinds of episodes scratched away at David's sensitive nerves. His depression dragged him down again, and he began to spiral into another self-reinforcing fugue state.

One morning in April, David decided he needed a mental-health break. He skipped work to mope at home for a day, lingering in bed. 'Thank god,' David wrote – because this random act of truancy meant he was there when the telephone unexpectedly rang.

It was Michael Jackson.

'We talked for an hour,' David wrote afterwards. 'He's adorable and wants me to visit one weekend.'

The previous July, in Philadelphia, Marlon, Michael and Randy Jackson had turned up backstage at one of Elton's tour performances. David, 'very up' that day, had snapped a few frames of the boys posing with Elton and then struck up a conversation with Marlon Jackson, who he'd thought was particularly 'sweet'. Marlon had asked David to 'send him some pics', so they'd exchanged details before David had turned his attention to Elton and Elizabeth Taylor.

Elton with Marlon, Michael and Randy Jackson in Philadelphia, July 1976.

Next morning, Marlon phoned David first thing to say he'd try to make the show that night. He did not make the show – 'shame really', David wrote – but Michael, his younger brother, turned up instead. David had spoken briefly with the eighteen-year-old before heading off to a pub to eat shepherd's pie with Elton's band. Evidently, this conversation – which was a passing thing for David, barely registered in his journal – had made quite the impression on Michael Jackson, because he soon called David for a follow-up chat. And then another one. These phone calls, David recalls, could stretch on for hours and had the meandering aimlessness of two teenagers talking about everything and nothing.

By the time Michael called David and caught him hiding at home from Bill King, they'd been talking sporadically for nine months. A bond of trust had developed between them. Now Michael asked David to come and visit him in person, in Philadelphia, where he was working with his brothers on *Goin' Places* for Epic Records.

David caught a train down on 23 April – a Saturday, so he could stay on for a few nights. Arriving at the recording studio, he found an unobtrusive spot in the corner and settled down to watch. Michael was doing vocals for the title track, which David thought was excellent, 'very disco'. Between takes, David passed the time by chatting to Dexter Wansel, the composer, whom he knew through Elton's entourage; he also spoke with the Jacksons' school tutor, who was fighting a losing battle to correct grammar in the song lyrics.

That evening, David accompanied Michael back to his hotel room, and the two of them sat up gossiping with Marlon into the early hours. The next day, the weather was miserable, so they settled in to watch *Roots* on television, then clowned around as Michael tried (and failed)

Michael Jackson's umbrella dance in a Philadelphia hotel room.

to teach David some dance moves.

On Sunday night, Michael picked up a yellow legal pad and sketched David's face in remarkable detail – the bump in his nose, the lines around his eyes, his unkempt beard and mussed-up hair – then signed the portrait with a decorative flourish as rain lacerated the city outside (which Michael also noted, along with the location, date and exact time: 9 p.m.). David, when Michael gifted it to him, was amazed at the likeness; he carefully tucked it away to frame and hang on his wall, where it would remain for many decades.

Michael's father, Joe Jackson, did not approve of his son's unusual guest. During the recording session, David had noticed that Mr Jackson acted 'a bit cold' towards him, refusing to shake his hand. This made David feel 'uneasy', a discomfort that was only exacerbated by another stand-offish encounter in the hotel lobby. But perhaps Joe Jackson also felt uneasy around David, who was, after all: white, thirty-seven years old, exhibiting all the telltale mannerisms of a gay man, and wielding a camera around two of his sons. In truth, David harboured no particular libidinous interest in Marlon. And he felt even less desire for Michael, whom he liked 'immensely' as a *friend*, because Michael was uplifting company, but who struck him as a young eccentric suffering from a serious case of loneliness.

David did wonder if Michael was gay. 'Still uncertain,' he confided in his diary. He yearned to ask outright, or at the very least to tell Michael about himself, so they could talk about 'the gay thing' openly and honestly. Maybe there was some stuff that Michael would want to get off his chest, David reasoned. Maybe what he needed was a sympathetic ear, somebody to listen to whatever might be confusing him on the threshold of maturity. Michael seemed closed up like a vice. Without exerting any pressure, David just made himself available, a reassuring, avuncular presence who was ready to talk. Later, Michael would recall about this period: 'I was searching, both consciously and unconsciously. I was feeling some stress and anxiety about what I wanted to do with my life now that I was an adult. I was analyzing my options and preparing to make decisions that could have a lot of repercussions.'

Back home in New York, David waited a few days, then decided to call Michael at the hotel to thank him for the weekend, which had bolstered his spirits. Joe Jackson answered and was 'cold as ice'.

David was appalled. He dashed off a letter to Michael and Marlon 'laying it all on the line' about their father's unnecessary behaviour. Michael soon phoned up to apologise. As David recalls, he said: 'This is why I have no friends.'

A few months later, in September, Michael would call David again with another invitation, this time to Brooklyn. Michael had been hired by Sidney Lumet to play the Scarecrow in *The Wiz*, an opportunity he would later describe as 'the most wonderful thing in the world'. Jackson loved *The Wizard of Oz*, had always wanted to act in a movie, and now 'got to be somebody else' and 'escape' through a character who could sing and dance – his two biggest passions. They were rehearsing just across the East River, at the Hotel St George in Brooklyn Heights.

When David arrived, Michael was practising his steps in the hotel's Colorama Ballroom with the sprawling cast. (Jackson would prove so superior to everybody else at mastering the complex choreography that Diana Ross, who was playing Dorothy, pulled him aside one day and suggested in no uncertain terms that he was making her look bad.) David watched from the sidelines, recognising several of the other performers from gay nightclubs around town. Then he joined Michael for lunch. While they were eating, Diana Ross walked up and asked Michael who his friend was. By way of introducing himself, David mentioned that his brother had once made suits for her on Savile Row.

'Oh,' Ross replied. 'I don't wear those any more.'

That evening also turned out to be Michael's nineteenth birthday party (though his actual birthday was a few days earlier). He was throwing it on the 107th floor of the World Trade Center, at a new restaurant called Windows on the World. The way Michael talked it up in advance, David imagined a lavish celebration with hundreds of guests. However, when he actually arrived, he found the party was a tiny affair: just Michael; two publicists from Epic, Steve Manning and Susan Blond; and himself, playing the role of Michael's close friend. David put on a brave face but found it quietly tragic.

After that, there were further late-night phone chats, another party at which David got terribly drunk and besieged the performer. ('Don't remember too much about it,' he wrote the next morning through a throbbing hangover. 'May have been embarrassing.') But Michael's life soon began to pick up velocity and drag his attention elsewhere. Though Michael remained warm and generous, extending invitations to events and performances, David fell increasingly out of touch.

The last time David would see Michael Jackson in person was November 1979, at Studio 54. *Off the Wall*, Michael's funk-pop masterpiece, had just been released; people everywhere were dancing to 'Don't Stop 'Til You Get Enough'. Catching sight of Michael from across the room, David muscled and pushed, trying to reach his erstwhile friend. To no avail. 'Couldn't get near Michael for the crowds,' he wrote. They'd had their vivid period of convergence, and then it was over.

———————

Studio 54 lifted its velvet rope for the very first time on 26 April 1977. Perhaps the most legendary nightclub ever, it was the unlikely creation of two middle-class Jewish friends from Brooklyn: Ian Schrager, a straight, conservative-looking lawyer searching for a good business prospect, and Steve Rubell, a gay restaurateur whose chain of steak joints had been struggling to turn a profit. One evening – or so the story goes – Schrager had gone with Rubell to Le Jardin, on West Forty-Third Street. Technically, Le Jardin was a gay club, but Schrager noticed that straight people were also standing in the queue, attracted by a kind of 'sexual electricity' that did not seem to exist anywhere *except* these dedicated gay spaces. 'It was like a Sodom and Gomorrah,' Schrager later recalled. 'There was frenzy on the dance floor, the music was reverberating around the room, they had lighting effects, and it was like – *boy!* – overwhelming.' Afterwards, Schrager told Rubell that he smelled an opportunity. The pair formed a partnership to open something of their own.

They soon took over an eleven-room mansion next to a municipal golf course in Douglaston, Queens. Though hardly the most ideal location in New York (or even in Queens), they spent $27,000 renovating the house and christened it the Enchanted Garden. Then they courted Carmen D'Alessio, a Peruvian nightlife promoter, to host theme parties that would attract a 'fusion' crowd of gays and straights, like the one at Le Jardin. D'Alessio scoffed: 'I said there was no way that I could get involved because I wouldn't take my crowd all the way to Queens, plus I didn't know any press out there.' Eventually, she relented; one of her more elaborate evenings, dubbed the 'Island of Paradise', featured hula girls, a seventy-pound roasted pig, and 'a fire dancer working himself into a charcoal-broiled frenzy'. It ended up in *Newsweek*.

Schrager would later claim that the Enchanted Garden became another victim of David Berkowitz, the Son of Sam, who was then stalking New York with a .44 calibre Bulldog revolver. 'It was hard to get people to come into a nightclub when someone was out there killing you.' (In all fairness to the Son of Sam, the Douglaston community was also less than enthused about the noise, and the City Parks Department soon issued an eviction notice.) But the Garden had been successful enough during its short run to embolden Schrager and Rubell to attempt a second, far more ambitious club in Manhattan – in the old CBS studio on West Fifty-Fourth Street that had once been used to produce *The $64,000 Question*.

Schrager, who was the creative in the 'marriage' between himself and Rubell, oversaw a six-week construction job. Carmen D'Alessio, however, would later claim that *she* did all the work, while Schrager and Rubell did 'nothing much' at all. 'They raised the money, but other than that it had definitely the taste of a woman who had been involved in fashion.' Either way, to overhaul the TV studio, a superstar team was brought in to conjure some magic: a minimalist interior designer, some restaurant architects, a florist, and two theatrical lighting experts who were responsible for *Chicago* on Broadway. The studio's existing lighting rig was retained, which allowed Schrager to transform the environment of the club continuously, unpredictably, like a dynamic stage set. Schrager also wanted 'serious sweaty dancing' to music you could feel in your bones, so he employed Richard Long, an audio maestro who was behind most of New York's best gay discos. Long installed enormous bass speakers around the floor, which would reverberate through your feet, and tweeter arrays along the ceiling to rain down the high notes. Schrager later said that 'the idea was to constantly assault the senses'.

David first visited Studio 54 at the end of July. Though it was then just three months old, the club had already established many of the hallmarks for which it would become legendary. Rubell, for instance, had begun standing outside on the street, sometimes on a stool, hand-picking people from the thirsty crowd to create what he called a 'tossed salad' of gays, celebrities, wise guys, street kids, gorgeous models and Eurotrash. Rubell did not want 'deadwood' floating around his club, or people from the outer boroughs and New Jersey – the reviled bridge-and-tunnel crowd. Once, two women turned up dressed as twin Lady Godivas accompanied by a live horse; Rubell rejected the women, but said yes to the horse. And not for the first time, either: Bianca Jagger had already sat astride a white one at her birthday party, creating one of the most indelible images of the decade.

Inside, a giant Man-in-the-Moon loomed high above the dance floor,

'I made the foolish decision to get on it for a few minutes,'
Bianca later told the *Financial Times*, annoyed by all the attention.

sniffing cocaine from a mechanised spoon. Confetti guns spewed glitter over the heads of revellers while busboys in tiny gym shorts shimmied their toned asses through a mezzanine bar. David, who went with Elton, and then with Elton and Rod Stewart, with whom he got 'totally wrecked and stayed until four', thought it was all 'so amazing'. He would go dozens more times over the next few years – taking THC at a Halloween bash; celebrating Rubell's birthday with Shetland ponies and a marching band – before the club finally lost its lustre in 1980, the year Rubell and Schrager were sentenced for tax evasion. 'You never knew who you'd see there,' David says – Liza Minnelli, Brooke Shields, Donald Trump. 'There was a beaded curtain that would go up and down. I remember lying on the dance floor looking up at it just before I passed out.'

One evening stands out as particularly notable in the annals of 1977: an album and book launch at Studio 54.

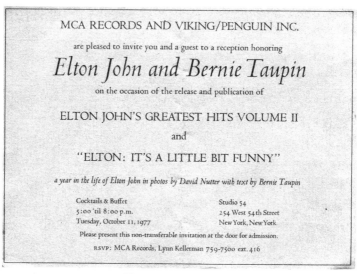

The launch invitation

The book, David thinks, had originally been Elton's idea. The earliest diary reference to it comes the same night Freddie Mercury told him off about his battered face. 'Bernie was lovely and wants to do book with me.' Running into David at the Queen after-party, Bernie Taupin had agreed to write the text; David would supply the photographs. After signing a contract with the Viking Press and Penguin Books, he would also finally receive some royalties for his work.

David had grand plans when it came to the book's presentation. Using the darkroom at King's studio, he made contact sheets and meticulous prints from his favourite negatives. He then took everything to Ruth Ansel, the former co–art director (with Bea Feitler) of *Harper's Bazaar* who had recently moved on to the *New York Times Magazine*. (David had met her through working with King.) Brilliant and provocative, Ansel had designed Richard Avedon's book on an avant-garde theatre troupe, *Alice in Wonderland:* the *Forming of a Company and the Making of a Play*. She was also responsible for an exquisite edition of Peter Beard's *The End of the Game*, about the fraught history of African wildlife. David wanted something just as ambitious for his photographs of rock stars: glossy black-and-white spreads arranged like an art catalogue; animated action shots contrasted with intimate close-ups. After he flipped through his portfolio in Ansel's apartment, Ansel agreed to take on the project.

However, when David shared his plan with the production team at Viking, they demurred. 'They said they wanted to use their in-house person,' he recalls. David felt powerless to take on a behemoth publishing company, so Ansel was out before she was ever officially signed. This 'in-house person' then reconceived the design as a madcap montage that was almost like a scrapbook or graphic novel. Bold, italicised type crawled across pages decorated with palm trees and place names. David's photographs were crammed together – four, five, eight to a page. In some instances, they were violently altered using correction fluid and a pair of scissors, so that Elton's disembodied head appeared to peek through the book credits. The intention was whimsical, but the result was amateurish. David hated it. He also hated the printing, which he thought used the wrong grade of paper stock. For some copies, the plates used in the offset printing process were not aligned properly, so final images were blurry. He grumbled about the cumulative degradation of his work, seeing it as a missed opportunity to make something truly beautiful. Yet for all its flaws, *Elton John: It's a Little Bit Funny* was a high-profile release that publicly validated David as a photographer. He liked what it represented in the abstract, if not on the actual page. It helped, too, that Elton decided to dedicate the book to him.

This book is dedicated to David Nutter
and to everybody else who picked me up off the floor!

On 11 October, David arrived at Studio 54 for a 5 p.m. cocktail reception with the media. The buzz in the club was loud and positive, though Elton, who'd just been inducted into the Madison Square Garden Hall of Fame, appeared for barely an hour before throwing a tantrum. 'It seems he still isn't used to either superstardom or his recent re-haired dome,' a journalist complained, 'because when photographers engulfed Elton on his entrance, he retreated to a backstage room for the duration of the event.' Not that David noticed; he later wrote that the spectacle was 'amazing': 'Elton walked out after five minutes and Bernie and I were left. Did an interview and had some pics taken. Book very well received.'

After the buffet, David raced home to meet a special guest who was accompanying him to the *proper* party. A few weeks earlier, he'd received a letter with some unexpected but delightful news: Tommy's situation had shifted in London, his prospects were now looking good again, and he was scheduled to arrive in New York in early October for a few days of work. Serendipitously, this meant he would also be able 'to go to the Ball!' David took a disco nap and then woke to receive his brother, who turned up carrying a brand-new black bespoke suit. David was thrilled – 'My suit sensational' – and put it on immediately.

A limousine arrived to collect them, along with a few more of David's friends. Around 11 p.m., it pulled up outside Studio 54. The street crowd parted like the Red Sea, and David marched his own personal entourage past the velvet rope.

Inside, the throng of partygoers was 'murder', David thought, jostling elbows as he shot for the bar – but also 'wonderful'. The Commodores were there, along with Andy Warhol, David Hockney, Dame Edna, Ellen Burstyn. 'They all came,' David would later write, delirious at the turnout. Michael Jackson was in town for a *Wiz* party and stopped by to say hello. Several members of Monty Python slinked around the room in drag. Elton reappeared in a velvet suit and newsboy cap (covering those tender hair plugs), and he mingled with his admirers until somebody grabbed him, hoisted him up by the waist, and swung him round and round in nauseous circles.

It is one thing to identify the most terrifying episode of a person's life; it is quite another to pinpoint the moment when a person is at their peak, happiest to be alive. For David, perhaps this comes close: 11 October 1977, publication day, sometime towards midnight, on the dance floor at Studio 54.

David and Tommy with *Elton: It's a Little Bit Funny.*

Tommy posing outside Kilgour, French & Stanbury on Dover Street.

13

ARE YOU BEING SERVED?

Of his miraculous, Lazarus-like comeback in 1977, Tommy would once explain: 'I applied to the largest textiles conglomerate in Britain, Lincroft Kilgour, and asked if I could sort of stand in their shop in Dover Street: Kilgour, French & Stanbury. And they said, "Yes, Tommy." And so I stood there. And Elton walked in, and Tim [Rice] and Andrew [Lloyd Webber] walked in, and it all happened.' This was a mostly accurate account, albeit a little burnished around the edges for dramatic effect.

Barry Grigg, father of David Grigg, whom Tommy had stayed with before moving to Chelsea, worked as a director at Lincroft Kilgour. After watching months of Tommy's failed scheming, Barry arranged for him to be hired in-house at Kilgour, French & Stanbury (which operated under the umbrella of Lincroft Kilgour). 'Kilgour needed a fresh face, so they brought him in,' David Grigg recalls. This extraordinary last-minute reprieve saved Tommy from imminent bankruptcy, assuaging his skittish lenders. It also restored him to the heart of the tailoring trade in Mayfair. Beginning in February, Tommy 'stood' in the showroom at No. 33a Dover Street . . . and he would continue to stand there for much of the next five years, a stretch of his working life that can be treated as discrete and self-contained, like, say, Picasso's Blue Period.

Kilgour, French & Stanbury was one of the most respected bespoke tailors in the Savile Row area ('and therefore the world'), rivalled at that moment only by Huntsman, Henry Poole and Hawes & Curtis. Founded in 1880 as T&F French, it catered to an exclusive clientele of aristocrats and social luminaries. In 1923, the original firm had merged with A. H. Kilgour – another tailor of considerable repute – to create the partnership of Kilgour & French. A few years after that, Kilgour & French had opened its doors to a pair of Hungarian brothers named Frederick and Louis Stanbury. Frederick Stanbury was 'an engaging personality who revelled in the creation of clothes', but Louis was considered something of a 'wild one' on Savile Row – meticulous, strict, and prone to displays of theatrical excess. One story has him wrestling with a coat in front of a customer, then stamping on it repeatedly like an angry child to illustrate his disgust at poor workmanship. 'I want a man to look a he-man,' he once told a writer. 'I like square shoulders, big chests and narrow waists.' (He also declared that 'a man's success with people depends on his tailor' – an overstatement that illustrated how seriously he took his role.) The Stanbury brothers introduced an attractive cut that soon became the house's signature style; for their effort, the firm was renamed Kilgour, French & Stanbury. Then, in 1970, it expanded yet again, this time to incorporate Bernard Weatherill, a tailor famed for equestrian and sporting wear. Indeed, by the time Tommy finally entered the picture in 1977, the business was like Frankenstein's monster, stitched together from multiple bodies and lumbering along with little sense of unified purpose. Its public image, however, remained all Hollywood grace: Fred Astaire in *Top Hat*, dancing in a Kilgour, French & Stanbury tailcoat with a white carnation threaded through his lapel.

Tommy told people that he felt privileged to become a member of the team at KFS. He meant it too. A journalist, observing him in Dover Street, noted that he seemed 'a shade awed' by his new surroundings. 'Tommy is sure that he'll fit in, he's only been there six weeks to date, but – *no* trouble.' Because Lincroft Kilgour was a giant conglomerate with smart people taking care of the money side of things, Tommy had high hopes for his future. 'I will not have the responsibilities of worrying about overheads and will get down to the business of creating my own look,' he said.

Still, it was a strange fit, KFS and Tommy Nutter – a 'piquant mixture', as *The Times* put it, of conservative old-timers and the iconoclast who had once opened a shop that aimed to supersede them. Capturing a widely shared opinion, Angus McGill in the *Evening Standard* commented that the 'hushed anonymity' of Dover Street was 'not the place you would expect to find the starry and very individual Mr Nutter'.

Tommy would have agreed with this assessment. Years later, he'd sit down to jot some preliminary notes for an autobiography in which he'd recall his entrance to KFS as an act of high-farce gate-crashing.

'He's not a member of the chorus – he's a STAR,' said Mr Tremble as he introduced the 'new boy' to Kilgour, French & Stanbury.

Miss Worth of the venomous tongue was writing out her tickets as usual, but [was] very much 'put out' by the arrival of the added member of staff. After all, things had been running very well without him. You could see the horror on her face as she conjured up the image of Elton John walking into such a hallowed establishment, perhaps waiting on the Chesterfield alongside Lord [?] for Mr Nutter to discuss his trousseau for a forthcoming tour . . .

This was Jubilee year, and I had been away from my own business Nutters of Savile Row for nearly a year now, and found that funds were becoming exceedingly low. Therefore it was a case of starting at the bottom again, and working my way up through the company which had in fact ruled the roost in the tailoring world for all the impresarios, actors, advertising [men] and the less conventional types of Savile Row client until I had opened my own shop in 1969. And this is where one starts.

Tommy knew that he needed to show some humility to the older staff at KFS. To avoid any repeats of the unpleasantness at Nutters, he declared his intention, straight up, 'to get in there and create an understanding with the cutters'. He emphasised that this was 'not a case of Tommy Nutter going in . . . to reorganise Kilgour and save it'. As a show of respect, a sign of his deference to tradition, he adjusted his personal style to something more serious-looking, subtle pinstripes and various shades of battleship grey. One observer would describe him as going from 'avant to old guard' almost overnight. Tommy also altered his tone towards the media. Gone were the bold prophecies of change; instead, he declared that the company's classic cut from the 1940s was now 'the new look'. He tightened the seat of the trousers to make them a little more flattering, yes, but the silhouette was left otherwise untouched: a drape suit, double-breasted, with built-out chest, moderate lapels, no flaps and no fuss. This he anointed the modified 'Robert Mitchum look', perhaps because the name emphasised continuity with a reassuring golden age. He did not want to frighten the horses straight out of the gate.

After a short run of this, however, when people had got used to his presence, when Tommy had worked out the hierarchy and who wielded the real power at KFS, he dropped the pretence and began to exert his true will. The Dover Street showroom was fusty and cluttered. Bolts of cloth were stacked up alongside a riot of leather goods, dressing gowns, umbrellas and ties. Workers tottered about with tape measures around their necks and pins sticking out of their mouths. It was all decidedly unglamorous – and Tommy yearned to fix it. On 11 August, he wrote to his brother about 'the new accessories department' that would sweep it all out for a much-needed fresh start. He had talked management into a radical makeover. 'The whole of the front area of the shop will be a sort of mini Gucci, and all the bespoke goes in to the back area. This has all been panelled and has chandeliers etc. – all very grand! I shall be flitting around posing and trying to get the whole thing together.'

So much for not reorganising Kilgour.

'We are slowly creating a new atmosphere,' Tommy boasted, barely seven months after first arriving. 'The stuffiness should soon go.'

***

It is difficult to know what the other members of staff really made of the 'new boy'. Michael Smith, a tailor who worked at KFS during Tommy's tenure, recalls him as 'just a figurehead'. Yet the directors of Lincroft

Kilgour were at least moderately aligned with Tommy's opinion of his own transformative abilities. With his star-studded contact list and media pull, he was brought in to 'add a new dimension' to the ageing clientele. Which he did, almost immediately: Elton John was indeed waiting on a chesterfield (having loyally followed him across from Nutters), along with Eric Clapton, Lord Montagu and the Marquess of Tavistock. Tommy could successfully instigate the makeover of the Dover Street showroom because the conglomerate directors saw him as a cash cow. As Angus McGill wryly observed, 'I understand they mean to use Nutter to cure the nation's balance of payments deficit.'

In fact, Lincroft Kilgour's plan for Tommy consisted of two parts. First, he would design for long-standing KFS customers ('they want only gradual change'), as well as his own loyal clientele ('*my* customers want *my* look and they trust me to give it to them'). In doing so, he would draw on and promote other subsidiaries within the Lincroft Kilgour group, including the cloth merchant Holland & Sherry.

Second and simultaneously, Tommy would also work to become, as he himself put it, 'the top menswear designer in Great Britain' – a natural successor to Hardy Amies, whom he suddenly began citing in interviews as his guiding light.

In 1959, Amies had signed on as a design consultant for Hepworths, a mass-production tailoring firm (called a 'multiple' tailors) that owned numerous stores across the country's high streets. Amies was already famous by then, having opened his atelier on Savile Row and made dresses for the queen. By enlisting his support, Hepworths hoped to borrow Amies's prestige to elevate the social value of its budget clothes – to, in effect, create an illusory link between the 'bank clerks and office workers' who patronised Hepworths and 'the world of corgis and garden parties'. Amies was a terrible snob, but he liked money, and he relished the opportunity to branch into menswear. 'Our courage paid off,' he later wrote. Though his initial designs were mostly unremarkable (featuring a masculine line 'a bit like an hourglass', in the words of Nik Cohn, and colours that ranged from drab grey to beige), they proved a sensation at the end of the austere 1950s. Starved of anything with even a little bit of shape, male customers could not get enough.

Hepworths watched its profits double in the space of four years to more than a million pounds. And Amies, having turned his name into a hot commodity, found himself enriched by more than a dozen new consultancy deals – including hats for Battersby, pyjamas for Bonsoir, sweaters and socks for Byford of Leicester, and men's gloves for Dent, Allcroft & Co. He 'virtually pioneered' the Chelsea boot for Clarks, according to Rodney Bennett-England; he also created an original clothing line under his own label, which was distributed by Genesco throughout the United States, Australia, New Zealand, Canada and Japan.

In short, Amies had elevated himself into a one-man brand of considerable international standing. This had been Tommy's goal for years, but now he had serious support behind him in the form of Lincroft Kilgour. 'What they want to do with me here is to turn me into the new Hardy Amies,' he said.

Once the makeover of Dover Street was finished, Tommy and his employers set out to pursue their objective aggressively. At the beginning of 1978, Lincroft Kilgour formed a limited company called Tommy Nutter Promotions. The directors then placed advertisements in industry trade publications that invited licensing proposals to use the Tommy Nutter label.

Tommy Nutter would like to work for you 24 hours a day!

In April, Tommy travelled to America with KFS cutters to collect new orders from their clients. In New York – between nights out with his brother to the Anvil or Cock Ring – he spent his free time trying to line up a deal between Tommy Nutter Promotions and a 'big name' department store like Saks Fifth Avenue. Tommy promised 'the traditional Savile Row suit', but slimmed down, with 'a little flair' to set the wearer apart from the crowd. Ideally, he wanted a dedicated 'Tommy Nutter shop' within one of these department stores for which he would personally design suits, shirts, ties and 'whatever else the store wants'. He visited Chicago, Los Angeles, San Francisco and Houston on the trip, telling wholesalers in each city that he would design in London but manufacture all-American. He received no enthusiastic bites.

More headway was made at home. The trade advertisements led to several letters of enquiry ('I must stress again that design is our main interest,' one buyer wrote, 'not just the application of a name on Tommy Nutter's merchandise') – and at least one serious offer, from the fashion retailer Austin Reed.

Austin Reed's flagship store was located on Regent Street, which positioned it, with fitting symbolism, right between Savile Row and Carnaby Street. Aimed firmly at the middle class, it offered quality and affordability, made-to-measure precision at the cost of ready-to-wear. It was a dependable source of sensible men's clothes, but it was not afraid to try new things, keeping up with the trends. In 1965, it had hired a fashion editor from *Town* magazine to launch an in-store menswear boutique called the Cue Shop, which offered everything from highwaymen coats to bell-bottom hipster trousers. The target demographic was the 'bachelor about town', those young executives with plenty of disposable income and a taste for extravagance. In this respect, Cue had proved a smart bet; by the time Tommy opened Nutters in 1969, there were fifty-six Cue Shops in Britain and plans for even more. Austin Reed had struck an ideal balance between tradition and fashion – had, in a sense, succeeded in doing exactly what Tommy had done, but at a price point that appealed to the everyman. There was an obvious symmetry of ambition between Austin Reed and the tailor.

In May, Tommy met with Graeme Tonge, controller for the Cue Shops, and came to an agreement. 'I was extremely pleased with our meeting yesterday and feel confident that we will produce a stunning collection,' he wrote to Tonge afterwards.

Tommy was decidedly less confident in another letter to his brother, admitting that he found the job of conceiving looks for a future season 'quite difficult', because he was used to working as though his designs were timeless. It required a serious adjustment to think up collections that would come and go with the brutal frequency of weather. Still, he seemed to be 'getting along quite well so far', and he'd just been given a tour around the Austin Reed factory in Kent, which delighted him. 'I felt like the Queen. All I needed was a bouquet.'

Samples for the Tommy Nutter collection went into production in

August. When they were finished, Tommy was 'absolutely thrilled' with the result. His intention had been to create 'the Savile Row cut' as ready-to-wear, extending the flattering benefits of bespoke to a wider audience: dropped shoulders, generous sleeves, a draped chest, narrow lapels and (because God is in the details) genuine horn buttons. His Cue range would also include cable-knit sweaters in Shetland wool, tab-collar dress shirts, and an entire line of fetching ties. A complete Tommy Nutter look.

Just before Cue unveiled the collection publicly the following March, for spring 1979, Tommy circulated a press release that summarised his grand (yet geographically muddled) vision like this: 'Shades in pale earth colours are reminiscent of the glamorous days of the 20s and 30s at Deauville, strolling along the Croisette before changing to visit the Casino.' He listed his inspirations as Rudolph Valentino, Clark Gable and Erté, the Russian-born French father of art deco. The unifying theme of everything was 'elegance', Tommy wrote – 'a new feeling for the British male'.

When it finally hit the streets, the Cue collection drew exactly the kind of attention that Tommy and his backers were hoping for. 'Not since Hepworths signed up Hardy Amies in the early 1960s and launched him on his "total man" package has any other British retailing group really attempted to repeat the exercise,' David Harvey wrote in *Men's Wear*. The reviews were favourable too. Sure, the Cue suits were understated for a Tommy Nutter production, even 'amazingly conventional'. But perhaps that was a good thing: you didn't need to be Mick Jagger to pull off these styles. In quick succession, Tommy was vaulted up the *Sunday Telegraph*'s 'IN' list. He was described by *Style* as one of the British menswear industry's 'leading lights', and as a 'shooting star' by *Tatler & Bystander*. Meanwhile, in a more ambiguous honour, *Harpers & Queen* placed him on a list of 'tradesmen grander than their customers'.

Tommy Nutter designs for the Cue Shop, 1979.

All this praise promised excellent things – as did the fact that Austin Reed had already secured his commitment for future seasons at Cue. Tony Holland, the chairman of Lincroft Kilgour, began to rub his hands together with avaricious excitement. 'Mr Holland has not lost sight of Austin Reed's financial links with the American clothing giant

Hart Schaffner and Marx, who themselves run an Austin Reed line in the States,' a journalist noted.

And yet, in Tommy's view, not all was as it should be in the world around him. He was not *content*. Partly this had to do with the Dover Street showroom, still frustratingly passé despite his best efforts to bring a bit of modern flair. More than once in letters to David, Tommy would liken KFS to *Are You Being Served?*, the BBC sitcom about an old-fashioned department store called Grace Brothers, populated by class-obsessed, clueless, petulant or mincing staff members who pepper their speech with double entendres and make constant mistakes. Because he was now an employee, Tommy was immersed in this stupefying atmosphere all day, every day, unable to escape.

But even worse – what was really bothering Tommy – was a kind of phantom pain: Nutters of Savile Row, still open and trading in 1979. As Tommy sought to leverage his name as an exclusive label, Edward Sexton and his cutters continued to use it freely on their windows just round the corner. People got confused; Tommy was annoyed. As soon as he arrived at KFS, he'd begun slinking past No. 35a to make surreptitious assessments of his old firm's health. 'I think the Nutters girls are now just beginning to feel the pinch – they are busy but I don't think that things are running too smoothly at the moment.' This bitter assessment, relayed to his brother in New York, was based on nothing more substantial than wishful thinking. In fact, Nutters post-Tommy was actually doing relatively well.

But it was no longer quite the same place that Tommy once knew. After his vanishing act, Edward had assumed the role of managing director, just as he'd wanted, and he'd reorientated the company away from an innovative fashion house towards a more dependable tailoring model. 'Savile Row is a fine line between fashion and tradition,' Edward explained to the writer Iain Finlayson. 'I am entirely practical: I was brought up in tailoring, and I have a commercial spirit. I enjoy designing innovative fashion, but it must be appropriate to our clients' personalities.' This reorientation – effectively choosing to be led by the client, rather than the whim of a lead designer – was exactly what Edward had been encouraging Tommy to do before their fateful rupture.

Nutters also *looked* different. The cutting room and fitting area had been enlarged, which necessitated a change in decor. Edward had hired a new freelance window dresser named Simon Doonan (the same young man who'd once watched Tommy walking around on his lunch breaks looking like 'an old illustration of art deco glamour'). As Doonan recalls, 'Somebody said to me, "Tommy Nutter's had a fight with his partner and left. And they need a person to do the windows now because Michael Long also left with Tommy out of solidarity." So I zoomed in there! I met Edward Sexton. Edward and I bonded immediately. He was hilarious – very cockney, very straight, but he knew Polari, too, because he learned it from Tommy. Everything was *bona* and *eek* . . .' Because Doonan was influenced by the punk movement – Malcolm McLaren and Vivienne Westwood were doing a brisk trade in safety pins and rubber ties over on the King's Road – he filled the windows of Nutters with a striking new aesthetic. In his most notorious display, rubbish bins and stuffed rats wearing diamanté chokers ('I just bought some trim from John Lewis and stitched it on myself') were arranged around beautiful bespoke dinner jackets. This kind of high/low tableau was so eye-catchingly deranged it would ultimately get Doonan hired in America, where he would go on to become the creative director of Barneys New York.

Tommy noted these adjustments at Nutters from a safe viewing distance. He was careful not to get *too* close, lest he stumble into an accidental encounter. If he spotted Edward walking towards him down the street, he crossed to the other side.

At KFS, to keep himself happy at the small desk where he was expected to spend most of his time, Tommy indulged in design follies. There was his poppy-red bespoke 'jogging suit' that was 'also suitable for discotheques' (£402). And a pair of pyjamas with a black bow tie and wing collar, adorned with £21,000 worth of antique jewel-encrusted crosses.

In another ensemble, Tommy paired white leather breeches with a slub silk jacket, evoking, as he told *Men's Wear,* 'a cross between Cecil B. DeMille and a jockey at a cocktail party'.

During warmer months, he took much-needed breaks to Saint-Tropez with Stewart Grimshaw, Simon Sainsbury and his new friend Amanda Lear. He also frequented the Embassy Club, London's answer to Studio 54, where Michael Fish now worked as a greeter. Tommy remained

The white leather breeches were left in the basement at KFS 'by a duke who changed his mind at the last moment'.

a committed devotee of gay nightlife – dinners at La Popote, a 'leather and chains' party, an Australian drag revue in Wimbledon. He dated a witty, blond twenty-seven-year-old solicitor ('very me!' he wrote to his brother) and then a six-foot, blond professional swimmer from the East End ('very me – won't last dear, but it's nice at the moment').

Throughout it all, one dependable pleasure remained a series of galas thrown by the Scottish luxury textile mill Reid & Taylor. The company's managing director, a flamboyant autocrat named John Packer, would convene a gathering of international buyers and designers at some iconic location around Europe – the Ca' Pesaro in Venice, say, or Schleissheim Palace in Munich. Guests would be flown in on a private Boeing 707, showered with Moët & Chandon, and beguiled by opera singers or the London Lassus Ensemble. Then there would be a catwalk show staged as a procession of dramatic scenes: blushing brides, followed by a hunting party pretending to shoot game birds above the head of Princess Margaret (the honoured guest). John Packer attended to every detail with the morbid fastidiousness of Stanley Kubrick. Of course, these gatherings, which could cost more than £100,000 (some £600,000 in today's currency) to stage, were little more than elaborate PR exercises intended to increase sales for Reid & Taylor and the designers who used the company's products. But Tommy valued the events for an entirely different reason. Once, after a gala in Munich, he would write a thank-you note to Packer laying out his thoughts:

> I think the nicest part about the whole jamboree was being transported from the humdrum saga of everyday life into a kind of dream world where reality became twinkling lights, glamorous people, exquisite cuisine, and, to cap it all, the heavenly strains of the most beautiful voices in the world . . .
>
> In these days, when most things seem to be a problem, thank god there is someone who can LIFT us out of the gloom to recharge our batteries so we can battle on in this extremely competitive world we all live in.

Perhaps 'gloom' was the most appropriate word to describe the dawn of the new decade. The Winter of Discontent had descended at the end of 1978, and since then Britain had experienced one convulsive shock after another. That dreadful season, one of the worst cold snaps since the Second World War, had coincided with a perfect storm of union strikes and go-slows, involving everyone from bakery workers to provincial journalists. Trains shut down because rail staff refused to budge on four separate days; rubbish piled up because binmen refused to clear it (including from Leicester Square); and, perhaps most famously, gravediggers declined to bury the dead in Liverpool until their demands were met. Some hospitals were reduced to taking emergency patients only, because fresh medical supplies could not get past the picket lines. When Labour Prime Minister James Callaghan, having just arrived home from a summit in the Caribbean, was asked by a reporter about this 'mounting chaos', Callaghan replied: 'I don't think other people in the world will share the view that there is mounting chaos.' This response was quickly paraphrased in popular imagination as the out-of-touch 'Crisis? What Crisis?', sealing Callaghan's fate. In 1979, his minority Labour government lost the general election, restoring the Conservatives to power and elevating Margaret Thatcher to the post of prime minister. Her economic policy reforms sent the unemployment rate soaring as the nation was exposed to the full shock treatment of Thatcherism.

At least publicly, Tommy professed to be unconcerned by the prospect of recession. In 1980, speaking on BBC Radio Brighton, he affirmed that no matter how bad things might get, people 'will still eat good food, buy nice cars. And they will buy nice clothes.' It was a commonly held assumption, one journalist wrote, that monetary stress encouraged men to retreat to more traditional modes of dress, that when times are hard 'there is nothing like a sober suit, conservative shirt, old school tie and short back and sides to persuade the bank manager that you are doing well'. But Tommy brushed this idea off like lint. Before a large audience of manufacturers in Cologne, he insisted that the opposite was true: the bowler hat, pinstripe suit and rolled umbrella – the British businessman's uniform – was 'officially dead' as a result of the worsening economic climate. It was a moment of *opportunity* for men's fashion, Tommy argued.

This unwavering optimism reflected Tommy's personality: he always leaned towards the sun. Yet it also showed just how emboldened he'd grown in the light of his recent achievements. The Cue Shop arrangement was still going strong a year after his inaugural collection. Following the lead of Calvin Klein in New York, he'd just introduced 'classic, respectable Savile Row jeans' – terracotta-coloured seams, with a signature 'N' stitched on the back pocket. And there was also, finally, an international franchise deal on the table: a five-year design contract with Daido Worsted Mills, the Japanese consortium, and an agreement to create two collections a year for Osaka's Hankyu Department Store. 'Is there an end to the success of Tommy Nutter at Kilgour, French and Stanbury?' asked one of the trade papers in August 1980. As far as anybody could reasonably tell, the answer appeared to be 'no'. Which is perhaps why Lincroft Kilgour now agreed to a terrifically risky proposition.

A draft of this idea can be found on a notepad among Tommy's papers, in his own unmistakable handwriting.

> Get rid of Are You Being Served? image in Savile Room and transform into SEPARATE boutique i.e. Elizabeth Arden ... Open up shop window as much as possible to encourage passing trade, although at the moment this is negligible. Eliminate as much office work and incoming telephone calls whenever possible. No typing in this area ... Umbrella stands to go ... Take out circular pouffe and re-design shop to incorporate two settees ...
> Have separate logo etc.

That is, have a separate logo for the Tommy Nutter ready-to-wear boutique that would devour a sizeable chunk of the Dover Street shop and offer limited-edition items in houndstooth tweeds, corduroy, bouclé, flannel and velvet cord.

To his credit, Tommy (referring to himself in the third person) did make a note about the dangers of going through with this plan.

> T. N. admitted not to have sufficient knowledge of running and stocking such a shop. Nutters Shirts opened and folded. If such a shop is to open an expert should be hired for . . . setting up.
>
> T. N. would promote.

But he thought it was a worthwhile gambit anyway.

> We need to get younger people in shop – Disco, Pop, Film people who have no time for fittings etc. At the moment <u>NONE</u> of those come in except the few who like bespoke clothes.

At the moment, <u>NONE</u> of the people Tommy saw as *his* people were coming in, and he was proposing a plan to rectify this. The Lincroft Kilgour directors apparently found his pitch thoroughly convincing, too, because they soon approved it. Tommy got his wish for a 'shop-within-a-shop' – the second major renovation of Dover Street he'd instigated in the past four years. Called 'Tommy Nutter for Kilgours', the boutique was launched in February 1981 with a reception at the Ritz, attended by none other than Cilla Black, who delayed an international flight to show up and support her friend. (Having recently given birth to her third son, Cilla moaned about her weight to a tabloid journalist while digging into 'second helpings of lamb and potatoes'.)

With typical hyperbole, Tommy immediately announced that Savile Row tailoring would never be quite the same again. His ready-to-wear line, one of the very first for a serious bespoke tailor, was positioned on a retail ladder below bespoke but above something like Austin Reed: pricey, but not eye-wateringly so. It was also branded with Tommy's subversive sense of humour. Many of the items – check jackets, elephant-cord trousers, Schiaparelli-pink silk ties – could be jumbled together and redeployed in multiple contexts, so Tommy named it his 'millionaire-on-the-dole' collection. As if to underscore the brazen jab at class snootiness in this title, he also affixed everything with an emerald-green tassel. Even press releases received this faux-aristocratic appendage, which made them look like regal decrees about sales trends in men's knitwear.

Finally, Tommy unveiled a print advertising campaign that gently mocked any KFS client who turned up his nose at the idea of ready-to-wear – and mocked, judging by the salesman's grim expression in the ad, any haughty staff member at Dover Street who might have resented having to sell it. The collection was simultaneously serious and ironic, Savile Row and 'Savile Row', elegant and winkingly self-aware as a per-formance of high-class elegance. In other words, camp.

'Tommy Nutter for Kilgours'

There is no doubt that Tommy could sometimes get a little carried away. For years, his more experimental designs had raised eyebrows in certain quarters; for every handful of admirers, he had at least one critic questioning his taste and intentions. But sometime around 1981, it became increasingly difficult to draw a steady line between his serious work and those light-hearted design follies. It was as though Tommy's self-indulgent tendencies went into overdrive. He became a parody of himself. He proposed, for example, a line of 'Rugged Couture' with serrated hemlines, which he conceived after catching a screening of *Jaws* on television.

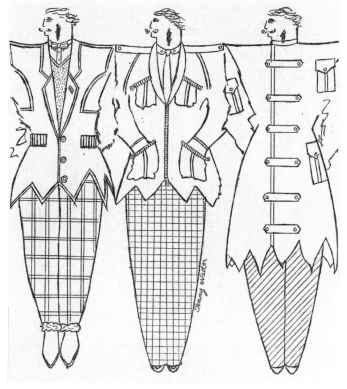

'Rugged Couture'

Then there was the Big Sweep for Men, as Tommy called it. 'Large cashmere blankets with fringing will be thrown with aplomb and gay abandon over the shoulder and SLASHED in at the waist with strong leather belts.' Modelling this dubious look for the *Evening Standard*, he freely confessed to 'feeling a little absurd' as he posed on the street outside KFS. Yet the outfit was treated sincerely by the columnist Liz Smith, who thought it made 'several strong fashion points', and then embraced by a pair of earnest reporters over in New York: 'Meticulously draped or artlessly flung about the shoulders, The Sweep is being worn by this city's most intrepid males – a phalanx of stylish d'Artagnans...'

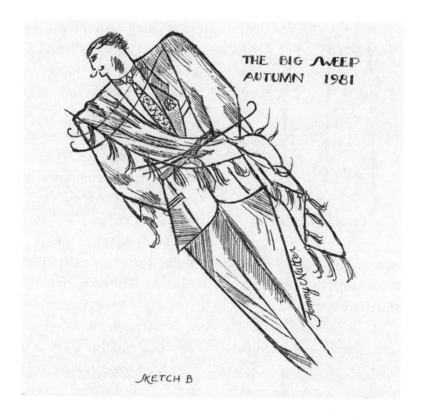

THE BIG SWEEP
AUTUMN 1981

SKETCH B

In April 1982, Tommy would even take a major international crisis and turn it into fodder for his sketch pad. As Thatcher was furiously dispatching her Royal Navy task force to snatch back the Falkland Islands from Argentina, Tommy alerted the media to his own aggressive 'Nautical Look', insisting that 'marine blue will be the new colour, with an armada of peaked caps angled jauntily. Not since the "Khyber Pass" look

'The Nautical Look'

has there been such an invasion on the male fashion scene'.

Years later, Tommy would admit that much of this stuff was just him 'having a bit of fun. In business you've got to lighten it a bit, whatever you do, so I used to write funny little press releases about whatever was current, and the press would pick up on it.' Be that as it may, Tommy's idea of *fun* required resources and time; time meant money; and money was running alarmingly low at Lincroft Kilgour in the early 1980s. Just five months after opening Tommy's 'shop-within-a-shop', the conglomerate directors released a statement about preliminary talks that 'may lead to the sale of a substantial part of the group'. Lincroft Kilgour's losses from the previous year had surpassed £425,000, and Tommy's efforts at KFS were hardly helping to turn the family's fortunes around.

Indeed, even Tommy could recognise that relations between him and the group had started to sour. He confided in a letter to David that he didn't think the second makeover of Dover Street had worked on any level: the showroom was still 'boring and old-fashioned', and now, with the deepening recession taking its heavy toll, there was a suffocating atmosphere of 'gloom' about the place (that word again). Really, the only thing that seemed to be going even remotely well was the Cue Shop collaboration. And Japan, which was 'enormous', Tommy wrote. 'They even have posters of the "old girl" all over the tube stations.'

トミー・ナター

In June 1982, Tommy flew to Japan to see for himself. His primary goal, he announced in a press bulletin that cast the voyage of 'Mick Jagger's tailor' as a monumentally important event, was to 'get all those Japanese businessmen out of their boring navy blue suits'. His luggage was crammed with schedules, to-do lists, letters of introduction, half-written speeches and costume changes. On the flight over, he nursed a fractured arm; a speeding motorbike had knocked him down the week before. This was an irrelevant detail he also offered to journalists, in case they wanted to write about his health.

The itinerary was dizzying: ten days of presentations and runway shows, train trips and planning sessions, and long, formal meetings. As Tommy glanced over an outline of the trip forwarded to him by the team in Japan, he added his own annotations: 'Mr Hori – whiskey', 'Mr Iijima – cigarettes', 'VIP', 'DEPART EXHAUSTED'.

Landing at Narita International Airport, he was immediately rushed away to a business dinner. The next morning, he was at the Foreign Press Centre for a rehearsal and two 'fashion spectaculars'. European models had been brought in for the shows because Tommy's angle (at his Japanese hosts' request) was that he was giving 'part of Britain's great heritage to Japan, where I know it will be appreciated'. This exoticised Britishness – a refreshing reversal from the usual Orientalism – was played up to an almost ludicrous extent, through stage projections of London icons (Big Ben and red phone booths) and gold-leaf stamps on all the press releases, which were written out in meticulous calligraphy.

Over in Osaka, Tommy attended a gala reception in his honour at the Hankyu Department Store. Then he delivered a lecture to 150 tailors, and posed for pictures with every single one of them. He travelled by train to Kyoto for a day of tourism, photographing a Buddhist temple, Japanese schoolgirls, more Japanese schoolgirls, and himself in a bathroom mirror. Amid all this, he was showered with gifts – a Minolta camera, bouquets of flowers – and treated like a visiting dignitary. This was deeply gratifying to Tommy, who had only recently complained that he'd 'never been a megastar in England. Always famous, but never a real megastar.' Now here he was, standing in a spotlight, basking in rapturous applause.

A gala reception at Hankyu Department Store, Osaka.

When Tommy returned to London on 9 June from this delirious vanity tour, he found himself unemployed. If that sounds abrupt – well, it was. And also not.

'He fell out with Kilgour because he thought it wasn't good for him, it was too restrictive, they wanted to control him,' remembers Alan Lewis. The partnership had always been a marriage of convenience, and now it was time to divorce. Lincroft Kilgour no longer wanted to bankroll Tommy, an expensive wildcard at a moment when every expense was being scrupulously appraised; and Tommy no longer wanted to work within the strictures of KFS, which was (he said) tying him down. Still, inevitable though it may have been, the parting seems to have caught him unprepared in the middle of 1982. 'He had no money at all when he came to see me,' Lewis recalls.

A bold entrepreneur from Manchester, Alan Lewis had made his money through property and finance in the wool textiles industry. Forty-four years old, he was a staunch Conservative, a fervent believer in Christian healing, and extraordinarily self-disciplined. 'Karate in the morning, weightlifting in the evening and no smoking, alcohol, or meat-eating in between,' as a journalist once put it. He could be ruthless when it came to business, buying and merging or breaking up companies, prioritising efficiency and results over all other concerns (including the workers). But he also liked to be seen on the social circuit, to have a good time, splash a bit of money about. And he knew how to *dress*, often in Tommy Nutter suits. So perhaps it was not so surprising that Tommy should suddenly gravitate towards him as a potential *deus ex machina*, despite being his polar opposite in nearly every way.

As Lewis remembers it: 'Tommy said, "I'm broke. I need some help. I think you're an honest man. Will you help me?"'

Lewis liked the tailor. 'So I said, "All right, I'll finance you."'

The handshake happened extremely fast. Just fourteen days after Tommy returned from Japan, Alan Lewis formed Fabricwood Limited and issued four shares: one (25 per cent) to Thomas Albert Nutter; and three (75 per cent) to a company named Alcrafield Limited, which Lewis had controlled since its incorporation in 1968. (Later, Lincroft Kilgour would also sell Lewis its Tommy Nutter Promotions, handing over several boxes of documents and ephemera.)

On paper, it sounded like an irresistible prospect. Through Fabricwood Limited, Tommy would have ready access to all of Lewis's other holdings – including, once the deal was finally approved by the Monopolies Commission, the world's second largest wool-textile group and a producer of luxury materials, Illingworth Morris.

But far more important, Lewis had something that Tommy desperately wanted, something Lincroft Kilgour had never been able to offer: a place on Savile Row. Recently, the businessman had acquired a vast showroom at No. 18–19. It was currently vacant.

Tommy made a public announcement in August that he was leaving the team at Kilgour, French & Stanbury. He maintained that this had been the plan for 'quite a while', that he'd merely been 'waiting for a suitable site' before he gave his notice and ventured out on his own. 'I'm getting some of the bright lights back into the street,' Tommy declared in September, hinting at 'a megastore'. He would open on 4 October, having been away from Savile Row for more than six years.

18-19 SAVILE ROW LONDON W1 · OPENING OCTOBER 1982

'18-19 Savile Row, London W1: Opening October 1982'

14

LOST BOYS

I.

It had not been until 1979, after what seemed like an eternity of Dantean torment, that David finally managed to break free from Bill King. The moment had come during a photo shoot with Patti LaBelle, though King's behaviour had been building towards some terrible crescendo for months. Not long before, for example, a fire had broken out in the studio's lift shaft; King had evacuated himself first, leaving the rest of the staff to potentially suffocate from smoke inhalation. That had been bad – but this, with LaBelle, was something else entirely.

David was assisting, as he often did when the big-name performers came in to be photographed. King snapped a few pictures of the singer. Everything was untroubled, going fine. But then King turned and, as though David were his co-conspirator, whispered 'a racist remark about Patti and her friends'.

David was horrified. If there was one thing he could never abide, not since his father's ignorant ranting back in Edgware, it was racism. Years of pent-up resentment suddenly came exploding out in a vitriolic rush. 'When I walked out of the studio for the very last time,' David recalls, 'Bill gave me a bottle of champagne, and I told him to shove it up his arse.'

Now, in 1982, David was working for the American photographer Art Kane, who in many ways was a much better fit than Bill King had ever been. A portraitist and bold visionary (and, arguably, one of the more underappreciated artists of the twentieth century), Kane's interests paralleled David's almost exactly. There was the experimentalism, for instance. Kane had pioneered the creative use of wide-angle lenses, distorting his subjects for poetic effect. He'd squeezed emulsion from the pods of unexposed Polaroid film to create ghostly abstractions. He'd perfected what he called the 'sandwich' image: multiple transparencies stacked together using tweezers and tape, so a black man's face appeared overlaid by metal grates, say, or Venice seemed to be sinking into the lagoon. (This was a different technique from the one David once used to put John and Yoko into the clouds, though the effect was comparable.)

At the same time, Kane had produced photo essays on poverty, Native Americans, the great American racial divide. He'd worked for all the major fashion magazines and done exquisite studies of rock stars: Jim Morrison, Bob Dylan, the Who. One of his most enduring pictures, *Harlem 1958*, showed fifty-seven giants of jazz, everyone from Dizzy Gillespie to Thelonious Monk, gathered around the stoop of a single brownstone. Andy Warhol once compared Kane to 'the sun', saying: 'Art beams his eye straight at his subject, and what he sees, he pictures – and it's usually a dramatic interpretation of personality.' David agreed with this assessment; he thought Kane was blindingly brilliant as a photographer, if a little more uneven as a boss.

Kane suffered from debilitating bouts of depression. In fact, the reason Kane had hired David in the first place was because he found him amusing; he insisted on calling him 'David Funner'.

Kane did not have his own darkroom and therefore had no need for a darkroom technician. So David was put 'in charge' of his studio at Broadway and Twenty-Eighth Street, a light-filled penthouse with glorious views over Manhattan. Once again, though, the job description did not really capture the job reality. David spent a great deal of time wrangling the studio bills (there never seemed to be enough money to go round), but he could also be called upon at any moment to fulfil some other function. On one occasion, the French fashion brand Cacharel commissioned Kane to illustrate a womenswear ad campaign – and then objected when Kane submitted photographs of burning giraffes, possibly inspired by Dalí. 'Art wouldn't go and see them,' David recalls. 'I had to go. The owner told me, "We can't have this kind of thing."'

On another occasion, Kane needed models for a *Vogue Italia* fashion shoot, so David was ordered to dress up as a Catholic priest. In the final photograph, David poses alongside a 'Hasidic rabbi' (one of his friends doing a favour) and Christie Brinkley.

David also typed scripts, because Kane was determined to break into show business. An original screenplay, *The Camoufleur*, was about Kane's wartime experiences in the 603rd Camouflage Engineers, a unit responsible for creating a 'ghost army' of fake, inflatable tanks, cannons, trucks and jeeps to bamboozle the Nazis after the invasion at Normandy. Another script, titled *Paper Dolls*, was a stage musical with book and lyrics by Kane, and music by the composer Michael Kamen. Also loosely autobiographical, *Paper Dolls* told the story of a photographer who gets swept up in New York fashion and disco. David, having added small edits based on his own life experiences as he typed, remembers it fondly: 'It probably could have been great.' (Neither script was ever produced.)

Meanwhile, David still chipped away at his own artistic projects on the side, though he'd never quite managed to leverage the moment presented by the Viking/Penguin book back in 1977. Perhaps he lacked the relentless ambition required to succeed as a creative in New York. David was too passive; rather than going out to seize opportunities, he tended to wait for them to come to him. Which, admittedly, they did – just not as often as he would have liked. Over the years, Elton had continued to rely on David's services for album covers and publicity shots. And every now and then, another request might filter through that led to paid work, or, at the very least, a strange encounter.

One that would haunt him for years happened not long after John Lennon's assassination. On the evening of 8 December, 1980, Lennon had been walking into the Dakota when a man named Mark David

Chapman stepped out and opened fire with a Charter Arms pistol. After news broke that John had died from his wounds – had been *murdered* – May Pang phoned David in hysterics, and Elton called him at 3 a.m., deeply unnerved. David was immediately beset by nightmares. 'Went to Dakota after work,' he'd written the next day. 'Eerie . . . Like a movie.'

The following April, David had been summoned back to the Dakota by a grieving Yoko Ono. Swearing him to secrecy, Yoko, knowing she could trust David, asked him if he was interested in working on the cover of her next album. As David recalls, she then pulled out a pair of glasses. John's glasses, coated with his dried blood. She placed the glasses near a window overlooking Central Park. 'She said, "What do you think I should use, a wide-angle lens? What kind of lens will you use?"' David swallowed his shock to offer a considered professional opinion.

According to his diary, David was still waiting for a follow-up call a week later. 'No word from Yoko – I'm sure it's off.' He'd never chased her about the job, once again allowing an extraordinary opportunity to slide away. But that June, David had been reminded of their discussion when he saw Yoko's *Season of Glass* in the record shop: a photo of Lennon's bloodstained glasses, perched on the windowsill alongside a glass of water. Yoko had picked his brain for technical details, David says, and then taken care of the final picture herself.

———

One day in September 1982, David was working in Kane's studio when he came across a discarded copy of *Time*. The cover showed a charging bull tangled up in reams of ticker tape, an illustrated commentary on the finance industry. This was hardly David's area of interest, but he opened the issue anyway. He thumbed past 'Wall Street's Super Streak', and 'Hope and Worry for Reaganomics', and past multiple cigarette advertisements, right up to the Medicine page, where he hit an article that stopped him cold.

It began suddenly, in the autumn of 1979. Young homosexual men with a history of promiscuity started showing up at the medical clinics of New York City, Los Angeles and San Francisco with a bizarre array of ailments.

Written by Claudia Wallis, the report was titled 'The Deadly Spread of AIDS', an acronym (acquired immune deficiency syndrome) that had only recently been coined by the Centers for Disease Control. According to the CDC, which was now monitoring the situation, Aids had been responsible for the death of at least 232 people in the past sixteen months – considerably more, Wallis noted, than certain other epidemics that had caused widespread alarm, including the 1976 outbreak of Legionnaire's disease in Philadelphia. Wallis quoted Dr James Curran, head of a CDC task force on Aids, describing it as 'a very, very dramatic illness' with a seemingly exponential spread.

In the beginning, when Aids seemed to be specific to gay men, 'our efforts were concentrated on trying to dissect out life-style differences', Curran continued. Researchers had started their search by examining the colourful particulars of gay sexual practices, including the use of amyl nitrite poppers as a muscle relaxant. But now there were signs of Aids elsewhere, beyond the gay community: in Haitians, haemophiliacs and heterosexual drug addicts. And so, Wallis wrote, scientists had come to suspect something new was responsible – sexually transmitted, perhaps also transmitted by blood – though nobody seemed to understand exactly how it worked. Attempts to identify a common infectious agent from various patients had so far been fruitless. 'It is not known whether there *is* a transmissible agent,' Curran said.

Wallis listed the early symptoms of Aids, which were not much different from those of a nasty cold. She noted that Aids seemed to have a curious effect on the immune system: patients showed unusually low counts of helper (CD4+) T cells, leaving them open to all sorts of infections healthy bodies would usually fight off. She reported that apprehension had swept the gay neighbourhoods of New York and San Francisco, that some gay men were no longer going out to clubs, effectively isolating themselves. After a grim discussion of current treatments for Kaposi's sarcoma (surgery, chemo), Wallis then tried to conclude her article with an upbeat note: 'immunologists, virologists and cancer experts agree that AIDS represents a remarkable experiment of nature'. Perhaps the syndrome, in the words of Pablo Rubinstein, an immunobiologist, could even 'teach us more about cancer and old, familiar diseases than we are able to fathom at this time.'

David put the magazine down. This was the very first time he'd heard of 'the AIDS', as he would describe it in his diary. He saw nothing upbeat about the implications.

A few weeks later, David woke up feeling unusually dreadful. He was freezing, and then he was hot, back and forth, hot and cold, in strange, alternating flashes. He wondered if this meant the flu again, which he seemed to contract with alarming regularity these days.

He climbed out of bed and pulled on his clothes. He headed downtown to work. Before long, he left the studio and returned uptown to bed, tucking an electric blanket under his chin.

The next morning, David found that he was too ill to even leave his apartment. 'Told Art it could be psychosomatic re: money issues, etc,' he wrote in his diary. He huddled under the blanket and willed his body to improve. He felt 'weak as hell', both physically and mentally. Even his dreams had stopped coming, which was 'very strange', because David usually dreamed so lucidly that he could recount them like other people discussed their waking life.

On 9 October, he started to vomit. 'Can't keep a thing down,' he wrote. He was wracked with 'awful pains'. He fretted – 'Getting worried' – and then vomited some more, for two days in a row. He cried off a friend's birthday party, a catch-up with Elton John. 'Have to see doctor,' he wrote to himself.

At the medical centre, Dr Schachtel took samples of his blood. After asking David to pee in a cup, Schachtel was alarmed by what he saw there. 'He didn't like colour of pee (very dark). Said "liver".'

Now David was seriously rattled.

But because there was nothing he could do until the test results came back, he staggered home on the shoulder of his room-mate, Kevin Bostick, who was tending to him like a dutiful nurse.

Kevin Bostick and David on Fire Island, June 1978.

David had first met Kevin back in 1978, when a mutual friend introduced them. There'd been a fling, though it hadn't lasted long before fizzling out. Kevin had a drug dependency – Tuinal and Seconal, sourced from the dealers who lurked along Fourteenth Street. David had found him impossible when he was high. ('Had row on the pier about drugs and money,' he'd once written in his diary. 'I threw money at K and it fell to the floor.') Yet even after their involvement ended, the two men had maintained a strong connection. David liked Kevin, who was sweet and well intentioned; and Kevin was attached to David, perhaps because David showed such a keen interest in his welfare. Soon David had started letting Kevin crash at his apartment when he needed somewhere to stay. Over time, Kevin crashed with increasing frequency, until he was living there full-time. This was an unplanned development, though not an unwelcome one. While Kevin could be challenging with his multi-day benders, he was loyal. Indeed, you could say that Kevin had gradually, without either of them quite realising it, become a kind of partner. David and Kevin did not have sex, but they provided each other with all the other things partners were supposedly good for: comfort, companionship, emotional support. And 'greens,' which Kevin now brought David on grocery runs in a bid to get his friend's strength back up.

On 12 October, David staggered back into Art Kane's studio. He thought he 'must be mad' to work, but there was 'so much shit to clear up', and Kane would only let it accumulate until David took care of business. He got as much done as possible before calling a cab and returning home to resume brooding.

It was not until 25 October, nearly two weeks later, that a definitive diagnosis finally arrived. Schachtel called to say that David had been slammed with 'a massive dose'.

Viral hepatitis, usually cleared with time.

This was excellent news, a huge relief. Yet beyond some light self-admonishment ('I have to be careful'), David didn't register much of a response in his diary. Perhaps he was distracted by the other developing news: 'Norman had called. He has to go into hospital to have lump removed on his neck. Sounds bad to me. Harry too is in hospital with fevers etc . . .'

Years later, David would say that he had 'a premonition' after reading the article by Claudia Wallis. That he'd sensed what was coming, immediately adjusted his sexual behaviour, and tried to warn his friends in New York, his brother in London. Although, by then it was already too late: the virus could incubate undetected for years. It was now just starting to wake up.

II.

At almost exactly the same moment that David began to feel ill, Tommy put the finishing touches on the most important event of his working life since the launch of Nutters in 1969. But perhaps a full description of the 'Grand Opening & Fashion Show', as his elaborate invitations called it, is best left to Annie Frankel, who attended the party, then went home and typed out (in green ink) a biting commentary of the whole episode for Tommy's private amusement.

Hello there Nutter fans everywhere,

It's Monday 4th October 1982, 8.30pm and my goodness the rain is pouring down ruining the makeup and hairdos before we even get started. It hasn't deterred the fashionable from coming to Mr Tommy Nutter's new and sumptious salon – ablaze with lights in the highest of tecs [sic].

And here is Mr Nutter himself approaching us with hysterical laughter (can't help but wonder why he always laughs like that whenever he sees us: could it be Petie's bow tie and my frock???). 'DARLINGS,' he screams, grabs hold of us and without a moment's hesitation throws us into little gold seats . . . 'At least I've got you firmly put in your places,' he grunts contentedly and disappears. This gives us the chance to look at all the other little gold seats and what is written on them. We are on the catwalk itself – my, my, what an honour – and directly opposite see the words 'Miss Cilla Black' planted on a chair.

And here she is: a little black-and-white Crêpe De Chine number, beautiful with a slit up the middle revealing one of the best pair of legs ever displayed.

. . . I note that the chair next to hers is marked 'His Grace The Bishop of Southwark', and ask my next-door-neighbour, who is called 'Guest of Mr Stewart Grimshaw', whether we also should grovel or prostrate ourselves or curtsy when his Grace arrives? No need to worry, however, because into the good bishop's chair drops Liz Brewer looking chirpy in red/gold/silver/green/blue/ yellow/mauve/pink frock, with shoes to match. 'What a good disguise,' says my neighbour, 'the bishop looks like Liz Brewer.'

. . . But now then what is this? Something is falling in the door . . . we can only guess . . . it's electric pink taffeta from

mouth to ankle . . . it's topped by a 4-foot hat with things hanging off it – also pink . . . it's got the most enormous pair of black brogues sticking out of its end . . . IT MUST BE WALKING CANDY FLOSS????? No. Wrong. It's Mrs Shilling (or maybe it's the missing bishop).

At this point we have all turned the colour of Mrs Shilling's dress – and as shiny – especially me and Cilla who are seriously concerned about the mascara. WE ARE MELTING. But it's time for the show to begin and a marvellous show it is too. W-o-n-d-e-r-f-u-l suits, jackets, woollies, trousers and coats fly past our eyes on spectacular models (quite obviously hand-picked by Tommy's discerning eyes): 2 lovely girls and the boys are to die [for] . . . Tommy's colours are just as glorious: greys/reds; browns/petrol/blues; greens/beige: STUNNING AND NOT EXPENSIVE.

And now it's over but not before a reluctant, bashful Tommy takes a curtain call to tumultuous, well-deserved applause. We get a chance to stretch our legs.

There are two quite separate stampedes taking place: 1) to get to Tommy and 2) to get to the free champagne. We've seen Tommy so we opt for the champagne. We are nearly trampled to death by those who are trying to get FROM the champagne to Tommy. We scratch and claw our way through Ossie Clark, Ricci Burns, Lady (looking bubbly) Rothermere, Stewart Grimshaw with yet two more guests: Jan de Villeneuve who looks just the same as she did ten years ago, and a very pretty anorexic lady looking alarmingly like a) Audrey Hepburn and b) [as though] she's going to drop dead from starvation at any minute, PLUS a whole assortment of long, tall, fat, thin persons who interfere just too much to allow the drunks among us to get to the bottle. Never mind. We go home.

Marvellous show Tommy.
WE'LL BE BACK.

Tommy's eponymous emporium announced itself loudly, with an electric-blue neon sign above the entrance. Five cream awnings were also stencilled with his name, in case there was absolutely any doubt about his triumphant return to Savile Row.

Through a glass door, up a short staircase trimmed with wrought iron and polished oak, the showroom – all 3,000 square feet of it – was covered with thick beige carpet. The walls and ceilings were joined together by soft curves, so there were very few sharp corners anywhere. Most of the lighting was recessed, flowing down or gushing up from beneath displays like water from a dozen hidden fountains. Persian rugs were juxtaposed with deep-padded sofas, tinted mirrors, copious amounts of chrome. One magazine would liken the decor to 'an elegant ocean liner', though perhaps there was also a touch of the starship *Enterprise* – a kind of retro-futurism about the place. 'I wanted it to exude quality, but not in a stuffy sort of way,' Tommy told one journalist. He told another that it was supposed to be an 'up-dated traditional look', featuring combinations 'that wouldn't normally be put together', which was, after all, the same approach he took to designing clothes. 'I wanted customers to be able to take one look at the shop and know immediately what type of clothes they would find here,' Tommy said.

Still, it was clear that there was also something a little off about the place. Despite Tommy's rapturous trumpeting in the press, the showroom design was not really his taste. Like a hermit crab, he'd scurried into an old John Michael shop; he'd made small cosmetic changes, adjusted the frontage, added his name in blazing neon, but left the major features mostly unaltered. This extended to the clothing too. 'They basically had all the old stock from the shop that had previously occupied 19 Savile Row,' recalls Catherine Everest (then Butterworth), Tommy's new assistant. 'Tommy was very unhappy about it, because it wasn't representative of his level of *style*.' As the offending knitwear and shirts were sold off to unsuspecting customers, the stock did not immediately replenish either, until the shelving displays began to look 'embarrassingly bare'. Tommy moved bolts of cloth around, 'trying to dress the shop up to look fuller than it actually was'.

Catherine Butterworth had responded to an advertisement in the

Evening Standard after recognising Tommy's name from back issues of *Vogue*. She understood where he'd come from, the glory of Nutters, and she understood what he was now hoping to achieve. 'Tommy looked at the shop – not like his last chance, but as an opportunity to become as big as he once had been,' Catherine says. Tommy's new head cutter, James Cottrell, a highly experienced coat maker from Kilgour, French & Stanbury, sensed something similar. 'I think he was trying to pick up the pieces from years gone by.'

Without Alan Lewis as his financier, Tommy would never have returned to Savile Row; he knew this and was eternally grateful for the chance. But he also got slightly more than he bargained for in their agreement. Lewis's approach to business that had made him so astonishingly successful elsewhere – backing a troubled venture and then 'turning it around' by reducing overheads, eliminating fat, pushing productivity – came as a shock to Tommy and his classically trained tailors. Lewis would pull up in a Rolls-Royce and walk into the shop wearing a large fur coat. He brought with him what Cottrell describes as 'relentless pressure'.

'How many orders have you taken?' Lewis might ask. 'How many are you getting out this week? Are they all going to go home?'

As Lewis himself remembers it, Tommy's business immediately began to haemorrhage money, 'a hundred thousand in the first two years'. So pressure was necessary to staunch the bleeding. His horsewhip attitude annoyed the workers, though, who were more accustomed to the vagaries of the bespoke trade, to building a clientele over time and then weathering famines and revelling in the feasts when they finally came. How many suits were they finishing up? 'It depends if the customer comes *in*,' says Cottrell. 'We just used to look at each other and think, "Oh, for Christ's sake."'

For his part, Tommy remained politely deferential towards Mr Lewis – or 'Alana', as he sometimes called him, less deferentially, behind his back. Still, shoestring conditions were not what Tommy had envisaged for his big Savile Row comeback, and he greeted the strictures and demands from above, invariably concerning money (always, his whole career, concerning *money*), with a disillusioned sigh. 'He wasn't really interested in money,' Catherine recalls. 'What did interest him was getting it right, the right suit. That was his thing: doing interesting designs.' In this regard, Tommy and Alan Lewis had a fundamental conflict. They would waltz around the situation for years, each one struggling to take the lead.

Tommy with James Cottrell, his head cutter.

At least there was the tantalising promise of future growth. The 1980s were shaping up to be a boom time for menswear. Tommy would later call it 'the suits revolution', explaining that 'everyone got back into wearing suits, the big suits, and it was a rebellion of sorts ... It became "new" to wear a suit.' Though unemployment was still high in 1983, inflation had fallen dramatically, and the recession was basically over. People began to accrue incredible levels of wealth, a grab that would only go into overdrive with the sudden deregulation of the financial markets in the middle of the decade. With new wealth came a desire to show it off, to *flaunt*. Aesthetics and materialism became even more entwined with social status, as Patrick Collins would note in the *Mail on Sunday*:

The Old Men bought their suits from Burtons, their hats from Dunns and their opinions from the *Daily Telegraph*. They drove elderly Daimlers, sitting alongside wives who wore long-serving sable and offered you pictures of their grandchildren.

The New Men are dressed by Mr Tommy Nutter. They wear built-up shoes for confidence and Cartier watches for show. They drive Italian cars with personalised number plates: computers on the dash board and Barry Manilow on the stereo. Their latest wife, who was once a beauty queen and wanted to be happy and own a health farm, sits in the back and pleads for their attention.

Suiting for the 'New Men' was a question of power: the 'power suit' signified success and self-determination. With the widespread adoption of centralised air conditioning, too, suits could be thinner, lighter and more comfortable, something you could wear to the office and then out to a nightclub. This shift from formality to versatility in men's suiting (which is what the so-called suits revolution was really about) was driven by the work of one figure in particular: Giorgio Armani. What Armani did was like 'cutting the buckles and taking the stuffing from a straitjacket', *Time* noted in a breathless cover profile of the Italian designer in 1982. An Armani suit was 'an epiphany of choreographed rumple', and wearing one brought 'an ease, the Armani ease', that was simultaneously sexy *and* sharp, formal *and* casual. Armani had re-imagined the suit as a kind of everyday, glamorous uniform. He'd then successfully marketed this vision to the masses via, for example, *American Gigolo*, in which Richard Gere modelled his clothes, looking louche yet devastatingly handsome.

Even Tommy had to admit begrudgingly ('I hate to mention it') that Armani had done something remarkable here. But he saw a natural affinity between their approaches to suits as a kind of lifestyle choice. 'Armani came along and was on my same wavelength,' Tommy once claimed. He was also determined to embrace the suits revolution in his own way, not through imitating Armani's successful style. As Aldo Fleri, a salesman at Tommy Nutter, explains, 'Armani used feminine fabrication – the suits are very soft, very flowy – whereas Tommy used masculine fabrication. He wouldn't put a crepe suit together, for example. It just wasn't him. He would put a Prince of Wales check together, or a chalk stripe: a very *masculine* type of look.'

A 1980s Tommy Nutter suit was something you could wear for business, but there was usually an irregular twist to it: emerald-green pinstripes on a navy background, say, or petrol blue in worsted flannel. 'I don't want to make everything too wild,' Tommy explained. 'I like a mixture. If you want to wear a classic, Savile Row cut, you can [buy ready-to-wear]. If you don't, then you can wear one of my bespoke designs.'

What characterised these bespoke designs was a no-vent jacket, because 'a gentleman never wears vents', and some seriously ambitious padding. Once, a journalist asked Tommy if he got many people coming in and asking for 'an Armani suit'. Tommy replied, 'Not really. My customers come because they want a suit that looks like a Tommy Nutter.' Then he squeezed both his shoulders to emphasise the point.

In recent years, Savile Row had come to prefer soft, 'ski-slope' shoulders, but with Tommy 'it was always a little bit of a battle to get the shoulders higher and wider', recalls James Cottrell. 'It was quite an exaggerated look.'

It was also divisive. On the one hand, Tommy's supporters were both vocal and socially prominent: Sir Roy Strong, director of the Victoria & Albert Museum, bought a grey horizontal chalk-stripe suit for

'A very masculine type of look.'

the museum's fashion collection, arguing that Tommy Nutter's menswear designs perfectly encapsulated the age. On the other hand, *GQ* would eventually compare a suit from Tommy Nutter to a Japanese limousine: 'very well-made, but a little other-worldly'. And other tailors on Savile Row, including some of Tommy's former employees, questioned the quality of his finish or muttered that his designs lacked the vigour and elegance he'd once achieved at Nutters with Edward Sexton.

But Tommy mostly ignored his detractors, making his suits as full and his shoulders as defiantly peaked as he wanted. Indeed, it became a good-natured joke among his staff that Tommy's own clothes made him formidable, a tank – and that, in modelling his ideal silhouette, which was like a capital letter *V*, Tommy had to turn sideways just to fit through the door.

Financial constraints meant that Tommy ran his new shop with a skeleton crew: a personal assistant, the bookkeeper, two salesmen, five or six tailors under the head cutter, and a rotating roster of outworkers to take care of trousers and waistcoats (coats being crafted on the premises).

Placing ads in the newspaper, Tommy carried out much of the hiring himself. This process led to some idiosyncratic combinations. One of the first salesmen he employed was David de Lacy Spiddal, a haughty, moustached Irishman who wore a fresh boutonnière in his buttonhole and adored the royal family. Another was Timothy Everest, a club kid with dyed hair who'd once dreamed of becoming a racing driver.

Tommy turned out to be remarkably good at keeping spirits high, and he was an excellent mentor to the younger members of his team. He was generous with his time, Timothy Everest recalls, inviting opinions and input and experimentation. 'Not a lot of leaders do that,' adds Aldo Fleri, who would arrange cloth samples on a table in the order and quantity he thought they should be ordered, then watch as Tommy came through and gently made corrections, dispensing advice like, 'A good contrast is better than a bad match.'

Almost immediately, Tommy opened his doors to students from the fashion colleges. John Galliano, studying at St Martin's School of Art, briefly appeared in 1983. He would come in to revamp the window displays with sack mannequins and straw boaters or observe the tailors as they conducted a fitting. Years later, Galliano would recall noticing that the sleeves of Tommy's jackets, lined up in rows on the display racks, 'all hung in a gentle arc rather than straight down'. This inspired him to experiment with cutting sleeves in a spiral, which further inspired him to cut entire garments in a spiral, which eventually became one of his signature techniques.

Also in 1983, Tommy welcomed a twenty-two-year-old intern named Sean Chiles. Another student from St Martin's, Sean came on as a kind of design assistant – 'not', he affirms, 'as a tailoring assistant'. The distinction was important.

With his background in fashion design as a point of comparison, Sean observed that Tommy had an unusual way of working. 'As a fashion designer like me, you arrive at your final designs through a process,' Sean explains. 'You have inspiration or an idea; you research and take it through experimentation and trial; you end up with your formalised concepts; and then you create it. Tommy didn't have any process like that. There were no mood boards or anything. It was about how he felt, what he knew, innovations *within* tailoring.' But Sean also sensed that Tommy was 'a designer inside', and Tommy seemed particularly amenable to design suggestions, filling in gaps in his own knowledge. Once, Sean took a sample of pinstripe cloth and placed a black bugle bead on every grey stripe to 'introduce texture and shimmer to the outfit'. Tommy loved it: a Savile Row suit overlaid, quite literally, with fashion. He immediately sold a full suit of the bedazzled cloth to Elton John that would feature, by the time it was completed, 1,009,444 black bugle beads painstakingly attached by hand. 'You sat down and body parts started rubbing – eventually the beads would either break or come off,' recalls James Cottrell, who was less enamoured with this particular example of men's couture.

Above all, what Sean appreciated about Tommy was his fondness for subversion. 'Finding ways of conning people into thinking that they were part of the Establishment, or that one of his suits was part of the Establishment, and yet he twisted it, or changed it, and it *wasn't*.'

This mischievousness could manifest in surprising ways. For instance, Sean's mother is Ann Mitchell, a stage and television actress then known for starring in *Widows*, an ITV drama about bereaved mob wives who pull off an armed robbery and then escape to Rio. Tommy was obsessed with the show, and he asked Sean if a meeting could be arranged with his mother. Sean complied. 'We had dinner a few times and became friends,' Ann recalls. 'And then, for whatever reason, the *Evening Standard* picked up that we were an item.'

The reason was this: Tommy had invited Ann to be his date to Elton John's thirty-sixth birthday party at a Chinese restaurant in Knightsbridge (the same party, incidentally, where Elton debuted his bugle-bead suit). Afterwards, Tommy circulated a press release stating that he and the actress had been 'seen' there together. When a gossip columnist from the *Evening Standard* called and asked him to elaborate on what he meant by 'seen', Tommy issued a further statement: 'You never know about romance. These things happen.'

The newspaper printed it under the headline 'Tailor-Made for One Another'.

This was all very deliberate on Tommy's part. And Sean's, too, because he was in on the gag. 'We did it together, created this idea that Tommy and my mum were an item.' Tommy had decided to manipulate the press, 'to subvert what was out there', Sean recalls, and he relished the idea that somebody might be gullible enough to pick up such a ludicrous story and make it public. Once a journalist did exactly that, Ann herself became another willing accomplice. 'I loved Tommy,' she says. 'And I was subversive too. If he wanted to do it, it was fine by me.'

One of the things that attracted Tommy to Ann Mitchell was the specific character she played on *Widows*: a resilient, working-class, innately tasteful woman named Dolly Rawlins, who reminded him in certain ways of his own mother.

But whatever happened to Dolly Nutter?

Her extended absence from this narrative is not an oversight.

Dolly had been absent – or sidelined, more accurately – from the lives of her two sons for a little over two decades by the early 1980s. She still saw them, of course, Tommy for dinners, David whenever he returned to London to do something for Elton. But they visited her like somebody might visit a family member in prison: regretfully, and a little stiffly, just to check she was soldiering on in an unfortunate situation. Christopher's sour tyranny had never really abated. In letters to David, Tommy had variously described the atmosphere of their parents' house as 'HEAVY!!!' and 'very Pink Flamingos'. Neither brother could stand to stay for long; visiting hours to see Dolly were inevitably short.

All that changed, suddenly, on 21 January 1983, with Christopher's death, at the age of seventy, from chronic obstructive pulmonary disease.

The death itself made no great impression on Tommy or David. Though Tommy remained with his mother throughout the first night to offer some comfort, he did not think to mention it to his close friends; he required no comfort for himself. And David greeted the news with similar equanimity. 'Feel bad for mum,' he wrote in his diary, though for himself, after the initial shock, he felt merely 'odd'. He would not fly back to England for his father's cremation.

Indeed, the death is only worth noting at all for the impact it had on Dolly's life. Her own mother, Lily (aka Nanny Bannister, aka Creampot Lil), had already passed away, and now her husband was gone as well. It was as though both the jailers had abandoned their posts.

Dolly embraced her new-found liberation. Sixty-six years old, she started what amounted to a second life. She immediately began to travel, something that Christopher had always resisted. She awakened a long-dormant creative side, filling page after page with rudimentary watercolours. ('They were kind of childish, but she loved doing it,' David remembers.) She sunbathed on park benches for hours at a stretch and visited seaside towns to stroll along the sand. Most important, she set about reasserting a familiar role in the eyes of her two sons as a woman of strength and open-mindedness – a woman whose mantra had once been 'I take people as I find them'. Though Dolly would always hold out hope that Tommy might find 'the right woman', she soon felt comfortable enough to take her to a gay restaurant with his gay friends for a very gay fortieth birthday party. Dolly became part of the clique.

'He loved his mother to bits,' recalls Aldo Fleri, who would get to know her well during her regular visits to the Savile Row emporium. 'I think she was one of the major things in Tommy's life.' Now that Christopher was gone, and Dolly could make her own decisions again, she would remain a significant presence until the very end.

III.

Worn by Elton John at Wembley Stadium, 1984.

When Elton John announced that he was going to get married, on Valentine's Day 1984, the general reaction was 'complete surprise'. Many fans thought 'that Elton John would never marry', the *Evening Standard* reported coyly, and yet here was a woman: thirty-year-old Renate Blauel, a sound engineer whom Elton had apparently met in a recording studio, courted in Montserrat, and then asked to be his lawfully wedded wife. Renate had 'heard all sorts of stories about Elton, that he's supposed to be bisexual', she admitted, but that didn't worry her 'at all'.

Tommy agreed to provide the groom's suit. 'You'd think I was making the wedding dress,' he later recalled. 'Newspapers and TV stations from all over the world kept calling and speculating about what

Elton was going to wear. Frankly, I didn't know, because I had hedged my bet a bit. I made Elton 20 outfits, two of each in case of mishap, in a wide range of primary colors, including orange and very bright yellows. With each outfit went the appropriate straw boater, shirt, tie and shoes. Elton took everything to Australia.'

Meanwhile, in New York, David received a cold call four days before the big event. Elton shared the news – 'What a shock,' David wrote – and then asked his friend to fly to Sydney so he could take photos at a church in Darling Point.

Dazed, David raced to the consulate to secure a last-minute visa.

After a marathon flight with stopovers in Los Angeles and Honolulu, and 'lots of dishing' on the plane with other transiting guests, he arrived on 13 February. 'Lots of press coverage already – front page of papers,' David observed. He checked into the hotel and then went out to buy a flashgun, scoping out the harbour city as he went: 'No attractive numbers.'

The next day, at Darling Point, St Mark's Anglican Church was decorated with hundreds of orchids and white roses. Thousands of fans waited outside, braving the drizzling rain to catch sight of Elton in his tailcoat. Technically, the wedding should have been illegal: Australian law required a thirty-day waiting period after registration to prevent 'immature people [from] making immature decisions'. But government officials had waived the rule, according to a spokesman for the New South Wales attorney general, because Mr John and Ms Blauel were obviously 'two mature people who had known each other for a long time'. (If they had declined to waive it, Elton had an alternative plan to marry on a chartered boat outside Australian territorial waters.)

In the church, David shuffled around the vestry, snapping photos as the couple took turns signing their names on the marriage certificate. The moment reminded him of John and Yoko in Gibraltar – only this time round was even more surreal. David barely knew what to say to Renate. He did not understand what Elton was doing, what he was trying to prove here. Given all that had happened over the past few years, it must have been another joke. Only Elton seemed serious, and the marriage was definitely real.

As the wedding party exited the church, an Australian onlooker yelled: 'Good on you, sport, you old poof! You finally made it!'

'It just goes to show how wrong you all were,' Elton yelled back.

David climbed aboard a bus that was ferrying guests between Darling Point and a decadent, £50,000 reception at the Sebel Town House, where he got blindingly drunk on Cristal champagne.

David, with peroxide hair, in Central Park.

A few weeks later, back in New York, David went to see a psychiatrist named Dr Harrison, who asked him to stop taking lithium. Art Kane had shepherded him onto the drug, David recalls. 'Art was the first person I knew who was manic-depressive' – meaning the first person he knew who was being *treated* for manic depression – 'and once, when he stopped taking his meds, he was bedridden, and I had to take his mail over to his flat. I began to identify with what I was seeing and went to see his doctor at Columbia-Presbyterian, who put me on lithium.' Having self-prescribed alcohol for years to deal with his mood swings, David now turned to the medical establishment. But lithium didn't work, except to assault his body with unpalatable side effects and cause him, in a moment of euphoric madness, to peroxide his hair. Dr Harrison submitted him to a psych test, recording his answers to hundreds of questions on audio cassettes. David was also given doses of cilobamine – the second of several drugs he would try over the following few years.

> Pamelor (nortriptyline)
> Vivactil (protriptyline)
> Marplan (isocarboxazid)
> L-tryptophan supplements
> Buspirone (for anxiety)
> Halcion (triazolam; to aid sleep)

David was depressed about money, always in short supply. He was depressed about his achievements, the slim prospect of a career kick-start in his mid-forties. He was depressed about his drinking, which he sensed was out of control, a vicious cycle. 'Must stop,' he wrote in his diary.

But what depressed him most was something else: the spectre of Aids, now prominent enough to cast a shadow over everything in his life.

The previous year, at the Institut Pasteur in Paris, Dr Luc Montagnier and his research team had examined a sample of lymph tissue from an unwell gay man and found evidence of a retrovirus. When the team successfully replicated their original experiment, Montagnier named it lymphadenopathy-associated virus (LAV). A short time later, at the National Cancer Institute in Bethesda, Maryland, Dr Robert Gallo announced that he had *also* isolated an infectious agent, which he was calling HTLV-III. These two discoveries (the catalyst for furious recriminations of theft and grandstanding between the two doctors) were, of course, one and the same: what would come to be known as HIV, the human immunodeficiency virus.

While that was going on, the public outside the medical laboratories was becoming increasingly terrified of infection. Even more than usual, gay men were being ostracised, even turning on one another. Vitriolic debates had broken out about sex in the bathhouses and whether public health authorities should close them; a Gay Men's Health Crisis hotline was flooded with daily calls from men who were unsure of how to effectively protect themselves. By the start of 1984, the CDC had compiled a list of 3,000 Aids cases in the United States, 1,283 of which had already resulted in death. And a new study conducted in Washington DC – a study of seemingly healthy gay men, of men who believed they were *fine* – suggested that some 60 to 70 per cent of the community was showing signs of infection.

An impending catastrophe.

David was not following the news about LAV/HTLV-III, though he was certainly immersed in the paranoia sweeping New York, where there were now more cases of Aids than anywhere else in the world. He worried about his own history of promiscuity. Did he have the HIV virus, still undiagnosed? Or was he destined to get it eventually? He'd already seen up close what happened to people who developed full-blown Aids, the horrifying, humiliating, protracted end.

Norman Joseph, a black Welshman whom David liked to call Shirley ('Bassey, of course'), had been the first of his friends to succumb. It started with lumps in his neck, then a stay in St Vincent's Hospital for serious pneumonia. 'Feel so sorry for him,' David wrote in his diary. 'He thinks he'll be out by Christmas but . . . that's wishful thinking.' David and Kevin went to visit, which was 'awful, because the nurses wouldn't go near him, and we had to force them to provide ice packs to try and get Norman's temperature down'. Norman was 'scared and weak', and the smell was nauseating. Suddenly, for seemingly no reason, the hospital transferred him to another in the Bronx. 'He had to pay [the] ambulance drivers 110 dolls,' David wrote indignantly. Norman seemed to rally his strength there, and he was even released for a time; but then there was a precipitous slide, he was back in the hospital, could barely stand, became rambling and incoherent. The superintendent of Norman's building changed the lock on his apartment, rendering him homeless. Norman's mother announced that she would not be holding a memorial, that she didn't want any 'fuss'. Eventually, a ventilator was the only thing keeping him alive. 'He didn't see or hear us,' David wrote. And then it was switched off.

The death had hit David hard. But there was no time, no mourning period, before one of his best friends, Bernard Roth, then fell sick with bronchitis on Fire Island; coughing and mucus and shortness of breath. One day, David received word that Bernard was suddenly being admitted into a hospital burns unit. David went to investigate and was instructed by the staff to put on a paper gown. 'Before I went into the room,' David recalls, 'the doctor pulled me aside and said, "Be prepared to be shocked." Then he said, "We haven't got a clue what we're doing here."'

Bernard had contracted an opportunistic lung infection. To treat it, the doctors dosed him with the antibiotic Bactrim. Bernard had reacted by developing a rare condition called Stevens-Johnson syndrome. 'All his skin fell off,' David remembers. It blistered up and sloughed away in gruesome sheets, until Bernard looked as though he'd walked through a fire. 'They had him wrapped up like an Egyptian pharaoh. His boyfriend burst into tears.'

When Bernard finally died, excruciatingly, at the end of 1984, David wrote in his diary that he 'didn't feel too bad'. This was not callousness, though, so much as David observing his own coping mechanism. He had now lost two friends. Over the following few years, there would be many more. By necessity, his emotional withdrawal would only grow stronger, more resolute and total as the weight of loss piled on top of him. Of Bernard Roth, David now wrote: 'He was dead to me a week ago.'

Tommy dancing with his friend David de Lacy Spiddal.

15

HUMDRUM LIFE

The crowd convened in Fulham's Eel Brook Common, opposite John Galliano's design studio. It was a brisk, blustery Sunday morning in April 1989. Clouds threatened rain with enough conviction that some people had brought their raincoats, though others were committed to their tutus and fairy wings, to showing off rainbow patch trousers, Comme des Garçons jackets, antique neck scarves and brown suede brogues. Roger Dack, the director of Fashion Acts, which had organised the event, strolled across the grass with a megaphone rallying his troops. Later, he would describe it 'the most chic walk ever'.

More than 900 marchers had turned up, pledging some £90,000. Or maybe there was 'nigh on 1,000 people from Britain's fashion industry massed together in a giant circus of noise and colour', and pledges totalled £800,000; estimates varied. The official route threaded up the King's Road, through Knightsbridge and Westminster, all the way over to Covent Garden, where the finishing line was a champagne reception at Tuttons restaurant. Bruce Oldfield stood at the front of the procession, itching to go; Galliano, lingering behind a battalion of strollers, brought up the rear. But first, before anyone could take a single step forward, 1,116 red balloons were released into the sky: one for every person in the country who had died from Aids-related causes.

Early in the epidemic, Aids had been dismissed by some members of the British public as 'an American problem' that would never creep its way across the Atlantic. Of course, it had already arrived; as early as 1982, a man named Terrence Higgins had collapsed on the dance floor at Heaven and died a few months later from *Pneumocystis* pneumonia. 'I hope you get very scared today because there is a locomotive coming down the track and it is leaving the United States,' Mel Rosen, an American Aids activist, warned at a conference in London the following year. By late 1985, there were 241 cases of Aids in Britain, and newspapers were reporting instances of 'scared' firemen and paramedics who were refusing to perform the 'kiss of life', lest they get infected. In 1987, as conservatives talked seriously about compulsory testing of all gay men and possibly even mass quarantine, the science correspondent of *The Times* wrote that 'leading specialists believe . . . between 40,000 and 100,000 people in Britain are now carriers'.

By the time the crowd had gathered in Eel Brook Common, the cumulative impact remained small compared to what was happening over in San Francisco and New York, but it was no less devastating for those personally affected. In the fashion industry alone, that meant designers, models, stylists, magazine editors, make-up artists, photographers, boutique owners, managers, agents, public relations professionals, and dressmakers, all either dying as a result of Aids or under ambiguous circumstances that strongly suggested Aids. Fierce stigma had stopped many people from naming the thing that truly ailed them.

As the red balloons drifted into the sky above Fulham, Tommy took swigs from a hip flask to fortify himself for the long march to Covent Garden. He was deeply ambivalent about the realities of disease. He tended to avoid seeing ill people as much as possible, and he joked about Aids – about looking '*AIDSy*' – as a way of masking his discomfort. Yet he'd been joining fundraisers like this one since Comptons of Soho, his favourite gay pub, had held a drag cabaret and charity auction to help fund the country's first purpose-built Aids ward, the Broderip in Middlesex Hospital. He wanted to help. He offered donations, money, sponsorship – anything he could. Tommy understood the gravity of the crisis confronting his community. Now in his mid-forties, he also understood that it might be his own crisis, too, given the arc of his personal history.

By 1989, Tommy's shop was doing a robust trade. Wendy Samimi, a sharp, sensitive woman with an eye for numbers (and Tommy's back), had shown up and streamlined how the business was being run. 'He started doing really well,' recalls Alan Lewis. 'Not millions, mind you, but a profit.'

Around half of his trade came from bespoke. From Bill Wyman, for example, who got married to the nineteen-year-old model Mandy Smith in a grey Tommy Nutter suit. And from Tom Jones, who declined to have his waist measured, insisting he was a perennial thirty-two inches. Christie Brinkley had worn a white Nutter tailcoat on the cover of *Playboy*. Divine, too, wore Tommy's suits when he wasn't in drag, though he didn't seem to understand how bespoke tailoring worked, telling people that Tommy kept a 'Divine-sized mannequin' in his back workroom.

Just a year earlier, Hollywood had come buying for Tim Burton's *Batman*, which was shooting about twenty miles west of the West End at Pinewood Studios. Bob Ringwood, the film's costume designer, conceived the Joker's outfits (aubergine and emerald green, square shoulders, tight waistcoats, baggy trousers), and commissioned Tommy to make them actually wearable for Jack Nicholson. 'I guess they came to see me because I specialise in those sort of clothes anyway,' he later said. 'They are Tommy Nutter looks from over the years.' (During production, the tailors had found Ringwood's sketches impractical to execute. 'You'd cut them and it was impossible, you just couldn't do it,' recalls Terry Haste. They'd had to improvise their way to the final fifty-three outfits, some of which sported hidden tricks or grossly elongated sleeves for optical effect.)

The other half of Tommy's business came through his ready-to-wear lines, which were manufactured in Italy using British cloth.* Beyond

---

* 'It's common knowledge that you can't get good ready-to-wear made in Britain,' Tommy complained, 'and that's why most of the top designers have gone to Italy where factories are streamlined for making a far superior garment. The only company you could have quality clothes made by in this country is Chester Barrie, but it's too expensive. Even my ready-to-wear is made in Italy which is sad and a complete contradiction of being a Savile Row tailor.'

his own showroom on Savile Row, the Tommy Nutter label could now be found at Fortnum & Mason, as well as Selfridges, which Tommy thought was extremely 'supportive of British fashion' and thus 'an ideal location to be in'. Indeed, ready-to-wear, once all but anathema on Savile Row, was now being offered by many of his most venerated neighbours. Once again Tommy had proven himself to be a trailblazer in the tailoring industry, and the National Federation of Merchant Tailors had recently acknowledged his foresight by offering him the post of guild president, a great honour that Tommy immediately declined. 'I couldn't be doing with all those golf weekends,' he later explained. 'Not me at all.'

And yet, despite all these successes and new accolades, Tommy was now treated by some people as redolent of another era, 'a relic of the Sixties'. Did this bother him?

'No,' Tommy said, when a journalist asked him this question – 'it is rather flattering to be talked about with legends, such as Mary Quant, who, like me, are still around. There were others who disappeared completely, some of them much bigger than I was. I think I survived because I seem to be on my own. There aren't any others around here who are quite like me.'

Tommy knew that he was 'on a level with the best' and that everyone important knew it as well. At the same time, he'd also come to recognise that a tension in the Tommy Nutter image had stopped him from achieving what he really desired, the global foothold that some, like Armani – and, a little closer to home, Paul Smith – had managed to secure. 'I fall somewhere in between being a fashion designer and a Savile Row tailor, which, I suppose, can be confusing,' Tommy finally acknowledged. 'They both fight against one another.'

Not long ago, that handicap would have frustrated him; he would have tried to overcome it through publicity and media outreach. Now, however, he seemed to shrug.

The staff could sense this mellowing, a letting-go of vaulting ambition. 'I think he was quite content to just exist and have his shop on Savile Row again,' recalls Wendy. As they went about their work, Tommy told her he'd been everywhere now and met everyone, done everything there was worth doing. 'He'd gone to parties in New York where Judy Garland was sat next to him.' What more could a man want?

Sometimes, strolling down Savile Row, Tommy would pass his old shop at No. 35a and catch sight of four familiar Corinthian columns framing a large wooden door salvaged from a house in Isleworth. Then he would clock his own name, stencilled on the plate-glass window – and wince, knowing there was still nothing he could do about it all these years later.

'Chittleborough and Morgan at Nutters' was now owned exclusively by his former assistant cutters, Roy Chittleborough and Joseph Morgan. Edward Sexton had left to start his own business at No. 37. Tommy had still not spoken to any of them since 1976.

He did have one important encounter that November, though, at an event called Fabric of the Nation, a fashion spectacular held at the Royal Museum in Edinburgh. The purpose of the event was to show off Scottish wools and fabrics; designers ranging from Oscar de le Renta to Jean Muir contributed a wide-ranging collection of clothes, made from locally sourced materials, that were put on public display in the main hall.

To attend a lavish opening gala, Tommy travelled up with Wendy and checked into the Caledonian, a former railway hotel near Edinburgh Castle. Unbeknownst to them, also staying there was Edward Sexton.

At one point, they all inadvertently converged in the hotel lounge. But instead of diverging immediately, as they might have done a decade ago, the erstwhile business partners sat down and began a polite conversation.

Tommy asked after Edward's family.

'We sat together for a long, long time talking and drinking,' Edward recalls.

Tommy was 'a bit regretful', says Wendy.

As was Edward. 'I could tell that we were both very sad any of this ever happened. He was saying, "You were my best cutter ever." '

An admission of sorrow, even a lament for missed opportunities – but no reconciliation. 'There would never be bygones,' says Wendy. The break was too traumatic to ever be forgotten.

A few months later, in July 1990, David flew to London for his own reckoning with the past. Lugging a gaudy purple suitcase, he took a car from Heathrow to Finchley Road, where his mother now lived. She let him in and brewed some tea in the kitchen so they could talk.

In some ways, the David who rang Dolly's doorbell that evening was the same one she'd been worrying about ever since he decamped to New York nineteen years ago. He was still disorganised, still susceptible to strange twists of fate. But age had greyed him, thinned his hair, and brought – if not peace, then at least a degree of much-needed stability thanks to three major changes that had occurred in David's life.

First, David was now on Prozac, a drug he found so miraculously effective he'd already converted several of his friends (including Elton John) and appeared on *Geraldo*, the tabloid talk show, trying to convert the depressed masses of Middle America.

Second, he was sober, which was maybe even more transformative. It had started back in 1986, when Kevin, David's room-mate, had found himself addicted to crack cocaine and tried to break free using Narcotics Anonymous. Being nosy, David had gone along to observe the meetings in Harlem. He didn't think of *himself* as an addict – he did not do crack – but he was impressed by what he saw at NA, the confessional storytelling and non-judgemental reassurance. It had lodged in his mind as an abstract idea, until, one morning, he'd been pouring a glass of Olde English 800 when he started to shake violently. His head pounded; he felt nauseous. He'd struggled to get the malt liquor down. And something suddenly flipped in his thinking. Was he actually an alcoholic? He was getting drunk every day, largely as a way of dealing with all his disappearing friends. So David had gone to another meeting, on 125th Street, and told his story, which had made him feel marginally better. Soon he'd started to attend multiple meetings a week,

NA and AA, all over the city – had reorganised his entire *life* around meetings, just as his life had once revolved around nightclubs. Eventually, he co-founded a new meeting, 'Recovery by the River', at the Riverside Church. Since then, Kevin had come and gone, struggling to keep clean without relapsing; but David had never wavered. Not one day since 19 May 1986.

The third major change was a career shift. David had fled the photography world completely. Had, in fact, become one of Mick Jagger's New York assistants.

'David was having a very bad time, an emotional crisis,' recalls Tony King, who'd also moved from working for Elton John to working for Jagger. 'So I went to Mick and said, "I'd like to give David Nutter a job." And Mick said to me, "Are you sure he's going to be OK?" Because he knew David through Elton, and knew that David was . . .' Going through a rough patch. Tony vouched for his friend – and David, after learning the ropes, had shown himself to be more than just 'OK'. He'd thrived in the position. He looked after Jagger's house on the Upper West Side, fed Jagger's cat, Calico, dealt with building contractors and deranged stalker fans, befriended Karis Jagger, one of Mick's daughters, and made sure that his houseguests had fresh milk in the fridge and clean sheets on their beds. He even helped Jerry Hall work on her British accent for a theatre audition.

Taken together, all these massive adjustments meant David, sitting opposite his mother at her kitchen table, was quieter and more reflective than he had once been. 'Sat up & chatted & talked of Wales,' he wrote in his diary.

A few days later, on 14 July, David took Dolly to Euston Station, where they boarded a train heading north on a route they'd last taken together some forty-five years before, under the clouds of war. The purpose of the trip was nostalgia, the return to a formative location that David yearned to see one last time with his elderly mother.

They arrived in Barmouth and checked into a small hotel. David took a look at the town library, once a school he remembered well. Then they crossed the Mawddach Estuary to wander the modest streets of Fairbourne. 'Lots of new houses rather spoiling the memory,' he wrote in his diary, though he was deeply moved to be there again. 'Am trying to soak up as much of this as possible – it's a lot to take in.'

That night, back in Barmouth, the town where his brother was born in 1943, David had a vivid dream. He still dreamed often, but this one was a little stranger than usual. He wrote it down the following morning.

> <u>Dream</u> of someone like Kev or Tommy spraying black spots on a clean white wall. I was furious and he attempted to clean some of it off, knowing I was mad.

The first black spot appeared on Tommy's leg: small, dark, refusing to heal.

Stewart Grimshaw first noticed it when they were summering together in Saint-Tropez. Other friends noticed because Tommy drew their attention to it, making light of what the mark could possibly signify. When Carol Drinkwater read an article describing Kaposi's sarcoma lesions, the reddish-purple patches often associated with Aids, she asked Tommy if he had anything like that. He replied, 'Yeah, yeah,' indicated his leg, and shrugged away the question. But then the spot got worse, his health took a turn, and ignoring it became impossible.

Many of the gay men Tommy knew went to St Mary's Hospital to be screened for sexually transmitted diseases. But Tommy refused; he hated being seen in that environment. Instead, he went to see Stewart, who, Tommy knew, had been actively involved in Aids awareness since the days it was known as the dreaded 'gay cancer'. As Stewart recalls, 'He came to me because he had loads of questions, and he thought I'd have all the answers.'

For example: How many people get over it?

Stewart told him that nobody 'got over it'.

And how long before . . . ?

That depends on your T cell count, Stewart said.

After Tommy exhausted his enquiry, Stewart convinced him to

follow up with a brilliant clinician named Brian Gazzard. Having encountered his first case of what became identified as Aids back in 1979,
Gazzard was one of the leading medical authorities in Britain. He'd
already seen hundreds of HIV-positive patients by the mid-1980s, and
more recently he'd been instrumental in setting up the Kobler Centre, a dedicated HIV/Aids research and outpatient clinic funded by a
combination of private donations and money from the National Health
Service. (Princess Diana had opened the day-care wing during a well-
publicised visit in 1988; it had been packed with patients ever since.)
The Kobler saw 'a never-ending procession', Gazzard recalls, and the
atmosphere was both depressing – with up to ten deaths a week – and
inspiring, because 'people were full of courage and determination'.

Tommy made an appointment to see Dr Gazzard, but he didn't want
to go alone. He asked Stewart to keep him company.

The doctor sat them down in a quiet office. He told them that some
people wanted to hear all the details, while others didn't want to hear
any of the details.

Tommy said, 'Tell me everything.'

'But that's not really what he wanted,' Stewart recalls.

What Tommy would have been told is something like this: That
there is no easy way to break bad news. That, according to his test results, he was HIV-positive, with a very low CD4 cell count. That he already had opportunistic infections, and there was a good chance he
would contract even more. That the treatments available to him were
limited – AZT, perhaps, though its effectiveness at prolonging life was
finite and accompanied by side effects. That most types of treatment
would focus on infections rather than the virus itself, which could not
be cured. That there would be ways forward, however, to remain in control of the situation. Because that was the most frightening thing for
patients newly cognisant of their status: the prospect of losing control.

Stewart listened carefully and understood exactly what was going to
happen to his friend.

Tommy also listened, silent until the doctor finished and asked him
if there was anything further he wanted to know.

Tommy thought for a moment. Then, Stewart remembers, he said,

'Yes, there is one thing I'd like to know. I'd like to know when *Mack and Mabel* is opening in the West End.'

Mack and Mabel was an American musical by Michael Stewart and Jerry Herman that had premiered on Broadway in 1974, but thus far failed to transfer to London except for a one-off charity performance at Drury Lane, in 1988. It told the tragic 'true' (heavily fictionalised) story of Mabel Normand, a working-class girl who became a glamorous star of silent cinema before sliding into scandal and ultimately dying from pulmonary tuberculosis at the premature age of thirty-seven. Tommy had acquired a cast recording, and declared to several friends that it was his new favourite show.

The doctor stared at Tommy.

'I truly think he thought that Tommy already had dementia,' Stewart recalls.

When Tommy arrived home that evening, he telephoned Carol.

'What is it?' Carol asked. She was standing in her upstairs bedroom.

'I've got Aids,' Tommy said.

Carol took a deep breath. 'Tommy, you've got to be positive.'

'*I just said that,*' he snapped. '*I am "positive".*'

Once Tommy knew for sure that he had HIV, his first response was to make jokes, and his second was to adopt a kind of optimistic denial. 'In the first six months, he was very sure that something would be done and that he would be OK,' recalls Tim Gallagher, one of his salesmen who had also become a close friend. 'I think he took it very well indeed.' Occasionally, Tommy called up Stewart to ask some more questions: *What about that new drug mentioned in the newspaper? What about this experimental form of treatment?* But mostly he preferred not to discuss the situation at all, carrying on as though absolutely nothing had changed. Which is not to say, however, that he wasn't affected. His assistant, Wendy, spent enough time with Tommy to notice cracks in the carapace. Despite his demeanour of cool unconcern, she could tell that he was rattled. 'Would it affect his brain? Would he get all the sarcomas? It could manifest in so many different ways – that's where his demons were about it.'

These demons manifested most clearly whenever it came time for another doctor's appointment, now regular and essential. Visiting the Kobler at St Stephen's meant Tommy could not pretend that everything was just the same; it forced him, for a few hours each month, to confront the full spectrum of Aids, from patients like him with mild ailments right through to those in terminal stages – his probable future. The days leading up to his treatments were 'awful', Wendy recalls, 'because he'd be hell at work. You could see it: ginning himself up to go. Really didn't want to go. Probably a bit angry. A bit hard on people, which was not like him.'

(From David's 1990 diary)

19 October: . . . Spoke to Tommy. Didn't sound too great. Peter Brown called too about the same thing.

25 October: Spoke to Mum who's going in hospital tomorrow [for a hip replacement]. Sounded fine really but Tom still confined to bed.

2 November: Elton had gone in to see Tommy and he looked awful. Doesn't sound good at all. Called Peter Brown and he sounded worried too.

3 November: Worried about Tom. Peter Brown had tried to call him but no answer.

4 November: Still worried about Tom. Feel helpless.

5 November: Called Tom and he sounded a lot better. Apparently Mum's up. Went so well that she'll be out Wednesday.

7 November: Called Mum and she's out of hospital. Operation a huge success. She said that Tom was much better . . .

At the end of 1990, while Tommy tried to recover from a skirmish with the flu, his staff on Savile Row worked furiously to finish a major order. The customer was Elton John, who'd also given up alcohol and shed five or six inches from his waistline, a stab at sobriety – at 'changing his image', as Tommy described it – that required the creation of an entirely new wardrobe. Despite his fragile health, Tommy threw himself into the challenge, focusing hard to deliver the goods: brocade waistcoats, country-squire jackets, and a dozen suits in the kind of 'quite brightish tweeds' that most of his regular customers still fled from.

In early January, Elton was spotted at Heathrow trying to check forty-one suitcases on a flight to Los Angeles. 'I suppose it is a lot to take on holiday,' he admitted to the press, 'but I like to be prepared for anything.'

Tommy deteriorated; the flu became pneumonia; by March, he was in the hospital struggling to breathe. 'Sounds awful, really,' David wrote in his diary, and word quickly spread among their friends in London and New York. Peter Brown called David and was 'very cagey about Tom'. Peter then asked Tony King, working with David, if David knew what the disease was – 'as if I was that naive,' David wrote. He was annoyed at being treated with kid gloves; he'd seen enough in his life and heard enough about what was happening with his brother to draw the logical conclusions.

By the time Tommy was finally well enough to be released, he'd lost an alarming amount of weight. To keep tabs on him, David started phoning the shop for meandering, seemingly pointless chats that were notable for their evasiveness, for all the things not being said. It would take until 7 May, after nearly two months of these calls, before Tommy 'casually talked about being positive'. *Casually,* David wrote in his diary, as though the simple fact had already been established between them and was barely worth acknowledging.

Dolly received even less in the way of notification. On 15 July, she called David to share some news that had just been communicated to her by Wendy: Tommy was suffering from a 'blood disease', she said.

David decided not to enlighten her further.

Tommy tried to steady himself and continue as the unofficial spokesman of Savile Row. He co-judged the annual all-industry Colour & Design Competition (CREATIVITY v COMMERCE) at the Grosvenor House Hotel. He offered suggestions to *The Times* on dressing for Royal Ascot: 'Perhaps a brocade waistcoat. But breaking away is very difficult . . .' He even went on the radio to rail against men in midlife crisis who resort to wearing 'dreadful' ponytails and sneakers with the 'nasty' tongues hanging out. The host asked Tommy what *he* was wearing; Tommy replied that he was wearing a brown lightweight wool three-piece Prince of Wales check double-breasted suit. 'In the old days,' he said, 'people used to dress for radio.'

On 17 October 1991, *Men's Wear* published an article titled 'Worth Its Weight' that had been written by Tommy. Given he mostly limited himself to quotes and press releases, this was unusual. It began with a bon mot from Oscar Wilde: 'A man's first duty is to his tailor. What his second is, nobody has yet discovered.' Then Tommy offered his own interpretation: 'Although this is a far cry from today's philosophy, where jeans, T-shirt and sneakers are *de rigueur*, a young man would be hard pushed to find a better investment than a hand-made suit, to give himself a lift up the ladder of success.'

He continued, 'It may sound snobbish, but once a man has worn a made-to-measure suit, he finds it very difficult to return to off-the-peg.' Besides the obvious superior quality, the reason for this had to do with its magical effect on a man's self-confidence. 'To the body it feels like a second skin while the mind is comfortable in the knowledge that it cannot be faulted,' he wrote.

Tommy was so committed to the idea that an 'immaculate suit' offers 'a psychological uplift' that he then took it to a curious extreme. 'Being better dressed' could boost morale, encourage spending, and revitalise the business community, 'thereby ending the recession'. If everybody simply *dressed* better, he wrote, then everybody would *be* better off. Start, Tommy suggested, with the current prime minister, shabbily attired John Major. 'Bring back the elegance of Anthony Eden and Harold Macmillan and see the world's confidence in Britain restored!'

This was an idealistic argument about the glamorous power of clothes, and it is difficult not to read its plea as something personal. Indeed, Tommy finished his essay by turning reflective.

He was 'very fortunate' to find himself in a position where he could 'combine high quality tailoring with design and flair'. It was this that had made his career 'so fulfilling', and he hoped that others could appreciate and safeguard the 'wonderful British institution' of Savile Row that had lifted him up and given him everything in life. 'It would be criminal to let it slip now,' he wrote.

But it wouldn't slip; Tommy's influence was too firmly rooted by this point. Just a few months later, a young man named Richard James would open his shop on the Row. 'The move will mean that I will be seen as a serious tailor as well as a designer,' he told the press, 'and I see this as the ideal move towards the market of the future.'

Over several decades, Tommy had worn down the division between tailoring and fashion. Now others would arrive in his wake to take bespoke in a whole new direction.

The tipping point came at a dinner for the National Federation of Merchant Tailors. Distressed about his appearance, Tommy was of two minds about whether to even attend. 'Everyone will be talking about me,' he told one of his friends. But then, they would be talking about him if he *didn't* attend, too, so he may as well go and try to control the situation. He took Dolly as his date and smiled amiably as they circulated through the crowd.

A few days later, word leaked out that Tommy looked 'haggard' at the trade dinner. 'That got into print somewhere,' recalls Christopher Tarling. Whispering tailors was one thing, but gossip published in the public sphere was quite another. 'Tommy heard and was deeply, deeply affected.' He could no longer convincingly sustain an illusion of wellness anywhere.

It was around this time that Tommy went to pay a visit to Alan Lewis. The financier already sensed that something was wrong with his chief designer. 'You could see it in his business, slowly but surely.' Tommy sat down and immediately broached the topic of money. 'He wanted to know about his pension,' Lewis remembers. 'Because he was obviously thinking he was going to be incapacitated. And that's when I said, "Look, what is it?" And he told me. And I said, "Well, I don't know anything about it. But I've got the best doctors and we'll send you to see them."'

Lewis assured Tommy that his pension was secure; they would continue paying out a salary 'to make sure he had the income to survive'.

And so, with that settled, Tommy decided to retire, in January 1992. Though perhaps 'retire' is not exactly the word for it. David scrawled it in his diary – 'Tom seems to be retiring' – but for many other people, including the ones who worked alongside him, it was more like a sudden self-banishment. One day Tommy Nutter was a vital presence on Savile Row, looming large in his eponymous shop at No. 18–19. And then he was gone.

***

Over in New York, David and Kevin bought a car – 'a real bargain with all the features' – and began to go on joyrides around Manhattan. They drove to Bloomingdale's, then down to Greenwich Village, then up to a coffee shop on Sixty-Ninth Street. 'Can't keep out of the car!' David wrote in his diary, though he left out the reason for his wild enthusiasm: having 'wheels', as he called it, was an effective distraction from everything else weighing on his mind. Being on the move was a way to change the subject, like changing cassettes in the tape deck.

Because it wasn't just Tommy in crisis at the moment. Now there were lumps on Kevin's face, a patch of something fungal blooming in his lungs. The doctors had also mentioned HIV-associated nephropathy – kidney disease, in other words. All grim news that made Kevin furious and David increasingly numb.

One day in March, needing to get away from it all, David and Kevin drove through a snowstorm across the Hudson River into New Jersey. They reached Richmond, Virginia, around 2 a.m. and continued on to South Carolina. They visited Augusta, Georgia, where they attended an AA meeting, and then Atlanta, where they attended an NA meeting. They drove all the way down to Jacksonville, Florida, pushing on until they reached St Augustine, where they fed breadcrumbs to some catfish. And then, finally giving up, they turned the car round and headed home to face the doctors.

Not long after arriving back in New York, David received another phone call from his mother. Dolly told him she'd just been to see Tommy in his flat; he was vomiting violently, she said, and she knew it was Aids. There was no need to hide it from her any longer.

Tommy's flat, at 27 Conduit Street, was so tiny and austere that people often professed surprise that he actually lived there. With a bedroom just big enough for the bed and a mahogany wardrobe, and a kitchenette where one person constituted a crowd, it was a far cry from the stylish pad he'd once shared with Peter Brown on the same street. Of course, Tommy preferred to see it a little more romantically. Since moving there in the late 1970s, he'd imagined the space as a kind of artist's garret and himself as the reclining figure in Bernard Buffet's *Homme couché* (1947), even writing on a postcard of the painting: 'T. N. in Conduit Street getting inspiration.'

Bernard Buffet, *Homme couché (Lying Man)*, 1947

Once it became clear that Tommy's health was in irreversible decline, that he would soon be spending almost all his waking hours inside the flat, Robert Leach, a close friend and stylist, decided to give the place a little makeover. He replumbed the bathroom with new brass taps. He kidnapped a couch from the Savile Row shop, reupholstering it in lush trellis fabric. He bought wallpaper from Osborne & Little and paint in shades of peach and pale green – art deco colours, to match all the art deco curios that Tommy had collected over the years and arranged around himself, shrine-like.

Following his retreat into the flat, Tommy was reluctant to receive any visitors, or at least he feigned reluctance when somebody asked. 'He said he didn't want to see anybody, but I could tell when he said it that he really *did*,' Robert recalls. Tommy was being treated with doses of AZT, which caused him to develop anaemia; after he was given a blood transfusion, Robert turned up uninvited on the doorstep. 'I'm really glad you're here,' Tommy told him. He was shaking, perhaps from shock. Robert just sat there and held him for a while.

Occasionally, when Tommy really needed help, he called Tim Gallagher, who had a spare set of keys. One evening, Tim came over to find Tommy sitting in the middle of the floor, his legs having given way beneath him. 'I can't get up,' Tommy said.

'There's no problem, Tommy,' Tim said. 'I don't care what you ask me to do. I'll do it for you.'

'Can you help me get up and back into bed?'

This was a shock: Tommy was a big man, over six feet tall, and Tim could just pick him up with one arm, as though he weighed nothing.

After a while, venturing outside the flat became potentially hazardous. When Tommy would try, wanting to go to Green Park to sit in a deckchair, his body sometimes revolted. 'He was so weak he would fall over in the street,' recalls Catherine Everest (née Butterworth), his former assistant. 'And people would not really help him because they thought he was drunk. I can remember him telling me that. He was near his flat in Conduit Street, and – he collapsed. "They almost stepped over me, Doll," he said.'

By June, David was beside himself, unable to think straight. He fixated on his new air conditioner, on some new carpet, on what Jagger should wear for an upcoming concert (a Morris dancer outfit, he suggested). It took John Reid to recognise what was happening and intervene. Elton's manager suggested that David fly to London at his expense to see Elton in concert at Wembley Stadium; while he was there, he might like to check in and see his unwell brother too.

David agreed to go on the twenty-fourth.

On 14 June, he wrote in his diary: 'Message on machine from Tom saying that I shouldn't come over. All a bit complicated.'

On 15 June: 'Spoke to Tom and he said he wouldn't mind seeing me.'

On 18 June: 'Carol called at 6 and was very teary. Said Tom was really bad and was rude to everyone. She doesn't think I should go.'

On 21 June: 'Very nervous about my trip.'

On the appointed day, 24 June: 'Into work in rain. Kev picked me up at 3. Home. Got ready. Drove to Newark. Flight cramped. No sleep.'

When David finally arrived in London, he did not go to the hospital where Tommy had just been admitted. Instead, he went to a 'boring' AA meeting, then collected his ticket from Reid and headed out to Wembley to watch a 'lacklustre' performance by Elton.

It was not until the next day that David worked himself up to visit the Cromwell in South Kensington. He went with Michael Long, one of their oldest friends, and carried a bouquet of flowers in his hand. As he stepped into the room, Tommy was curled up on the bed, looking, David thought, exactly like a victim at Bergen-Belsen: eyes sunken, face emaciated, wasting to nothing, his breath an audible rasp.

David was horrified. He stayed just long enough for Tommy to tell him, 'They're waiting for me onstage at *Mack and Mabel*.' Then David quietly left.

David knew this would probably be the last time he saw Tommy alive, though he did not record how he felt after leaving the hospital. What he wrote was: 'Michael dropped me in Piccadilly and I sat in a rehearsal of Judas Maccabaeus at St James's Church.'

This was not quite as dissociative as it might seem. *Judas Maccabaeus* is a three-act oratorio composed by George Frideric Handel. Handel was David's favourite composer – favourite, in no small part, because Handel had once worked as house composer at Cannons, the stately country home of James Brydges, 1st Duke of Chandos, in what would eventually become modern-day Edgware. In other words, Handel had once written music in the very place where David and Tommy grew up, which was a fact that David cherished as somehow significant, a ghostly connection between the composer, his brother and himself. Sitting in a pew at St James's Church, he was now listening to an echo of their childhood.

When Tommy was still mobile, only approaching the late stage of his illness, Stewart Grimshaw had taken him to inspect the London

Lighthouse in Notting Hill, a residential hospice for people with Aids who wanted to die as gracefully as possible. Tommy had taken one look around at all the gay men and announced that he 'couldn't possibly' live there.

The Cromwell, in South Kensington, was a private hospital used only infrequently by people with HIV/Aids. It was also the kind of place where a person could go to hide from public scrutiny. Tommy was admitted on 24 June; he would stay there for the next fifty-five days.

Because it was private, Tommy's room was more like a hotel suite than a hospital ward, offering a spacious bathroom and modern furniture. By the time he actually arrived, though, Tommy was only vaguely aware of his commodious surroundings, and sometimes it would seem to him more like a nightmare place. 'He would go through periods where he'd say, "There's a man in my bathroom,"' Wendy recalls. 'He was very scared of this man in his bathroom.'

These hallucinations would confuse the people who now came to pay their final respects. For example, Tommy told Aldo Fleri that helicopters were flying out of a cupboard at the end of his bed. When Timothy Everest came to visit, Tommy invited him to climb onto the bed, lifted off in his own 'helicopter', and flew them away down the Thames. On another occasion, Tommy insisted to Robert Leach that Tina Turner's wig was hidden somewhere in the room and that they should try to find it; when Robert got up to leave, Tommy said, 'I'm not coming out tonight, but I'll come out *tomorrow*.'

In mid-July, during a moment of lucidity, Tommy requested to see Valerie Garland and Cheryl De Courcey, the glamorous 'Garland Sisters' he and David had grown up with back in the 1950s.

Dolly made the call. She told them, 'Listen, he has his own lifestyle.'

'That's all she said,' Valerie recalls. 'And then she said that he was dying of HIV and that he wanted to see us.'

The sisters braced themselves and went to the Cromwell together. They sat around him and tried to think of things to say. 'It was like talking to a skeleton,' Valerie recalls. 'But he was still smiling. And that's when he turned and said, "You know what I should have done? I should have grown up and married *you*."'

Tommy with Valerie Garland on a speedboat in the Channel Islands, 1960.

Dolly refused to leave the hospital. She ate and slept there and kept constant, vigilant watch over her ailing son. For David, who'd returned home to New York almost immediately following his visit, his mother became a set of eyes and ears and emotional responses, a way to monitor from afar the minutiae of his brother's condition. 'Spoke to Mum,' he wrote in his diary. 'Tom may have TB. She sounded worried.'

'Spoke to Mum and Tom still won't eat. He'll stay in the hospital. I fear the worst. She sounded very shattered.'

'Spoke to Mum who sounded frustrated. Doctors won't tell her anything.'

'Spoke to Mum. She said that Tom was looking "grey" – they had made him do a will.'

When it came to people outside the 'family' – a circle that encompassed, beyond herself and David, several of Tommy's most intimate friends – Dolly was more like an unyielding gatekeeper. She revealed nothing and, as his health became increasingly precarious, admitted fewer and fewer visitors. The actress Ann Mitchell was gently denied:

'I always felt – although we all longed to see him – that it was his way of protecting his friends. He wanted our memories of him to be pristine.' And Louise Aron, the woman who'd once picked up men for Tommy in the Rockingham, found herself shut out after Dolly hung up the phone. 'She thought I was press,' Louise recalls. Recently, a series of premature, ghoulish eulogies had started to appear in newspapers with headlines like: 'Fashion King Nutter Fights for His Life', and 'Tailor to the Stars Dying of AIDS: Tommy Nutter Has "Days Left"'. So Dolly was understandably wary of people she thought might be journalists. 'Of course,' Louise continues, 'Dolly phoned me back up again and said, "Louise, I'm really sorry. It was so long ago!" But even then, I couldn't see him.'

One person who was admitted into the suite was Cilla Black, who came on 3 August with Bobby Willis and Peter Brown. Cilla had wanted to visit earlier, writing a card to Tommy scrawled with the lyrics to one of her songs.

> *Other eyes see the stars up in the skies,*
> *but for me they shine within your eyes*

She was frightened, though, of how she might react when confronted with his terrible appearance. For moral support, Cilla waited until Peter flew over from New York so they could all go together: a reunion to evoke the old, happier days of dinners at San Lorenzo.

Tommy's mind was wandering when they walked into the room. 'Look who's here,' Peter said. 'Do you know who it is?'

Tommy opened his eyes and turned to Cilla. 'It's Barbara Windsor,' he whispered. Barbara Windsor was a petite actress who started her career starring in the *Carry On* franchise.

Peter guffawed; his patronising query had revived Tommy's mordant wit. But Cilla was so grief-stricken she barely heard a word.

It was Dolly who stepped in to offer some comfort.

Wendy was standing in Tommy's room. 'You could see that he wanted to go,' she recalls, 'but his mother was sitting *right there*.' Tim Gallagher came in to say hello, and Wendy asked him to take Dolly out to the hospital cafe 'for a cup of tea'. Once they left, Wendy walked over, sat down by the bed, and took hold of Tommy's hand.

Tommy said, 'Oh, I've been a naughty boy, haven't I?'

'Don't be silly,' Wendy said. 'We've all been naughty.'

He was fading in and out of consciousness. Even the bedsheet was too heavy for him now.

'It's OK,' Wendy said. 'You can go. You don't have to hang in there. I know you're only fighting it because Dolly is here.'

On 16 August, Tommy's heart stopped beating.

Then it started again.

Then it stopped, definitively, on 17 August, 1992, at 1.20 a.m. The cause listed on the death certificate was 'Bronchopneumonia'. He was forty-nine years old.

Dolly was alone at the Cromwell when it happened. Tim Gallagher had left a few hours earlier to get some sleep, though he couldn't sleep and was sitting up at home when the phone suddenly rang. 'I haven't called anybody else,' Dolly told him. 'Can you come back to the hospital?' She didn't have to say that Tommy had died.

Tim returned to the hospital and made his way to Tommy's room. When he got there, Dolly was standing sentinel, silent, and Tommy was a husk on the bed.

Dolly handed Tim two pennies. 'Can you put these on his eyes for me?' she asked. An old custom so the dead can pay the ferryman to take them across the River Styx.

Tim put the pennies over Tommy's eyes.

Then he ordered a cab and accompanied Dolly back to her flat on the Finchley Road. 'She hadn't slept in two nights,' he recalls. 'She was very upset, but then she calmed down. I think, in some ways, it was a big relief. Because the last few days – even the last weeks – were something that I wouldn't wish on anybody. It was a relief he had finally gone.'

About a year before the end, when Tommy was still feeling good enough to talk about himself, he sat down with a journalist named Thom O'Dwyer, a friend and great admirer ('When you met Tommy, you couldn't help but fall madly in love with him'). O'Dwyer had once covered Tommy's exploits as an editor at *Men's Wear,* and now he edited a glossy trade magazine called *HeLines.*

This wide-ranging interview, which O'Dwyer would title 'The World According to Tommy Nutter', covered Tommy's modest beginnings, his first encounter with the Beatles, his thoughts about the so-called Peacock Revolution, the evolution of men's fashion through the 1970s, the rise of designer labels, his own worst sartorial offences (particularly around the Falklands War in 1982), and his hopes for the future, where Tommy intended to go next, 'possibly into Europe and America . . .'

It is an extraordinary document, the closest thing Tommy ever came to producing a memoir. But two passages stand out as particularly striking.

> **TO'D:** What really, really makes you happy, Tommy?
>
> **TN:** If you want an honest answer, it's really nothing to do with work. What makes me happiest is watching *Coronation Street.* The poet John Betjeman once said, 'It's like a half hour of sheer bliss,' and I couldn't agree more. You're in a totally different world, and I just find myself absolutely glued to the television set those three times a week . . . I must say, material things have never really been that important to me. I have a nice handful of friends that I have accumulated over the years, and they keep me happy. Really, my happiest moments, I suppose, are trying to relax after business. Oh, and Sondheim musicals – that's my other favourite thing in life. I look forward to any new musical he might be making. I must finally say, though, my work and the business in general brings me enormous satisfaction. I have been incredibly lucky, and I

do love it. Just think, I could have ended up being a plumber's mate for my entire life.

T'OD: So then, what makes you unhappy?

TN: It's difficult to say. I don't dwell on things, you see, so I try not to get myself into a position where I would feel sad or unhappy. I am obviously acutely aware of all the terrible things in life, but I always try to not let things get me down. Everybody worries, but you must keep on going. That's the whole point, I guess. There really isn't anything too devastating in my life. Sure, everybody has been through a lot, but you've just got to get on with your own humdrum life.

The Aids Memorial Quilt
BLOCK NUMBER 02640

David Nutter in London, 1958.

epilogue

DAWN BLACK

One autumn evening not too long ago, I rang the buzzer for David Nutter's apartment on the Upper West Side. A hesitant voice crackled over the intercom, asking me to wait, so I settled down on the stoop and plumped my orange silk pocket square. What had David decided to wear? There had been hand-wringing in his emails, because what did anyone wear to a party for the Rolling Stones?

I checked the invitation on my phone, noting the address. Then there was a gust of warm air as the building's door opened behind me. I stood up and turned to find David, smiling broadly, in a tweed jacket with contrasting patch pockets and pagoda shoulders so pointed they could have doubled as weapons. Gorgeous, bizarre; one of Tommy's old numbers.

'Ready,' David said.

I hailed a cab on Central Park West.

The event was the New York launch of *Exhibitionism*, a sprawling, self-indulgent roadshow of Stones memorabilia. The press release promised 'over 500 original Stones' artifacts, with striking cinematic and interactive technologies offering the most comprehensive and immersive insight into the band's fascinating fifty-year history'. David had been invited to the opening as a guest of Charlie Watts; I was going as a guest of David.

The cab shot down Manhattan to the West Village, where Washington Street was already a clogged artery of black Escalades. We pulled up round the corner and made the final approach on foot to the entrance of Industria, collecting holographic VIP passes that flashed alternating images of the Stones' trademark tongue-and-lips and a woman's crotch.

Inside, the exhibition, spread over nine galleries, was either breath-taking or soporific, depending on your feelings about the band: guitars entombed in glass cases, a faux recording studio, a re-created Edith Grove flat the boys had once shared early in their career. It was deeply, weirdly reverent; even dirty dishes were carefully placed in the sink like holy objects. David had seen much of the inventory before – including, on one wall, some Andy Warhol lithographs that Jagger had kept stashed in his basement for a decade. 'I had to take them to Sotheby's once,' David mentioned nonchalantly as we drifted past.

Eventually we reached the costume gallery, the main reason I had come in the first place. The room, filled with mannequins made up to resemble individual band members, reminded me of the tomb of Qin Shi Huang, terracotta warriors lined up in extravagant dress. There were feathers and sequins, pirate puffs, military gear, Mr Fish, Ossie Clark, Alexander McQueen . . . and Tommy Nutter. A red-and-gold pinstripe coat with lapels the size of banana leaves, made for Mick Jag-ger in 1971. A grey three-piece pinstripe suit, made for Charlie Watts in 1975. Both outfits were unmistakably Tommy. Standing before them, David slipped into quiet contemplation.

Once we were finished with the show, we crossed the street to a cavernous warehouse for the after-party. David was fatigued; several people had already recognised him and stopped us to reminisce about the old days. But we loitered for a moment, hoping to catch Watts or his assistant, to thank them for the invitation.

Then David spotted him: Mick Jagger, shooting through the crowd in a wide arc.

I had never seen anything like it. Adults who, only a few minutes earlier, had seemed reasonable and rational, now suddenly staggered like animals in rut, frenzied by the pheromone-like charisma of this single man.

Having witnessed this spectacle countless times before, David was unmoved. Still, an unexpected opportunity had presented itself here.

David had not seen Jagger for years – not since the performer had sold his mansion and departed New York at the end of the 1990s.

Leaving me standing where I was, David drifted across the room, calculating Jagger's trajectory. He found the right spot and waited patiently until Jagger, moving fast, started to approach. And then there was a moment, the rock star catching the eye of this bespectacled old man, now seventy-eight years old, gaunt and grey and almost swallowed up by his strange tweed coat, when Jagger's PR rictus gave way to a smile that was genuine.

'David!' Jagger barked, reaching out to grasp a well-padded shoulder. David nodded. 'I'm still alive.'

***

After Tommy's death in August 1992, David immediately returned to London to attend the funeral at Golders Green Crematorium, and to help Dolly with the emotional process of packing up Tommy's flat. He returned again, two months later, for a public memorial service at St George's Church, just up the road from Savile Row. Before a room filled with friends, admirers, tailors, clients, extended family, and at least one well-dressed pew of Tommy's ex-lovers, Peter Brown delivered the eulogy, and Cilla Black read an abridged excerpt from Chaucer's *Canterbury Tales*.

> *He was a true, a perfect gentle Knight . . .*
> *And certainly a man has most honour*
> *In dying in his excellence and flower,*
> *When he is certain of his high good name;*
> *For then he gives to friend, and self, no shame.*

At the end of the service, all stood as a full choir performed part of Handel's *Messiah*. David had selected the oratorio for his brother, though listening to it brought him little solace in the moment.

When David flew home to New York, there was no time to grieve. Kevin's kidney function had fallen below 20 per cent. His morale had fallen even lower, into deep despair, and nothing David could do or say made any difference. Kevin had given up; becoming increasingly lax with his dialysis treatments, he died less than seven months after Tommy, on 6 March 1993. The newspaper notice described him as 'Beloved son of Shirley Edward and Wilson Bostick. Dear friend of David Nutter.'

And then, in quick succession, due to Aids or other unexpected causes, David lost several more friends, his doctor at Columbia-Presbyterian, his dentist, his psychiatrist, his sponsor – and his mother. Dolly had always worshipped the sun a little too ardently; she sat on a park bench working on her tan right up until the moment she was diagnosed with malignant melanoma, in 1995. She was seventy-nine years old.

In the span of just a few years, David's immediate family was reduced to several boxes of personal effects shipped over and stacked up against a wall in his apartment. Most of his close friends became statistics in the epidemic. He did not get another room-mate after Kevin was gone. He stopped going to London with any regularity. He remained sober, always, but also gave up the sobriety meetings, tired of watching others relapse, fail, disappear. He closed up into himself, becoming reclusive, hard to reach, and let a decade drift by, then a second one.

I once asked David what he was most proud of in his life. We were sitting in my apartment drinking coffee, and I was hoping he would offer some reflective statement about a photographic career that was as beautiful as it was haphazard, almost accidental.

Instead he said, 'Probably surviving, because nobody else did.'

I was stunned, unsure how to respond.

To fill the silence, David continued: 'People sometimes talk about "survivor's syndrome". Well, it's not very comfortable, you know. People think you should feel lucky, that you should be grateful that you're still around. But it's not that easy. You expect to have all your friends with you. I did everything they did – maybe *more* than they did, reading back over those diaries. Yet I didn't get it. All of them got it. But not me. That's a very strange feeling. It was particularly strange a few years back, when I finally did return to NA after twenty years of not going to meetings. It was like in those science-fiction movies where they put somebody to sleep for a century, and then, when they wake up again, everything's different, and everyone familiar is gone.

'I was at a meeting on Saturday – a meeting for gay men – and the guy speaking was an ex-DJ. He mentioned this club. I'd started to think I'd *imagined* this club. But it existed! Afterwards, I went up to the ex-DJ and said, "It's so great to hear you speak, because I sometimes doubt half the stuff that happened to me. I often wonder if there is anybody else still alive who remembers what really happened."'

The Aids crisis destroyed a generation of designers, actors, dancers, writers and artists, from Freddie Mercury to Rock Hudson, Peter Allen, Bruce Chatwin, Denholm Elliott, Robert Mapplethorpe, Keith Haring, Perry Ellis, Liberace, Halston, Anthony Perkins, Rudolf Nureyev, Peter Hujar, David Wojnarowicz, Derek Jarman, Alvin Ailey, Kenny Everett, Antony Hamilton, Bill King . . . the list goes on – and then, of course, there are countless others, too, less famous but no less worthy of consideration. The Aids Memorial Quilt, conceived by Cleve Jones in 1985, now features more than 48,000 panels of three feet by six feet, the size of an average grave. Each one, painstakingly sewn and embroidered and spray-painted by friends and family, represents achievements, hopes, aspirations, connections, dramas, thoughts, dreams – a fully formed, three-dimensional life.

When I set out to write this book, one of my main intentions was to show the richness behind just one panel, excavating the lost history of Tommy Nutter, whose contribution to some of the most iconic styles and pop imagery of the twentieth century is woefully underappreciated, and whose influence lingers today on Savile Row, where tailoring firms are now like couture houses, releasing collections and appointing creative directors.

As a writer, it was deeply satisfying to gather anecdotes, trawl archives, read old newspapers, and then assemble all the pieces into a coherent whole. However, somewhere along the line it also became clear to me that this book was more than just an exercise in historical preservation – more, even, than just a tribute to a fascinating man.

For David, it was therapeutic.

David Nutter came to my apartment almost every week for more than a year to turn over his memories. Later, he read each successive draft of the manuscript, recalling more things about himself and his brother to add to the mix, and I watched as he went from guarded support to cautious optimism to, eventually, rapturous enthusiasm. In the end, it became as much his project as it was mine.

I would never presume to claim that working on it gave David any lasting psychological comfort. But it certainly removed some of the doubt he was feeling. Because it did happen, all of it.

David Nutter in New York, 2016.

NOTES

This book is based on interviews with more than seventy people, conducted mostly in person in London and New York. David Nutter spoke to me for more than a hundred hours. He also handed over seventeen of Tommy's scrapbooks; dozens of letters; innumerable invitations, sketches, photographs and negatives; and every single personal journal he kept between 1973 and 1992 (minus two missing volumes from the 1980s).

I consulted several archives during my research: the British Film Institute, for three videos of Tommy; the British Library, for several rare audio recordings; the John Stephen collection in the Archive of Art & Design at the Victoria & Albert Museum (which also has more than a dozen original Nutters suits); National Museums Scotland; the Tate Archive; the London College of Fashion (for more Nutters suits, on loan from Alistair O'Neill); and the private archive at Beaulieu House, with thanks to Lady Fiona Montagu and the National Motor Museum staff. Besides David Nutter, the richest source for Tommy Nutter material is the Archives of J&J Crombie Ltd. Almost everything of note concerning his career from 1980 onwards can be found there.

For the sake of concision, I have chosen to list the main interviews I relied on for each chapter at the outset, rather than reference every single detail drawn from interviews throughout. Direct quotes that are not specifically referenced below are drawn from this original reporting. Similarly, because David Nutter's journals are not available to the public, I have not referenced specific dates.

Sources held by David Nutter are marked 'DN'.

Sources held in the Archives of J&J Crombie Ltd are marked 'JJC'.

PREFACE

Interviews with: Garry Clarke, David Nutter, Peter Sprecher.

ix 'in-built feeling for clothes': Tommy Nutter, quoted in Janet Buckton, 'Nutter's the Name They're All Crazy About', *Coventry Evening Telegraph*, 26 August 1980.

ix 'as established and as important': Geoffrey Aquilina Ross, 'Who Needs Shows When You're Your Own Shop Window?', *Evening Standard*, 21 March 1973.

ix 'irreverent approach': Tommy Hilfiger, 'My London: Tommy Hilfiger', *Evening Standard,* 12 October 2017.

x has acknowledged his influence: Confirmation from Tom Ford came via Richard Buckley, email, 28 January 2016.

x 'Tailor to the Stars': Thom O'Dwyer, 'The World According to Tommy Nutter', *HeLines*, 1991.

ONE: ESCAPE ARTISTS

Interviews with: John Cross, Cheryl De Courcey, Simon Doonan, Carol Drinkwater, Valerie Garland, Bertram Keeter, Val Simpson Kindell, Robert Lipscombe, David Nutter, Maureen Tough.

3 'Somebody told me the other day': Tommy Nutter to David Nutter, letter, 14 August 1975. DN.

4 'a Botticelli youth': *Herrenjournal*, October 1970.

4 'living, breathing embodiment of Peter Pan': Thom O'Dwyer, 'The World According to Tommy Nutter', *HeLines*, 1991.

4 known for industry and manufacturing: 'Places in Brent: Kilburn', printed by the Grange Museum of Community History and Brent Archive.

6 'made such an impact': Stephen Pile, 'Three Faces of Steve', *Sunday Times*, 29 May 1983. The story was elaborated on by David Nutter in our interviews.

6 'It's all quite likely': Tommy Nutter to David Nutter, letter, 14 August 1975. DN.

8 mass graves and the incineration of bodies: Richard M. Titmuss, *Problems of Social Policy* (London: H. M. Stationery Office, 1950), 13.

8 typhoid fever, unchecked civil disorder, and so much material damage: Ibid., 14–15.

8 150,000 units per week: Ibid., 6.

9 The first day of evacuations focused solely on schoolchildren: Niko Gartner, *Operation Pied Piper: The Wartime Evacuation of Schoolchildren from London and Berlin 1938–1946* (Charlotte, NC: Information Age Publishing, Inc., 2012), 59.

9 barrage balloons bobbed in the sky: Ibid., 57.

9 mothers with young children became a priority: Ibid., 59–60.

9 1.47 million people: Titmuss, *Problems of Social Policy*, 101.

9 80 per cent of evacuated mothers: Gartner, *Operation Pied Piper*, 80.

9 enlisted in the army for DOW: Christopher Nutter's army service record (No. T/231825), held by the Army Personnel Centre – Historical Disclosures Division. All of Christopher's postings during the war are drawn from this record.

10 Tennyson wrote part of 'In Memoriam' in Barmouth: Alison Harrison, *The Light of Other Days: A Brief History of Friog & Fairbourne* (Wales: Y Dydd Press, 1966), 41.

10 'a polyglot assembly': Ibid., 47.

11 Polish Commandos billetted: Ibid., 49–50.

12 fought in the Great War and Second Boer War: Christopher Nutter's Military History Sheet, accessed via Ancestry.com, 21 November 2015.

14 'To have been consigned to the limbo': Peter Laurie, *The Teenage Revolution* (London: Anthony Blond, 1965), 41.

14 'the school for kids that don't stand much of a chance': Keith Richards, quoted in Stanley Booth, *The True Adventures of the Rolling Stones* (Chicago: Chicago Review Press, 2000), 51.

14 'desperately': Tommy Nutter, interviewed on *My Kind of Music*, BBC Radio Brighton, 20 September 1980.

14 75 to 80 per cent of students: Dominic Sandbrook, *Never Had It So Good: A History of Britain from Suez to the Beatles* (London: Little, Brown, 2005), 395.

15 'My parents put me on to a council school': Tommy Nutter, *My Kind of Music* interview.

15 'the bright but the unacademic': George Melly, *Revolt into Style: The Pop Arts in Britain* (London: Allen Lane, 1970), 131.

15 'to everybody's amazement': Tommy Nutter, *My Kind of Music* interview.

16 'Art in those days': Ibid.

16 'My parents, bless them': Tommy Nutter, quoted in O'Dwyer, 'The World According to Tommy Nutter'.

16 'all those butch things I couldn't bear': Ibid.

18 'It leads us to feel': Virginia Postrel, *The Power of Glamour: Longing and the Art of Visual Persuasion* (New York: Simon & Schuster, 2013), 6.

19 skipping classes to make the matinees: Tommy Nutter, *My Kind of Music* interview.

19 'a decent job': 'A Nutter Among the Pinstripes,' *Cambridge Evening News*, 14 March 1973.

19 'It really wasn't me': Tommy Nutter, *My Kind of Music* interview. Tommy also discusses the toilet bowls in 'Tommy Nutter for Cue at Austin Reed', press release, March 1979. DN. Several of his friends recalled the horror in our interviews.

19 'My parents': Tommy Nutter, quoted in Geoffrey Aquilina Ross, 'Who Needs Shows When You're Your Own Shop Window?', *Evening Standard*, 14 March 1973.

20 'Your starting pay': K. D. Wilcox (Ministry of Works), to Tommy Nutter, letter, 2 February 1960. DN.

20 'practically insane with boredom': 'There's Nothing Naff About Nutters', *Evening Standard*, 1 November 1969.

20 staring at the scratched surface of his wooden desk: 'The Ministry of Works Was Not for Me', *Men's Wear*, 16 April 1970.

20 Post Office Tower: Jonathan Glancey, 'Why We Love the BT Tower', *Guardian*, 9 November 2001.

20 'I shall never forget my first suit': Tommy Nutter, quoted in 'Tommy Nutter for Cue at Austin Reed', press release, March 1979. DN. See also: Aquilina Ross, 'Who Needs Shows'; David Taylor, 'Pop Goes the Whistle and Flute', *Punch*, 30 March 1977; John Hemsley, 'The £500 Suit That Made Me Look Fat', *The Reading Chronicle*, 6 January 1979; and Janet Buckton, 'Nutter's the Name They're All Crazy About', *Coventry Evening Telegraph*, 26 August 1980.

20 'dismal': Tommy Nutter, quoted in O'Dwyer, 'The World According to Tommy Nutter'.

20 'SAVILE ROW TAILORS': 'Situations Vacant', *Evening Standard*, 8 November 1960.

20 'or at least my mother did': Tommy Nutter, *My Kind of Music* interview.

21 'Come on': Ibid.

21 'Unfortunately I have no experience': Tommy Nutter to The Manager (G. Ward & Co.), letter, 9 November 1960. DN.

21 'their feeling was one of amazement': quoted in 'The Ministry of Works Was Not for Me'.

21 'I knew from a little boy': quoted in Hemsley, 'The £500 Suit.'

TWO: THE GOLDEN AGE

Interviews with: Angus Cundey, Rupert Lycett Green, Joseph Morgan, Eric Musgrave, John Pearse, Andrew Ramroop, Henry Rose, Edward Sexton, Manny Silverman. Special thanks to Tom Arena and Dominic Sebag-Montefiore.

23 'packed tight': Colin MacInnes, *Absolute Beginners* (London: MacGibbon & Kee, 1959), 66. My description of Soho c.1960 is derived from interviews with people who remember it (John Pearse, Manny Silverman); and Dan Farson, *Soho in the Fifties* (London: Michael Joseph Ltd, 1987).

23 'errand boy-trotter': Tommy Nutter, quoted in Thom O'Dwyer, 'The World According to Tommy Nutter', *HeLines*, 1991.

25 'takes longer than to train a brain surgeon': Robert Bright, quoted in Geraldine Ranson, 'A Stitch in Time', May 1988. The source and exact date of this article, which I found clipped in Tommy's scrapbooks, is unclear. Angus Cundey discusses the length of training required to become a cutter in 'National Life Stories: An Oral History of British Fashion', archived in the British Library.

25 'They used to say': Robert L. Green, quoted in Prudence Glynn, 'Fashion: The Mogul of Menswear Surveys His Territory', *The Times*, 23 May 1972.

27 'get rid of it': Cundey, 'National Life Stories'.

27 'must be able not only to cut': *The Dictionary of English Trades, 1804*, quoted in Richard Walker, *The Savile Row Story: An Illustrated History* (London: Prion, 1988), 38.

28 turn him into Cary Grant: Marion Hume, 'Perfectly Suited,' *W*, 25 February 1988; Betty Goodwin, 'Savile Row Tailor Re-Creates Cary Grant Look in Miniseries About Heiress', *Los Angeles Times*, 15 May 1987.

28 'A man should look': Hardy Amies, *ABC of Men's Fashion* (London: V&A Publications, 2007), 11.

28 'I started off picking up pins': Tommy Nutter, quoted in Robert Colacello, 'Tommy Nutter the Tailor', *Interview*, August 1973.

28 docked his pay in penalty: Prudence Glynn, 'The Construction Business', *The Times*, 21 November 1972.

28 'I think they were rather desperate': Tommy Nutter, interviewed on *My Kind of Music*, BBC Radio Brighton, 20 September 1980. He discusses his duties in Glynn, 'The Construction Business', and Janet Buckton, 'Nutter's the Name They're All Crazy About', *Coventry Evening Telegraph*, 26 August 1980.

28 'I was so keen': Tommy Nutter, quoted in O'Dwyer, 'The World According to Tommy Nutter'.

29 esteemed clientele: 'Tommy, the Natty Nutter', *Financial Times*, 16 September 1978.

29 'rather an old-fashioned company': Tommy Nutter, quoted in Buckton, 'Nutter's the Name'.

29 'His clothes seemed to melt': Virginia Woolf, *The Second Common Reader* (New York: Harvest Books, 2003), 150.

30 preach it authoritatively on BBC Radio: *Man's Hour*, BBC Radio 4, 1 April 1987. This was an April Fool's Day edition of the long-running program me *Woman's Hour*. Archived in the British Library.

30 'how to actually make a jacket': Tommy Nutter, quoted in O'Dwyer, 'The World According to Tommy Nutter'.

30 'From Our Estates Correspondent': 'Multi-Storey Car Park Proposal', *The Times*, 14 March 1962.

31 'To see the family inheritance': Cundey, 'National Life Stories'.

31 'the very end of the Golden Age': Tommy Nutter, quoted in O'Dwyer, 'The World According to Tommy Nutter'.

32 'mass of rents and patches': Edward, Duke of Windsor, *A Family Album* (London: Cassell, 1960), 37.

32 'Poole': Ibid.

32 Gieves had even filled a yacht: 'A History of Gieves and Hawkes', (gievesandhawkes.hk/history-article.php). Accessed 10 July 2016.

32 'even when out shooting': Edward, Duke of Windsor, *Family Album*, 30.

32 forty suits and twenty pairs of shoes: Eric Musgrave, *Sharp Suits* (London: Pavilion Books, 2013), 62.

32 'the robes of nine British': Walker, *Savile Row Story*, 54.

33 would one day become known as the dinner jacket: My understanding is based on a discussion with Angus Cundey at Henry Poole & Co. Stephen Howarth also discusses the origin and competing theories about how it came to be called a 'tuxedo' in *Henry Poole: Founders of Savile Row: The Making of a Legend* (London: Bene Factum Publishing, 2003), 58–60.

33 spinach down his starched front: Edward, Duke of Windsor, *Family Album*, 39. This book is an excellent source for Edward VII's innovations, though I also consulted Christopher Hibbert, *Edward VII: The Last Victorian King* (New York: St. Martin's Press, 2007), 176.

33 tailors from Paris and Vienna would trail him: Edward, Duke of Windsor, *Family Album*, 35.

34 'He was a good friend': Ibid.

34 stretched beyond capacity during the conflict: Walker, *Savile Row Story*, 92.

34 at least forty: Musgrave, *Sharp Suits*, 66.

34 'constrictions of dress': Edward, Duke of Windsor, *Family Album*, 105.

34 'striptease act': Ibid.

34 'tyranny of starch': Ibid., 107.

34 'I was in fact "produced"': Ibid., 114.

35 vaporised ten entire firms: Walker, *Savile Row Story*, 104.

35 'placed her typewriter on some debris': Ibid.

36 'sitting in secret': Ibid., 109.

36 'as though it came from Chanel': Nik Cohn, *Today There Are No Gentlemen* (London: Weidenfeld & Nicolson, 1971), 40.

36 'The exasperating thing': Rodney Bennett-England, *Dress Optional: The Revolution in Menswear* (London: Peter Owen, 1967), 51.

37 'the garb of ghetto rebellion': Walker, *Savile Row Story*, 106.

37 The youths became known as Teddy boys: I consulted numerous sources on the Teds, the best of which are Richard Barnes, *Mods!* (London: Eel Pie Publishing, 1979); Stanley Cohen, *Folk Devils and Moral Panics* (New York: St. Martin's Press, 1972); and Geoffrey Aquilina Ross, *The Day of the Peacock: Style for Men 1963–1973* (London: V&A Publishing, 2011), which was particularly good for sartorial pointers as well as being my original source for the idea that Teddy boys represent the emergence of modern teenagers in Britain (p. 32).

37 'The lack of parental authority': George Melly, *Revolt into Style: The Pop Arts in Britain* (London: Allen Lane, 1970), 34.

38 'the exquisitely prosaic city suit': Pearl Binder, *The Peacock's Tail* (London: George G. Harrap & Co. Ltd, 1958), 28.

38 'As far as setting men's fashion goes': Judy Innes, 'Now What's New from the LAND OF MOD?', *Daily Mail*, 12 February 1964.

38 'It is ridiculous': Cecil Beaton, quoted in Walker, *Savile Row Story*, 117–18.

39 'some deposed Slavic': Cohn, *Today There Are No Gentlemen*, 165.

39 'Although I actually loved': Tommy Nutter, quoted in O'Dwyer, 'The World According to Tommy Nutter'.

39 bright tie or outrageous pocket handkerchief: Tommy Nutter, undated notes for an autobiography. DN.

39 'I was moving right away from all the stiffness': Tommy Nutter, quoted in O'Dwyer, 'The World According to Tommy Nutter'.

THREE: YOUNG METEORS

Interviews with: Geoffrey Aquilina Ross, Louise Aron, Christopher Brown, Cheryl De Courcey, Carol Drinkwater, Valerie Garland, Kim Grossman, Stuart Hopps, Chris Hughes, David Nutter, Adrian Rifkin, Christopher Tarling, Vicki Wickham.

41 Gaumont State: Details including the building's height and auditorium capacity are drawn from the database of the Theatres Trust (theatrestrust.org.uk). Accessed 27 July 2017.

42 contributed vocals and harmonica: Stanley Booth, *The True Adventures of the Rolling Stones* (Chicago: Chicago Review Press, 2000), 69–70.

43 'The up-to-the-minute': Mike McGrath, 'Casual Column', *Top Boy*, 1964.

43 'no problem' . . . 'as well as all the teenage market magazines': Mike McGrath, quoted in Paul Anderson, *Mods: The New Religion* (London: Omnibus Press, 2014), 37.

45 'Apostle of the Mods': Geoffrey Aquilina Ross, *The Day of the Peacock: Style for Men 1963–1973* (London: V&A Publishing, 2011), 41.

45 take his white German shepherd: Richard Weight, *Mod: A Very British Style* (London: The Bodley Head, 2013), 76.

45 painting the shopfront canary yellow: Aquilina Ross, *The Day of the Peacock*, 42. This book is an excellent source for the particulars of Carnaby Street fashion. See also John Reed, *John Stephen: The King of Carnaby Street* (London: Haus Publishing, 2010).

45 a sleek £6,000 Rolls-Royce: 'Rolls-Royce' (small news spot), *Daily Mirror*, 19 June 1964.

45 'Man is asserting': 'The Fashion Dictators,' *Daily Sketch*, 23 September 1964.

45 'There was no fashion': John Stephen, quoted in Aquilina Ross, *The Day of the Peacock*, 41.

45 'new and exciting world': Mike McGrath, quoted in Anderson, *Mods*, 36.

46 'red hot boxer of the Sixties': Ibid., 37.

49 a porcelain vase: Barry Miles, *London Calling: A Countercultural History of London Since 1945* (New York: Atlantic Books, 2011), 53–4.

49 Regency wallpaper, leather armchairs and a large white piano: Matt Houlbrook, *Queer London: Perils and Pleasures in the Sexual Metropolis 1918–1957* (Chicago: University of Chicago Press, 2006), 84.

49 their own take on the neo-Edwardian look: Shaun Cole, *'Don We Now Our Gay Apparel': Gay Men's Dress in the Twentieth Century* (New York: Berg, 2000), 23.

49 'piss-elegant and full of queens': Simon Raven, quoted in Hugh David, *On Queer Street: A Social History of British Homosexuality 1895–1995* (London: HarperCollins, 1998), 165.

49 'Top drawer queers' . . . 'closet of closets': Barry Miles, *London Calling*, 54.

50 aversion therapies: Alkarim Jivani, *It's Not Unusual: A History of Lesbian and Gay Britain in the Twentieth Century* (London: Michael O'Mara Books Limited, 1997), 122.

51 The judge had understood what would happen: Ibid., 123.

51 'new drive against male vice': David Maxwell Fyfe, quoted in Peter Wildeblood, *Against the Law* (London: Weidenfeld & Nicolson, 1955), 46.

51 the first year after Maxwell Fyfe's appointment: David, *On Queer Street*, 164.

51 'In public terms': 'A Social Problem', *Sunday Times*, 1 November 1953.

51 'wretched business': Lord Montagu of Beaulieu, *Wheels Within Wheels: An Unconventional Life* (London: Weidenfeld & Nicolson, 2000), 95.

51 'the same place that Sir Walter Raleigh': Ibid., 103.

51 'I felt bemused and helpless': Ibid., 104.

52 'than any other since the days of Nero': Wildeblood, *Against the Law*, 40.

52 'I am no more proud of my condition': Ibid., 2.

52 'a searing episode': Lord Montagu of Beaulieu, *Wheels Within Wheels*, 95.

52 'caricature of justice': B. A. Young, quoted in Ibid., 122.

52 'If two chaps carry on like that': Unnamed taxi driver, quoted in Wildeblood, *Against the Law*, 65.

53 'homosexual behaviour between consenting adults': Report of the Committee on Homosexual Offences and Prostitution (London: Her Majesty's Stationery Office, 1957), 115.

53 first piece of progressive policy: Jivani, *It's Not Unusual*, 115.

53 'classless spirit': Mary Quant, *Quant by Quant: The Autobiography of Mary Quant* (London: V&A Publishing, 2012), 68.

55 'This three-part, hot-gospelling hymn': 'Exciting Dancers in British Debut,' *The Times*, 6 October 1964.

56 'The word "charismatic"': Christopher Tarling, quoted in Stuart Husband, 'Rock on Tommy', *Independent on Sunday*, 5 March 2006.

58 'Your weekend at gay Paree': 'Chow' (no other name is given) to Tommy Nutter, letter, 20 May 1964. DN.

58 'drop sequins': Ibid.

60 'I don't know, really': Tommy Nutter quoted in 'Tommy Nutter', *Style*, 23 May 1970.

62 more than a dozen handwritten missives: Names are withheld, as some of the men are still alive. DN.

63 'one of life's flitters': Christopher Tarling, quoted in Husband, 'Rock on Tommy'.

FOUR: THE NEW ARISTOCRATS

Interviews with: Geoffrey Aquilina Ross, Louise Aron, Peter Brown, Angus Cundey, Carol Drinkwater, Catherine Everest (née Butterworth), Tom Gilbey, Rupert Lycett Green, David Grigg, Kim Grossman, Carlo Manzi, David Nutter, John Pearse, Edward Sexton, Joan Sexton, Manny Silverman, Christopher Tarling, James Vallance White, Judith Wright (née Allera).

66 'In those days it wasn't all that easy': Tommy Nutter, quoted in Thom O'Dwyer, 'The World According to Tommy Nutter', *HeLines*, 1991.

67 'the fabric you wore': Edward Sexton, quoted in Stuart Husband, 'Rock on Tommy', *Independent on Sunday*, 5 March 2006.

68 'little suits': Tommy Nutter, quoted in O'Dwyer, 'The World According to Tommy Nutter'.

68 'It was all very well': David Taylor, 'Pop Goes the Whistle and Flute', *Punch*, 30 March 1977.

69 'boring establishment': Edward Sexton to Alan Lewis, letter, 1 June 2000. JJC.

71 'If I don't get whistled at and jeered': Michael Fish, quoted in Nik Cohn, *Today There Are No Gentlemen* (London: Weidenfeld & Nicolson, 1971), 145.

71 'for a man to wear about the house': Geoffrey Aquilina Ross, *The Day of the Peacock: Style for Men 1963–1973* (London: V&A Publishing, 2011), 113.

71 'a phenomenon': Anthony King-Deacon, quoted in Ibid., 108.

71 'high priest': Hardy Amies, *The Englishman's Suit* (London: Quartet Books, 1994), 32.

71 'without losing' . . . 'I felt I could': Tommy Nutter, quoted in Rob Ryan, 'Tommy Nutter: Well Bespoke', *Arena*, September 1989.

71 Tommy asked Michael Fish for a job: Geoffrey Aquilina Ross, 'Who Needs Shows When You're Your Own Shop Window?', *Evening Standard*, 14 March 1973; Taylor, 'Pop Goes the Whistle and Flute.'

71 'One feels almost a fool': Clement Freud, quoted in Aquilina Ross, *The Day of the Peacock*, 73.

74 'a comely youth from Edgware': Cohn, *Today There Are No Gentlemen*, 164.

74 'got into the whole scene': Tommy Nutter, quoted in Janet Buckton, 'Nutter's the Name They're All Crazy About', *Coventry Evening Telegraph*, 26 August 1980. Tommy also mentions the Ad Lib Club in 'Tommy, the Natty Nutter', *Financial Times*, 16 September 1978.

74 'It was where everybody went' . . . 'paid dividends': Tommy Nutter,

quoted in David Spark, 'The Stars Follow Tommy When It Comes to Fashion', *Evening Mail*, 1 June 1979.

75 'I supervised and conducted': Peter Brown and Steven Gaines, *The Love You Make: An Insider's Story of the Beatles* (New York: New American Library, 2002), 160.

75 more West End than Bebington: Ibid., 57. See also Cilla Black, *What's It All About?* (London: Ebury Press, 2003), 145: 'He spoke real posh, much posher than Brian.'

75 'very special' . . . 'I remember thinking': Brown and Gaines, *The Love You Make*, 57.

76 'psychiatric grounds': Ibid., 55.

76 an initial encounter: Mark Lewisohn, *Tune In: The Beatles: All These Years, Volume 1* (New York: Crown Archetype, 2013), 272.

77 'more popular than Jesus now': John Lennon, quoted in Maureen Cleave, 'How Does a Beatle Live? John Lennon Lives Like This', *Evening Standard*, 4 March 1966. Lennon's comments about Christianity in the article were republished around the world.

77 'It was ten o'clock on Friday night': Brown and Gaines, *The Love You Make*, 246.

77 *Juke Box Jury*: Ibid.

77 'I said to break down the doors': Ibid.

79 retreated into the closet: James Hogg and Robert Sellers, *Hello Darlings!: The Authorized Biography of Kenny Everett* (London: Bantam Press, 2013), 87. Peter discusses his relationship and break-up at length in this book, as well as his encounter with Tommy Nutter the day after Brian Epstein's death.

81 'physical satisfaction in the saddest of ways': Brown and Gaines, *The Love You Make*, 50.

81 'I have had Miss B. here': Tommy Nutter to David Nutter, letter, 3 July 1978. DN.

82 nearly £500,000 on a five-storey town house: Brown and Gaines, *The Love You Make*, 283. All of the descriptive details of Apple Corps are drawn from here.

83 an experimental track: The most detailed breakdown of the 'Hey Jude' recording schedule is in Mark Lewisohn, *The Complete Beatles Chronicle* (New York: Harmony Books, 1992), 291–2. I also consulted Bob Spitz, *The Beatles* (New York: Little, Brown and Company, 2012), 782–4, 791–2.

83 'I was always a bit in limbo': Paul McCartney, quoted in *The Beatles Anthology* (San Francisco: Chronicle Books, 2002), 297.

84 'the most incredible song': Tommy Nutter, interviewed on *My Kind of*

Music, BBC Radio Brighton, 20 September 1980. Peter's recollection of this event was corroborated by Catherine Everest, who heard it from Tommy himself in the 1980s.

84 'I don't know, I can't say why they did it': Tommy Nutter, quoted in Cohn, *Today There Are No Gentlemen*, 164–5.

85 oysters from Brittany, caviar from the Garonne: Anne Mason, 'Dining with Madame Prunier in London', *The Age* (Melbourne), 9 February 1960.

87 'In a once sedate world': Piri Halasz, 'You Can Walk Across It On the Grass', *Time*, 15 April 1966.

88 he'd routinely thrown her out of the Lewis's department store: Black, *What's It All About?*, 144–5.

88 'I watched her move': Brian Epstein, *A Cellarful of Noise* (New York: Doubleday & Company, Inc., 1964), 63–4.

89 'When an acquaintance had come up to me': Black, *What's It All About?*, 152.

89 'a big star': Tommy Nutter, *My Kind of Music* interview.

90 'It's going to be terribly posh': Cilla Black, quoted in 'Cilla of Savile Row', *Sunday Express*, 22 December 1968.

INTERLUDE: CILLA AND BOBBY GET MARRIED

Interviews with: Peter Brown, David Nutter, Judith Wright (née Allera).

91 'I guess it's on': Cilla Black, *What's It All About?* (London: Ebury Press, 2003), 172.

91 £8 burgundy dress, hastily shortened: 'Cilla Gets Married in an £8 Dress,' *Evening Standard*, 25 January 1969.

FIVE: DISCOTHEQUE IN A GRAVEYARD

Interviews with: Louise Aron, Peter Brown, Angus Cundey, Simon Doonan, Carol Drinkwater, Tony King, Carlo Manzi, Joseph Morgan, David Nutter, Edward Sexton, Joan Sexton.

99 'Thomas Nutter is opening': 'Back to Square . . .' *Daily Mirror*, 12 February 1969.

99 'elegant with a touch of the sombre': Stanley Costin, 'Bespoke Tailor', *Men's Wear*, 27 January 1972.

100 'People seem to think that our shop': Tommy Nutter, quoted in Prudence Glynn, 'The Construction Business', *The Times*, 21 November 1972.

100 'a riot of Royal Purple': Stephen Higginson, 'The Changing Face – and Pace – of Savile Row', *Men's Wear*, 18 January 1973.

100 'the idea of an "old look"' . . . 'show what we do': Tommy Nutter, quoted in Ibid.

100 'a lot more relaxed': Tommy Nutter, quoted in John Walker, 'Mr. Nutter (Aided by Cilla) Taking a Gamble in Savile Row', *Daily Sketch*, 9 January 1969.

100 'something different': Tommy Nutter, quoted in 'Men in Vogue', *Vogue*, March 1969.

101 a group of Americans knocked on the door: Cilla Black recalled this incident during her opening-night address of 'Tommy Nutter: Rebel on the Row', an exhibition at the Fashion and Textile Museum, London, on 20 May 2011 (youtube.com/watch?v=xZpHNUsnHDs). Accessed 2 March 2016.

101 Apple Corps doorman in a Nutters frock coat: Jimmy Clark, the Apple doorman, can be seen wearing a Nutters frock coat in *Let It Be* (1970) during the rooftop concert sequence.

102 wish him goodnight: Tommy Nutter, interviewed on *My Kind of Music*, BBC Radio Brighton, 20 September 1980.

102 'a bunch of East End gangsters': Cilla Black, quoted in Stuart Husband, 'Rock on Tommy', *Independent on Sunday*, 5 March 2006.

102 'I've never seen such big candles': Ibid.

103 'masses of shape and flare': Tommy Nutter, undated notes for an autobiography. DN.

104 'deep, deep': Ibid.

104 'gallant Nutter character': Fiona MacCarthy, 'The Secret Life of Beau Nutter', *Guardian*, 4 August 1969.

104 'an eccentric mix': David Taylor, 'Pop Goes the Whistle and Flute', *Punch*, 30 March 1977.

104 '"New Look" for menswear': Tommy Nutter, undated notes for an autobiography. DN.

104 'louche-but-sharp flamboyance': Stuart Husband, 'Rock on Tommy'.

104 'I thought I would play things down': Tommy Nutter, undated notes for an autobiography. DN.

105 'should be as brief as wit': Hardy Amies, *ABC of Men's Fashion* (London: V&A Publications, 2007), 119.

105 'Imagine this': 'Welsh Savile Row Subversive Tommy Nutter Remembered by the Pembrokeshire Tailor Who Knew Him Best', *Wales Online* (www.walesonline.co.uk/lifestyle/fashion/welsh-savile-row-subversive-tommy-1810946). Accessed 17 September 2015.

106 'The customers were complaining': Tommy Nutter, quoted in Aileen Doherty, 'Gentleman Jackson!', *Daily Mail*, 17 December 1984.

106 'They are as big-mouthed as anyone': John Lennon, quoted in an un-titled newspaper clipping reproduced in the sleeve notes of *Wedding Album*, released on 20 October 1969 by Apple Records.

107 John and Yoko arrived in Gibraltar: Ray Connelly and Sam White, 'It's a White Wedding for John and Yoko!', *Evening Standard*, 20 March 1969. Bob Spitz gives the time as 8.30 a.m. in *The Beatles* (New York: Little, Brown and Company, 2012), 826.

107 'an actress, painter and maker of a film': 'John Lennon Flies 2000 Miles to Marry Quietly', *The Times*, 21 March 1969.

107 a coat that was made ... from human hair: Connelly and White, 'It's a White Wedding'. The coat is plainly visible in several photos, although the true provenance of its hair is impossible to verify.

107 spent a restless night: Ibid.

110 'Marvellous tailor' ... 'Tommy Nutter is': Hardy Amies, quoted in Walter Logan, 'New, Exciting Tommy Nutter', source unclear (trun-cated press clipping), undated, *c*.1971. DN.

110 'Savile Row is a street of bespoke tailors': Hardy Amies, *The English-man's Suit* (London: Quartet Books, 1994), 33.

111 'When I opened up in my own right': Tommy Nutter, quoted in Thom O'Dwyer, 'The World According to Tommy Nutter', *HeLines*, 1991.

111 'was regarded with suspicion': Doherty, 'Gentleman Jackson!'

111 'It's amazing, but since we set up': Tommy Nutter, quoted in Costin, 'Bespoke Tailor'.

111 'In fact, they were rather nice': Tommy Nutter, *My Kind of Music* inter-view.

111 'Nutters is going to be extremely successful': Robert Valentine, quoted in 'Nutter's Open Their Doors', *Tailor & Cutter*, 21 February 1969. For a good overview of Valentine's career, see his obituary in *The Times*, 12 November 1994.

111 'stylish brick': '... Shops', *Men's Wear*, 22 May 1969. Angus Cundey credited Nutters as the inspiration for this drastic change at Henry Poole & Co. during our interview.

111 'I would like to see this stuffy image': Angus Cundey, quoted in 'Trying to Change an Image – Without Losing Quality', *Men's Wear*, 23 April 1970.

112 'Savile Row today is in a rare state': Richard Walker, 'Lincroft Doyen in the New Style of Savile Row', *Daily Telegraph*, 25 June 1971.

112 'making a comeback': John Walker, 'Mr. Nutter (Aided by Cilla) Tak-ing a Gamble in Savile Row', *Daily Sketch*, 9 January 1969.

113 'Don't ask me for a list of names': Tommy Nutter, quoted in 'There's Nothing Naff About Nutters', *Evening Standard*, 1 November 1969.

113 'Are you sure the sleeve's not wrinkled?': Tommy Nutter, quoted in MacCarthy, 'Secret Life'. All quotes concerning MacCarthy come from this article.

SIX: A COMPLETE LOOK

Interviews with: Manolo Blahnik, Peter Brown, Roy Chittleborough, Garry Clarke, Mel Furukawa, Stewart Grimshaw, Joseph Morgan, Prince Rajsinh of Rajpipla, Edward Sexton, Joan Sexton, Peter Sprecher, Christopher Tarling, James Vallance White, Judith Wright (née Allera), Zance Yianni.

115 'Come on' . . . 'not posing for Beatles pictures': John Lennon, quoted in Bob Spitz, *The Beatles* (New York: Little, Brown and Company, 2012), 842.

115 didn't feel like wearing shoes: *The Beatles Anthology* (San Francisco: Chronicle Books, 2002), 341–3. Most details about the *Abbey Road* shoot are drawn from this book, which features primary interviews with the group members, Derek Taylor and George Martin. I also examined Linda McCartney's behind-the-scenes photographs.

116 the business Tommy had expected in a year: Deborah Murdoch, 'How Tommy Whizzed into Savile Row,' *Daily Mail*, 20 January 1970. Tommy made the same claim in 'The Ministry of Works Was Not for Me, Savile Row Was', *Men's Wear*, 16 April 1970.

116 470 of them to Americans: 'It's Much Nicer at Nutters', promotional booklet, 1970. DN.

116 'It's been very hard work': Edward Sexton, quoted in Pamela Buonaventura, 'Tommy Nutter', *Style*, 23 May 1970.

116 'I haven't been for ages': Tommy Nutter, quoted in Ibid.

116 Johnny Carson on *The Tonight Show*: 'It's Much Nicer at Nutters'.

116 'Mrs Ronald Reagan': Ibid.

116 eight summer suits: 'Up at Citizen Stigwood's Place', *Evening Standard*, 8 March 1969.

117 Provans: Details come from Derek Granger, 'Obituary: Fergus Provans', *Independent*, 28 August 1997. I also drew from conversations with Prince Rajsinh of Rajpipla and Stewart Grimshaw.

118 made a signature out of braiding: 'The Sun Shines on Braided Suits,' *Style*, 30 May 1970.

118 'A tailor should not be scared': Tommy Nutter, quoted in 'The Ministry of Works Was Not for Me'.

119 'the place for men's clothes' . . . 'now in the class': Murdoch, 'How Tommy Whizzed into Savile Row'.

119 'one of the best': Douglas Hayward, quoted in 'Cottage Pie in Mayfair', *Evening Standard*, 4 April 1970.

120 'the way I like to see them' . . . 'It's very nice': 'It's Much Nicer at Nutters'.

120 'a comprehensive cross section of the public': 'The Ministry of Works Was Not for Me'.

120 At least two of them were over seventy years old: Murdoch, 'How Tommy Whizzed into Savile Row'.

120 he did a double take: Peter Sprecher, recorded interview with Dominic Sebag-Montefiore, 20 May 2011. This whole exchange comes from this interview, supplemented with my own phone interview with Peter Sprecher on 26 April 2016.

121 Henry George Poole had been a young dilettante: My account is based on Richard Walker, *The Savile Row Story: An Illustrated History* (London: Prion, 1988), 50–3. See also Stephen Howarth, *Henry Poole: Founders of Savile Row: The Making of a Legend* (London: Bene Factum Publishing, 2003), 25–8.

122 'definitely not the kind of tailor': Pamela Buonaventura, 'Tommy Nutter,' *Style*, 23 May 1970.

123 'part engineer, part scientist': Edward Sexton, quoted in Stuart Husband, 'Rock on Tommy', *Independent on Sunday*, 5 March 2006.

123 all of them under thirty: John Walker, 'Mr Nutter (Aided by Cilla) Taking a Gamble in Savile Row', *Daily Sketch*, 9 January 1969.

123 they'd all lived within the limitations: 'It's Much Nicer at Nutters'.

124 Polari: A good overview and short glossary is provided by Alkarim Jivani, *It's Not Unusual: A History of Lesbian and Gay Britain in the Twentieth Century* (London: Michael O'Mara Books Limited, 1997), 14–15. Much of the Polari popularised in Britain came via a BBC Radio programme, *Round the Horne*, which was broadcast between 1965 and 1968. The scripts read like a Polari dictionary: see Barry Took and Mat Coward, *The Best of Round the Horne* (London: Boxtree, 2000).

126 'a director of Nutters': Tommy Nutter, quoted in Murdoch, 'How Tommy Whizzed into Savile Row'.

127 original abstract paintings: Tommy discusses the sitting-room decorations in Buonaventura, 'Tommy Nutter'.

127 a tweed knickerbocker suit: 'Thomas Nutter' (news spot), *Daily Mail*, 16 October 1970.

127 'It turned out just the way you'd expect': Aileen Mehle, 'Suzy Knickerbocker', syndicated society column, 24 October 1970.

127 awkward-looking threesome: A photograph of the trio descending the stairs at the Plaza Hotel appears in *Herrenjournal*, October 1970.

128 'a cheery, cheeky, insouciant sort of look': 'Checking Out the Men', *Vogue*, November 1970.

128 'Many Savile Row tailors': Tommy Nutter, quoted in 'Now It's Savile Row's Turn to Diversify', *Men's Wear*, 17 December 1970.

129 chrome scaffolding: Anne Trehearne, 'New Shop for Show-Offs,' *Evening Standard*, 11 December 1970.

129 'There's no limit to what we'll sell': Tommy Nutter, quoted in 'New Nutter Shop to Open in Savile Row', *Men's Wear*, 19 November 1970.

129 Tommy's particular taste: The Nutters Shirts stock was described to me by Christopher Tarling. It is also sketched out in several articles: 'New Nutter Shop to Open in Savile Row'; 'Xmas Opening for Nutters', *Style*, 21 November 1970; Trehearne, 'New Shop for Show-Offs', *Evening Standard*, 11 December 1970; 'Shirts in Savile Row', *Men's Wear*, 17 December 1970; and Stanley Costin, 'Tommy Nutter – New Boy in Savile Row', *Men's Wear*, 27 January 1972.

129 'full wardrobes with a complete look and style': Tommy Nutter, quoted in 'New Nutter Shop to Open in Savile Row'.

SEVEN: BLOW-UP

Interviews with: Peter Brown, Stewart Grimshaw, Kim Grossman, Carlo Manzi, David Nutter, Edward Sexton, Joan Sexton, Christopher Tarling.

131 'The common denominator of all the winners': Eugenia Sheppard, 'Inside Fashion', *New York Post*, 11 January 1971.

131 'A Gentleman's Year': 'A Gentleman's Year', *Vogue*, January 1971.

131 it had been coming for a while: Peter Brown and Steven Gaines, *The Love You Make: An Insider's Story of the Beatles* (New York: New American Library, 2002), 348.

132 'a mausoleum just waiting for a death': Ibid., 324. In his book, Peter discusses the dirty work he did for Klein at length, including the mass firing: 'I unhappily agreed to do the job only because I hoped the news could be delivered with kindness and dignity, instead of from Klein's mouth' (p. 322).

132 'I have had an experience which has been invaluable': Peter Brown, quoted in Frankie McGowan, column, *Evening News*, 27 January 1971.

132 Cilla threw her friend a farewell party: Ibid.

132 '[Peter] is, at 33, unmarried': Ibid.

133 'unusual' ... 'desperately untidy': Bridie Mullen, quoted in Yvonne Thomas, 'The Other Man in Bridie's Life', *Evening Standard*, 6 January 1971. All details about Tommy's new flat come from this article and its accompanying photographs.

134 a patent violation: 'Cut on the Cross – Patent Violation', *Men's Wear*, 4 March 1971. Tommy models his Bermuda shorts in a news spot in *Men's Wear*, 18 February 1971.

134 A new Andy Warhol exhibition: Warhol exhibition catalogue (London: Tate Gallery, 1971).

134 'world of death and flowers': Andrew Causey, 'Warhol's World of Death and Flowers', *Illustrated London News*, 6 March 1971.

135 suicide thwarted by a low tide: In 'Rock on Tommy', *Independent on Sunday*, 5 March 2006, Stuart Husband quotes Tommy as saying, 'I had a vague idea of drowning myself, but the tide was out.' The provenance of this quote is not entirely clear; I was unable to find it anywhere else.

135 a hospital microphone so sensitive: Mark Lewisohn, *The Complete Beatles Recording Sessions* (London: Hamlyn, 2004), 174.

138 'The group is over': John Lennon, interview with Jann S. Wenner, 'Lennon Remembers, Part One', *Rolling Stone*, 21 January 1971.

139 'We paled visibly and our jaws slackened a bit': Paul McCartney, quoted in *The Beatles Anthology* (San Francisco: Chronicle Books, 2002), 347.

139 'monument to psychedelia': Richard Neville, *Hippie Hippie Shake: The Dreams, the Trips, the Trials, the Love-Ins, the Screw Ups . . . The Sixties* (London, Bloomsbury, 1995), 1.

140 all in a single issue: *Oz* No. 26, February 1970.

140 'bare-chested long-hair': Neville, *Hippie Hippie Shake*, 180.

140 'It will look way out': Ibid., 172–3.

142 'Some of us at Oz are feeling old': *Oz* No. 26, February 1970.

142 'On my left knelt Berti': Neville, *Hippie Hippie Shake*, 204. All details of the backyard scene, including David behind his tripod, come from this source.

143 police raided the Oz offices: An excellent overview of the *Oz* trial appears in Barry Miles, *London Calling: A Countercultural History of London Since 1945* (New York: Atlantic Books, 2011), 299–309.

143 'The five charges against the three men': 'Carnival Atmosphere Outside Court for Start of Oz Trial', *The Times*, 23 June 1971.

143 'obscene court room dramas': Neville, *Hippie Hippie Shake*, 224.

144 'a touch of reefer madness in the dock': Ibid., 1.

144 'Neither do I': Judge Michael Argyle, QC, quoted in 'Carnival Atmosphere Outside Court for Start of Oz Trial'.

144 'Gobbling, going down': George Melly, quoted in Miles, *London Calling*, 302–3.

144 'It couldn't be about the alleged pornography': George Melly, quoted in Neville, *Hippie Hippie Shake*, 295.

144 'Festival of Light': Amy C. Whipple, 'Speaking for Whom? The 1971 Festival of Light and the Search for the "Silent Majority"', *Contemporary British History* 24 (2010), 319–39.

144 'Operation Rupert': Lucy Robinson, *Gay Men and the Left in Post-War Britain: How the Personal Got Political* (Manchester: Manchester University Press, 2011), 72. Details of the GLF rally assault come from here.

144 Reverend Father Fuck: Miles, *London Calling*, 305–6.

145 'Roast pig, roast pig, roast pig': Neville, *Hippie Hippie Shake*, 3.

145 'It's like 1940 here' . . . 'gonna be America's': Ray Coleman, *Lennon: The Definitive Biography* (New York: HarperPerennial, 1992), 565–6.

147 'the Rome of today': Ibid., 566.

EIGHT: PICCADILLY TOM

Interviews with: Geoffrey Aquilina Ross, Peter Brown, Carol Drinkwater, Rupert Lycett Green, David Grigg, Joseph Morgan, John Reid, Neil Sedaka, Edward Sexton, Joan Sexton, Christopher Tarling.

149 'It seems that at the moment we are in a transitional stage': Karl Dallas, speaking in 'Towards 2001: Fashion Marketing', *Tailor & Cutter*, 26 March 1971. The panel consisted of Karl Dallas, Barry Grigg, Gordon Deighton, Eric Joy and Tommy Nutter. All quotes in this section come from the transcript, which is extremely long and discursive. For clarity, I have condensed and edited, though I have not changed any direct quotes or altered the meaning of the discussion.

150 An irascible, brilliant craftsman: My understanding of Eric Joy is due to Rupert Lycett Green, who worked with him at Blades. Further evidence of his tetchy nature can be found in Jonathan Aitken, *The Young Meteors* (New York: Atheneum, 1967), 265: 'This country has got just as many stuck-up and snobbish young people as it ever had,' Joy said. 'Look at me. If ever there was a bloke who ought to be a beneficiary of the classless society it's me . . . Whenever anyone starts telling me about the classless society, I just crease up.'

152 up to nine hours at a stretch: 'Blackouts Will Total Nine Hours Daily,' *Guardian*, 16 February 1972. The details about trains, banks and milk deliveries also come from here.

152 'little notette': Tommy Nutter to David Nutter, letter, 17 February 1972. DN. The featured notes come from this letter.

152 'She became very tanned': Tommy Nutter to David Nutter, letter, undated, c.August 1972. DN.

152 'Hope you are working hard': Tommy Nutter to David Nutter, letter, January 1973. DN.

153 'Not much trade': Ibid.

153 'If you have any ideas': Ibid.

153 'Do we have to mention that?': Tommy Nutter, quoted in Geoffrey Aquilina Ross, 'Who Needs Shows When You're Your Own Shop Window?' *Evening Standard*, 21 March 1973.

154 he was named in the annual World's Best Dressed List: Stanley Costin, 'Tommy Nutter – New Boy in Savile Row', *Men's Wear*, 27 January 1972.

154 'label' . . . 'status symbol': Geoffrey Aquilina Ross, 'You Too Can Win at Clothesmanship . . .', *Evening Standard*, 23 February 1972.

154 'far too flashy' . . . 'look like Andy Capp': Tommy Nutter, quoted in Aileen Doherty, 'Gentleman Jackson!', *Daily Mail*, 17 December 1984. Tommy mentions the rhinestones in Alan Cartnal, 'A Return to Male Glamour', *Los Angeles Times*, 21 November 1975.

155 'It was a big job': Tommy Nutter, quoted in Aileen Doherty, 'Gentleman Jackson!'

155 'I was rather upset': Tommy Nutter, interviewed on *My Kind of Music*, BBC Radio Brighton, 20 September 1980. Elton appeared as Donald Duck in Central Park on 13 September 1980. Bob Mackie was responsible for the costume.

156 'All of a sudden Jagger just walked up': Tommy Nutter, quoted in Cartnal, 'A Return to Male Glamour'.

156 Jagger elbowed his way through a mosh pit: The most vivid account of the Jagger wedding is 'Mick Jagger Rocks His Own Wedding Reception in Saint-Tropez', *Rolling Stone*, 10 June 1971.

157 Bianca wore white Yves Saint Laurent: Bianca Jagger describes her own wedding dress in 'Bianca Jagger Remembers Yves Saint Laurent', *Guardian*, 14 December 2008.

157 'Jagger look': Austin Reed press release surveying Tommy's career and achievements, March 1979. DN.

157 'When I first said I wanted to go to Tommy': Bianca Jagger, quoted in Molly Parkin, 'Sparkling Bianca', *Sunday Times*, 27 August 1972.

158 numerous fittings: Ibid.

158 an eighth of an inch shorter: Tommy notes this in Robert Colacello, 'Tommy Nutter, the Tailor', *Interview*, August 1973.

158 'It was part of my liberation': Jagger, 'Bianca Jagger Remembers Yves Saint Laurent'.

159 'just like a man's': Tommy Nutter, quoted in 'Nutter's New Man', *Yorkshire Post*, 28 April 1982.

159 She took Tommy's own jacket: Tommy Nutter, *My Kind of Music* interview.

159 'We've been making some lovely clothes': Tommy Nutter to David Nutter, letter, undated, *c.* August 1972. DN.

159 at the Oval watching a cricket match: Photograph in the Hulton Archive, Getty Images, #2633097.

159 'discussing life': 'Eye', *Women's Wear Daily*, 16 November 1972.

159 'I can't stand by her': Marina Schiano, quoted in Rosemary Kent, 'Eye View: Camping Out', *Women's Wear Daily*, 13 November 1972. Bianca's attire at the art exhibition is also noted here.

159 'Bianca arrives at a Vogue studio': Anthony Scaduto, *Mick Jagger: Everybody's Lucifer* (New York: David McKay Company, Inc., 1974), 371.

160 'I certainly don't want too many': Tommy Nutter, quoted in 'Nutters Attract Women's Press to the Row', *Men's Wear*, 7 September 1972.

160 'harder to please' . . . 'around the place': Tommy Nutter, quoted in Felicity Green, 'Tailor Made for Joan', *Daily Mirror*, 3 October 1972. See also Prudence Glynn, 'The Construction Business', *The Times*, 21 November 1972, in which Tommy is quoted as saying: 'Bill Blass, the American designer, complained that last time he was in, the shop was full of women.'

160 'Every young boy's dream': Tommy Nutter, quoted in 'Tommy Nutter, Tailor to the Famous', *Honey*, December 1975. He credits this phone call with putting him 'on the road to fame' in John Hemsley, 'The £500 Suit That Made Me Look Fat!', *Reading Chronicle*, 6 January 1979.

160 'She's so magical': Tommy Nutter, quoted in Colacello, 'Tommy Nutter, the Tailor'.

160 'Bianca has been around this week': Tommy Nutter to David Nutter, letter, 14 August 1975. DN.

161 Bianca Jagger dangling off his arm: Aileen Mehle, 'Suzy Says', syndicated society column, 21 April 1973. Mehle gives a guest list and says Peter paid for it all. Further aesthetic details (the bouffant hairdos, etc.) come from several photographs of the party. DN.

161 all of them were stolen: Timothy Everest recounts the story in Stuart Husband, 'Rock on Tommy', *Independent on Sunday*, 5 March 2006.

NINE: LIBERTINES

Interviews with: Peter Brown, Jimmy Clark, Simon Doonan, Carol Drinkwater, David Grigg, Lady Fiona Montagu, Joseph Morgan, David Nutter, Edward Sexton, Joan Sexton, Christopher Tarling.

163 'Dear David': Tommy Nutter to David Nutter, letter, undated, *c.* April 1973. DN.

164 junkies and homeless camps: A vivid picture of the East Village circa 1971 is painted in Ada Calhoun, *St. Marks Is Dead: The Many Lives of America's Hippest Street* (New York: W. W. Norton & Company, 2016), 165–89.

164 $2 'contribution': David could not recall the exact amount. This detail (and several others) comes from Tim Lawrence, *Love Saves the Day: A History of American Dance Music Culture, 1970–1979* (Durham, NC: Duke University Press, 2004), 1.

165 'Once you walked into the Loft': David Mancuso, quoted in Tim Lawrence, 'Love Saves the Day: David Mancuso and the Loft', *Placed*, 2007. (www.timlawrence.info/articles2/2014/1/4/love-saves-the-day-david-mancuso-and-the-loft-placed-2007). Accessed 9 September 2016. To understand the original Loft, I consulted several sources beyond David Nutter's vivid memory. Another interview with Mancuso was conducted at the Red Bull Music Academy on 10 June 2016. A good oral history taking in the Loft is Lisa Robinson, 'Boogie Nights', *Vanity Fair*, 6 January 2010. A writer who goes by 'Apollo' has produced an excellent and extensive personal history, 'House Music 101', which is archived online (www.livingart.com/raving/articles/housemusic101-07.htm). Accessed 10 September 2016. 'Issue 7' deals directly with the Loft.

165 male models posing with a transgender Puerto Rican dancer: Michael Gross, *Focus* (New York: Atria Books, 2016), 204–5. Gross's chapter on Bill King is one of the few comprehensive biographical examinations that exist on the photographer. Another is Stephen Fried, 'Fashion's Dark King', *Vanity Fair*, August 1994. However, David Nutter questions the accuracy of some of Fried's claims.

166 'became a different, much less nice person': Erica Crome, quoted in Gross, *Focus*, 206.

167 there was always the Sanctuary: I cross-checked David's memories of gay clubs in the early 1970s with several sources. For the Sanctuary, see Bill Brewster, *Last Night a DJ Saved My Life: The History of the Disc Jockey* (New York: Grove Press, 2014), 142–5. For the Tenth Floor, see Lawrence, *Love Saves the Day*, 75–81. A good source for archived memories of clubs that would otherwise be forgotten is www.disco-disco.com. Accessed 2 December 2016.

169 'discotheque pour monsieur': 'Small Talk', *Interview*, July 1973.

169 'I'm here promoting my name': Tommy Nutter, quoted in Robert Colacello, 'Tommy Nutter the Tailor', *Interview*, August 1973.

169 'a mix of everything': Ibid. Tommy also discusses the new style in 'Nutter's New Phase', *Men's Wear*, 25 November 1977. In notes for an unwritten autobiography, Tommy cites *The Sting* and *The Great Gatsby* (released in 1973 and 1974 respectively) as influences on this evolving style. DN.

170 'I suppose they'll shove me': Tommy Nutter, quoted in Colacello, 'Tommy Nutter the Tailor'. All quotes and details from the Colacello interview come from here.

171 the Continental Baths: A fascinating first-hand account of what the baths were like in their heyday is Richard Goldstein's 'A Night at the Continental Baths', *New York*, 17 September 1973. Tommy had visited just two months earlier.

172 watching soap operas: Tommy notes this in Colacello, 'Tommy Nutter the Tailor'. David Grigg bought him the wine each day as part of his shop duties.

172 sweaters purchased at the Chelsea Antiques Fair: Tommy mentions this in 'Tommy Nutter', *Style*, 23 May 1970.

173 Ian McKellen in the pages of *Vogue*: *Vogue*, July 1973.

173 eight-week stage spectacular: Cilla Black, *What's It All About?* (London: Ebury Press, 2003), 212.

174 'in a world being overtaken by blue denim': Tommy Nutter, quoted in Walter Logan, 'Letter from London Notes a Revolution' (syndicated article), 11 August 1973. DN.

174 'I know people can't believe it': Tommy Nutter, quoted in Geoffrey Aquilina Ross, 'Who Needs Shows When You're Your Own Shop Window?', *Evening Standard*, 14 March 1973.

174 'Perhaps, if clothing is an indicator of national spirit': 'British Tailoring Died a Bit (But Not Totally) with the End of Swinging London', *Financial Post*, 12 May 1973.

175 'I felt it only right to compose a few lines': Edward Sexton to David Nutter, letter, January 1974. DN. Reproduced with permission from Mr Sexton.

176 a time-honoured practice for Savile Row: Walter Logan, 'English Tailoring Firm Moves to U.S. Market' (syndicated article), 31 March 1974.

177 'It overlooks the sea': Tommy Nutter to David Nutter, letter, 9 October 1973. DN. Tommy seems to have found this flat as early as May 1973, according to a letter that month from Christopher Tarling to David Nutter: 'Tommy's going to buy a flat in Brighton. He's seen one he likes and he's trying at the moment to get a mortgage.' Edward claims he helped Tommy secure the mortgage.

178 'I love it': Tommy Nutter, interviewed on *My Kind of Music*, BBC Radio Brighton, 20 September 1980.

178 threatened rent increase: 'Savile Row Cut-Up over Rising Rents', *Evening News*, 9 September 1974.

178 Brighton had been a refuge for queer people: A good starting point for the queer history of Brighton is Rose Collis, *The New Encyclopedia of*

Brighton (Brighton: Brighton & Hove City Libraries, 2012). In 1989, a group of local gays and lesbians also founded 'Brighton Ourstory' to collect and preserve material about the town's LGBTQ past. Unfortunately, the initiative closed, though some of the history is still available online (www.brightonourstory.co.uk). Accessed 3 June 2016.

178 could not have cared less about the trial: 'The first thing he did when we started dating was to give me a book about the trial,' said Lady Montagu. 'But I wasn't interested in his sex life – I was far more worried that he had so much energy and I was afraid I wouldn't be able to keep up with him. I think part of the reason he married me was that I was non-judgmental, and he ALSO thought I'd be good for Beaulieu.' See Wendy Leigh, 'Lady Montagu of Beaulieu: I Had Three Nervous Breakdowns Trying to Run My Estate', *Telegraph* (www.telegraph.co .uk/finance/property/period-property/11993816/Lady-Montagu-of -Beaulieu-I-had-three-nervous-breakdowns-trying-to-run-my-estate .html). Accessed 14 November 2015.

179 'men and girls came and went': F. Scott Fitzgerald, *The Great Gatsby* (New York: Scribner, 2004), 32.

179 a habit of flouting social hierarchies: Lord Montagu, quoting Peter Wildeblood, owns up to and discusses this personality quirk in his *Wheels Within Wheels: An Unconventional Life* (London: Weidenfeld & Nicolson, 2000), 99.

179 Their matching Nutters suits: Details about the suits come from the Beaulieu archive (National Motor Museum), which still has them in storage. The archive also supplied me with an undated clipping about the ball from the *Daily Mirror*. Lady Fiona Montagu loved her suit so much she would continue to wear it intermittently for decades, disguising moth holes with sticking plaster and white chalk.

180 a schedule of the night's festivities: Carol Drinkwater has kept the black matchbook.

181 disqualified from the Charleston competition: Nigel Dempster, 'Great Gatsby! What This Quartet (And I) Did at the Weekend', *Daily Mail*, 21 October 1974.

181 'A lasting memory for all of us': Ibid.

TEN: MUSCLE QUEENS AND MOZART RECORDS

Interviews with: Peter Brown, Tom Gilbey, David Grigg, Bertram Keeter, Tony King, Joseph Morgan, David Nutter, John Reid, Jackie Rogers, Edward Sexton, Joan Sexton.

183 signed the lease on a loft of his own: According to his diary, David signed on 9 September 1974.

186 'We thought we'd do a number': John Lennon, quoted in David Buckley, *Elton: The Biography* (Chicago: Chicago Review Press, 2007), 178.

186 guests like Uri Geller: Ibid.

187 once been occupied by Valentino: David describes it as the 'Valentino building' in his diary, as does Prudence Glynn in 'Gentlemen's Agreement', *The Times*, 25 January 1975.

187 'Peacock Revolution' . . . 'a remnant sale': Hardy Clarke, 'The Year of the Drainpipe', *Evening News*, 9 January 1975.

187 'moderation will return to men's fashion': Rupert Lycett Green, quoted in Ibid.

187 'Fashion doesn't exist': Michael Fish, quoted in Geoffrey Aquilina Ross, *The Day of the Peacock: Style for Men 1963–1973* (London: V&A Publishing, 2011), 136.

189 a trio of shows premiering simultaneously: A copy of the opening reception invitation is held by David Nutter.

190 brown suit with beige rolled lapels: Erma Bombeck, 'Suited for a Gallery', At Wit's End (syndicated gossip column), 20 March 1975. A small note on the exhibition can also be found in the *Daily News Record*, 29 January 1975. A picture of Tommy at the gallery, taken a few days after the reception, is held by Getty in the *New York Post* Archive (#532198470).

190 'Were Tommy not such a sensible person': Glynn, 'Gentlemen's Agreement'.

191 approved of and encouraged by Yoko herself: See May Pang, *Instamatic Karma: Photographs of John Lennon* (New York: St. Martin's Press, 2008), xiii. Yoko Ono offers a corroborating account in Philip Norman, *John Lennon: The Life* (New York: HarperCollins, 2009), 712.

191 'I needed a break': Yoko Ono, quoted in Chrissy Iley, 'Yoko Ono: "John's Affair Wasn't Hurtful to Me. I Needed a Rest. I Needed Space"', *Telegraph* (http://www.telegraph.co.uk/culture/photography/9160041/Yoko-Ono-Johns-affair-wasnt-hurtful-to-me.-I-needed-a-rest.-I-needed-space.html). Accessed 27 March 2016.

193 he was alone in the apartment: Though David has no recollection of it, his diary entry for 5 March 1975 suggests that Tony King and John Lennon may also have been present for part of the shoot: 'Tony was there and so was John. Did job well. Many laughs. Lovely atmosphere.'

194 'rather reminiscent of Little Bo Peep': 'Teddy Boy Bridegroom Steals the Show', *Bath and West Evening Chronicle*, 26 March 1975.

194 'a few subdued gasps': Ibid.

194 'today's best young designer': Anna Harvey, quoted in 'Presentation', *Brides & Setting Up Home*, June 1975.

194 'Teddy Boy bridegroom': 'Teddy Boy Bridegroom Steals the Show'.

194 'played with my knee': Tommy Nutter to David Nutter, letter, 3 April 1975. DN.

194 'Ms Nakatsu' . . . 'quite a few lady clients': Ibid.

195 'a little holidayette' . . . 'look after them': Ibid.

196 'quite chubby, really': Tommy Nutter to David Nutter, letter, 8 July 1975. DN.

196 'Trying hard to think of a new look': Ibid.

197 'we have gone open plan in the shop': Tommy Nutter to David Nutter, letter, 14 August 1975. DN.

197 'Young David': Ibid.

197 'No special friends around': Ibid.

198 a rock photographer of drag bands like the Cockettes: Sherill Tippins, *Inside the Dream Palace: The Life and Times of New York's Legendary Chelsea Hotel* (New York: Houghton Mifflin Harcourt, 2010), 310.

198 beaten to death: 'Information Needed', *Village Voice*, 27 January 1975. David notes the murder in his diary on 26 November 1974.

199 'Sorry to hear about all your predicaments': Tommy Nutter to David Nutter, letter, 8 July 1975. DN.

200 a Pioneer Stereo System: According to David's diary, John tells him he has something for him on 15 September: 'I stayed in but it never came.' It arrived a few weeks later, on 8 October: 'It's rather beautiful but needs wires and a cartridge.'

200 first rock concert to be held there: Terry O'Neill, *Two Days That Rocked the World: Elton John Live at Dodger Stadium* (New York: Antique Collectors Club, 2015), 137.

200 a mansion that had once been owned by Greta Garbo: Buckley, *Elton*, 204.

201 110,000 people: O'Neill, *Two Days*, 31.

201 'what it must have looked like from Elton's perspective': Ibid.

202 'It seems so old-fashioned today' . . . 'very lucky': Tommy Nutter, quoted in Alan Cartnal, 'A Return to Male Glamour', *Los Angeles Times*, 21 November 1975. Tommy also discusses his plans for a Beverly Hills store in 'Lookin' Good', *Flighttime* (Allegheny Air System), February 1976.

202 just moved into a tiny bedsit: Tommy gives the date that he assumed residency of the flat as October 1975 in a letter to the landlord, 'Mr Lodge', sent 28 May 1976. JJC.

203 'I expected to see people dancing': Tommy Nutter, quoted in Cartnal, 'A Return to Male Glamour'.

ELEVEN: THAT WONDERFUL SUMMER

Interviews with: Peter Brown, Roy Chittleborough, Jimmy Clark, David Grigg, Stewart Grimshaw, Wendy Kavanagh, Tony King, Joseph Morgan, David Nutter, John Reid, Edward Sexton, Joan Sexton, Zance Yianni.

205 'Christmas season': Bernie Taupin and David Nutter, *Elton: It's a Little Bit Funny* (New York: The Viking Press, 1977), 10.

207 'I get depressed easily': Elton John, quoted in 'Elton John: The Lonely Love Life of a Superstar', *Rolling Stone*, 7 October 1976.

208 'that he might open a Nutters branch here': David Barritt, 'Suits Are Back, Says Dictator of Savile Row', *Sunday Times Magazine* (Johannesburg), 7 March 1976.

214 'I'm definitely leaving': Tommy Nutter, quoted in 'Final Cut', *Daily Express*, 7 May 1976.

214 'took a year off': Janet Buckton, 'Nutter's the Name They're All Crazy About', *Coventry Evening Telegraph*, 26 August 1980. Tommy offers a similar comment in an Austin Reed press release, March 1979. JJC.

214 'I felt that I'd achieved everything': Tommy Nutter, interviewed on *My Kind of Music*, BBC Radio Brighton, 20 September 1980. Tommy was already laying the groundwork for this narrative in his first *Daily Express* comment: 'I feel I've exhausted the made-to-measure business and want to try something different – selling everything from shirts and luggage to colognes.'

215 'There was jiggery-pokery going on': Tommy Nutter, quoted in Richard Walker, *The Savile Row Story: An Illustrated History* (London: Prion, 1988), 123.

215 'down and out': Tommy Nutter, quoted in 'Tommy Nutter: Well Bespoke', *Arena*, September/October 1989.

215 'I had reporters chasing me': Tommy Nutter, quoted in Walker, *Savile Row Story*, 123.

215 'Cutters can turn squabblesome': David Taylor, 'Pop Goes the Whistle and Flute', *Punch*, 30 March 1977.

216 'top model': The only written record of Tommy referring to Antony Hamilton comes in a letter to David dated 14 November 1978: 'I have found a new little friend . . . He is a solicitor, 27 years-old, blondish – very me. We'll see! I am not getting into a Tony Hamilton situation, I think. This one does not have aspirations as far as being a top model is concerned.'

217 Bang!, on Charing Cross Road: Details of Bang!, which opened in 1976, come from Luke Howard, 'Nightclubbing: Gay Clubbing in '70s London', *Red Bull Music Academy Daily*, 7 May 2013 (http://daily.red

bullmusicacademy.com/2013/05/coming-out-ball-70s-gay-clubbing
-in-london). Accessed 16 August 2016.

INTERLUDE: LOUDER THAN CONCORDE

Interviews with: Tony King, David Nutter, John Reid.

218 an exhausting schedule of twenty-nine performances: Bernie Taupin and David Nutter, *Elton: It's a Little Bit Funny* (New York: The Viking Press, 1977), 26.

218 'brown ale and cheese sandwiches': Ibid.

218 'really sincere' . . . 'not a trace of arrogance': From a review in *Sounds*, quoted in David Buckley, *Elton: The Biography* (Chicago: Chicago Review Press, 2007), 213.

219 Elton's US tour: Taupin and Nutter, *It's a Little Bit Funny*, 68.

219 137,000 people: Ibid., 131.

TWELVE: THE VELVET ROPE

Interviews with: Chris Albertson, Peter Brown, David Grigg, Stewart Grimshaw, Tony King, David Nutter, John Reid.

227 at least thirty-six people had already died: David Oestreicher, 'New York Declared a Disaster Area', *New York Daily News*, 30 January 1977.

227 Crisco Disco: David's memories of the club are augmented with details from www.disco-disco.com, an excellent archive of defunct New York nightlife. Accessed 4 September 2016.

228 Oh-Ho-So: David omits the venue's name in his diary entry. This detail, as well as the names of other guests, comes from Jon Tiven, 'Queen's Live Act Stuns City', a 1977 concert review (www.queen archives.com/index.php?title=Queen_-_XX-XX-1977_-_Circus_-_Madi son_Square_Garden). Accessed 12 March 2017. A review of the first Queen performance is John Rockwell, 'Rocks: Quartets', *New York Times*, 7 February 1977.

229 'My dear – what a calamity': Tommy Nutter to David Nutter, letter, 22 February 1977. DN.

229 'rent and all out-goings': Tommy Nutter to 'Mr Lodge', letter, 28 May 1976. JJC. In this letter, Tommy explains the relationship between the shop and the flat, and requests to transfer the lease into Edward's name.

230 'They are very kind': Tommy Nutter to David Nutter, letter, 18 October 1976. DN.

230 'Madame Pam is back in business': Ibid.

231 'marvellous offer' . . . 'very shady': Tommy Nutter to David Nutter, letter, 3 November 1976. DN. Peter Brown recalls: 'I didn't think they were trustworthy. They had a shop on one of the main shopping streets in Beverly Hills, and the idea was that we would take it over. But then the deal became really kind of odd.'

231 'This might come off': Ibid.

231 'The JR thing': Ibid.

231 'almost going crazy': Ibid.

231 'When I bought Brighton': Ibid.

232 'I have put Brighton on the market': Ibid.

234 'Is he still mainlining?': Tommy Nutter to David Nutter, letter, 11 August 1977. DN.

237 'I was searching': Michael Jackson, *Moonwalk* (New York: Harmony Books, 2009), 134–5.

238 'the most wonderful thing': Ibid., 135.

238 'got to be somebody else': Ibid.

238 pulled him aside one day: Ibid., 136–7.

239 'sexual electricity': Ian Schrager, interviewed by Alec Baldwin, *Here's the Thing* (podcast), WYNC, 12 May 2015.

239 'It was like a Sodom and Gomorrah': Ian Schrager, quoted in Bob Colacello, 'Anything Went', *Vanity Fair*, March 1996. Colacello himself was a frequent visitor to Studio 54.

240 spent $27,000 renovating: Ian Schrager, *Here's the Thing* interview.

240 'fusion': Ibid.

240 'I said there was no way': Carmen D'Alessio, quoted in Tim Lawrence, *Love Saves the Day: A History of American Dance Music Culture 1970–1979* (Durham, NC: Duke University Press, 2004), 232.

240 'a fire dancer working himself into a charcoal-broiled frenzy': Maureen Orth, 'The Disco Craze', *Newsweek*, 8 November 1976.

240 'It was hard to get people': Ian Schrager, *Here's the Thing* interview.

240 the City Parks Department soon issued an eviction notice: Lawrence, *Love Saves the Day*, 270.

240 'marriage': Ian Schrager, *Here's the Thing* interview.

240 'nothing much' . . . 'They raised the money': Carmen D'Alessio, quoted in Lawrence, *Love Saves the Day*, 271.

240 theatrical lighting experts: Colacello, 'Anything Went'. Most details about the interior renovation come from this article.

240 'serious sweaty dancing': Ian Schrager, *Here's the Thing* interview.

241 'the idea was to constantly assault the senses': Ian Schrager, quoted in Colacello, 'Anything Went'.

241 'tossed salad': Hasse Persson, quoted in Peter Conrad, 'Studio 54: Heady Daze of Disco Decadence – In Pictures', *Guardian*, 15 March 2015. Persson's photographs of Studio 54 offer extraordinary insight into the look and atmosphere of the club during its heyday. See Hasse Persson, *Studio 54* (Stockholm: Max Ström, 2015).

241 'deadwood': Steve Rubell, quoted in Lawrence, *Love Saves the Day*, 275.

241 yes to the horse: Ibid.

244 'It seems he still isn't used to either superstardom': Kris DiLorenzo, 'Manhattan MADNESS', *Rock Around the World*, December 1977.

244 'to go to the Ball!': Tommy Nutter to David Nutter, letter, 31 August 1977. DN.

245 somebody grabbed him: DiLorenzo, 'Manhattan MADNESS'.

THIRTEEN: ARE YOU BEING SERVED?

Interviews with: Simon Doonan, David Grigg, Robert Leach, Thom O'Dwyer, Tim Rice, Edward Sexton, Michael Smith.

247 'I applied to the largest': Tommy Nutter, interviewed on *My Kind of Music*, BBC Radio Brighton, 20 September 1980.

247 a stretch of his working life: Much of the Kilgour, French & Stanbury archive was destroyed by a fire in the 1980s. However, a trove of documents and ephemera (letters, receipts, press releases, speech drafts, potted histories, architectural plans, promotional photography, sketches, button samples and some emerald-green tassels) related to Tommy's involvement with KFS, were inherited by J&J Crombie Limited after Tommy entered into partnership with Alan Lewis in 1982.

247 one of the most respected bespoke tailors: Marie Scott, 'Living Down a Name in the Staid Seventies', *The Times*, 5 October 1977. As Scott writes, KFS 'is one of the four finest men's tailoring establishments in the Savile Row area – and therefore the world – and shares top billing only with Huntsmans, Henry Poole's, and Hawes and Curtis. Of the latter three the first is the most expensive, the second enjoys the imperishable fame of having "started" Savile Row, and the third dresses the men of the Royal Family.'

248 'an engaging personality': Richard Walker, *The Savile Row Story: An Illustrated History* (London: Prion, 1988), 98.

248 'wild one': Rodney Bennett-England, *Dress Optional: The Revolution in Menswear* (London: Peter Owen, 1967), 63.

248 wrestling with a coat in front of a customer: Walker, *Savile Row Story*, 98.

248 'I want a man to look a he-man': Louis Stanbury, quoted in Bennett-England, *Dress Optional*, 64.

248 'a man's success with people': Ibid., 66.

248 Fred Astaire in *Top Hat*: Walker, *Savile Row Story*, 98.

248 'a shade awed': David Taylor, 'Pop Goes the Whistle and Flute', *Punch*, 30 March 1977.

248 'I will not have the responsibilities': Tommy Nutter, quoted in 'US Will Be Top Priority for Nutter at Kilgour's', *Men's Wear*, 3 February 1977.

248 'piquant mixture': Scott, 'Living Down a Name'.

249 'hushed anonymity' ... 'not the place': Angus McGill, 'Power of the Pinstripe', *Evening Standard*, February 1977.

249 'He's not a member of the chorus': Tommy Nutter, undated notes for an autobiography. DN.

249 'to get in there and create an understanding': Tommy Nutter, quoted in 'US Will Be Top Priority for Nutter at Kilgour's'.

249 'not a case of Tommy Nutter': Ibid.

250 'avant to old guard': Addis Durning, 'From Avant to Old Guard', *Daily News*, 5 November 1977.

250 'the new look': 'Nutter Item', *Women's Wear Daily*, 14 February 1977. See also Jack Hyde, 'Nutter's New Phase', *Men's Wear*, 25 November 1977.

250 tightened the seat of the trousers: Suzy Menkes, 'From £50 to £300, a Suitable Case for Investment', *The Times*, 5 May 1981.

250 'Robert Mitchum look': Tommy Nutter, quoted in Taylor, 'Pop Goes the Whistle and Flute'. This is the earliest recorded reference to the 'Mitchum look' I could find, though Tommy goes on to use the description several more times. For other examples, see: Scott, 'Living Down a Name'; Albert Morch, 'By Appointment to Her Majesty – And the Royalty of Rock', *San Francisco Examiner*, 15 May 1978; and an Austin Reed press release, May 1979. JJC.

250 'the new accessories department': Tommy Nutter to David Nutter, letter, 11 August 1977. DN.

251 'add a new dimension': Durning, 'From Avant to Old Guard'.

251 'I understand they mean to use Nutter': McGill, 'Power of the Pinstripe'.

251 'they want only gradual change': Tommy Nutter, quoted in 'Tommy Nutter', *Tatler & Bystander*, May 1978.

251 'the top menswear designer in Great Britain': Tommy Nutter, quoted in 'US Will Be Top Priority for Nutter at Kilgour's'.

251 Hardy Amies ... as his guiding light: See Ibid.; 'Tommy Nutter', *Tatler & Bystander*; David Harvey, 'The Marketing of Tommy Nutter by Austin

Reed', *Men's Wear*, 18 January 1979; and Janet Buckton, 'Nutter's the Name They're All Crazy About', *Coventry Evening Telegraph*, 26 August 1980.

251 'bank clerks and office workers': Nik Cohn, *Today There Are No Gentlemen* (London: Weidenfeld & Nicolson, 1971), 72.

251 'Our courage paid off': Hardy Amies, *The Englishman's Suit* (London: Quartet Books, 1994), 31.

251 'a bit like an hourglass': Cohn, *Today There Are No Gentlemen*, 73.

252 more than a million pounds: Amies, *The Englishman's Suit*, 31.

252 a dozen new consultancy deals: The noted examples come from Bennett-England, *Dress Optional*, 55. Amies gives a figure of fifteen licensing deals in *The Englishman's Suit*.

252 'virtually pioneered': Bennett-England, *Dress Optional*, 55.

252 his own label: Amies, *The Englishman's Suit*, 35.

252 'What they want to do with me here': Tommy Nutter, quoted in 'Tommy Nutter', *Tatler & Bystander*.

252 'big name' . . . 'whatever else the store wants': Tommy Nutter, quoted in Patrick McCarthy, 'Nutter to Crack the States', *Men's Wear*, 14 April 1978.

253 'I must stress again that design': A. B. Andrews to A. H. Lewis, letter, 9 May 1978. JJC.

253 launch an in-store menswear boutique: Geoffrey Aquilina Ross, *The Day of the Peacock: Style for Men 1963–1973* (London: V&A Publishing, 2011), 78; Shaun Cole, *'Don We Now Our Gay Apparel': Gay Men's Dress in the Twentieth Century* (New York: Berg, 2000), 72.

253 'bachelor about town': Marnie Fogg, *Boutique: A '60s Cultural Phenomenon* (London: Mitchell Beazley, 2003), 68.

253 fifty-six Cue Shops in Britain: Ibid.

253 'I was extremely pleased': Tommy Nutter to Graeme Tonge, letter, 20 May 1978. JJC.

253 'quite difficult' . . . 'I felt like': Tommy Nutter to David Nutter, letter, 3 July 1978. DN.

253 production in August: Tommy Nutter to Cowan Jamieson, letter, 17 August 1978. JJC.

254 'absolutely thrilled': Tommy Nutter to Ron Hescott, letter, September 1978. JJC.

254 'the Savile Row cut': Tommy Nutter, quoted on an Austin Reed press release, 'Tommy Nutter Designs for the Cue Shop', 1978. JJC.

254 'Shades in pale earth colours' . . . 'a new feeling': Tommy Nutter Promotions Ltd press release, 1979. JJC.

254 'Not since Hepworths signed up Hardy Amies': Harvey, 'The Marketing of Tommy Nutter'.

254 reviews were favourable: See, for example: Ann Boyd, 'How Nutters Came Off the Peg', *Observer*, 14 January 1979; Harvey, 'The Marketing of Tommy Nutter'; Irene Morden, 'Why Tommy's Ready to Wear a Big Smile', *Evening Argus* (Brighton), 19 March 1979; 'Fashion Diary', *Evening Standard*, 26 March 1979; 'Suitable Nutter Gets His Mass Cue', *Yorkshire Post*, 28 March 1979; and Jessica Barrett, 'Oh, Man! He's Got Elegance', *Evening Times*, 17 April 1979.

254 'amazingly conventional': Morden, 'Why Tommy's Ready to Wear a Big Smile'.

254 'IN' list: Nigel Dempster, 'The Ins and Outs of Our Social Minefield', *Sunday Telegraph Magazine*, 11 March 1979.

254 'leading lights': 'Nutter Heads Up UK Design Boost and Points the Way', *Style*, April 1979.

254 'shooting star': 'Shooting Stars,' *Tatler & Bystander*, March 1979.

254 'tradesmen grander than their customers': 'Tradesmen Grander Than Their Customers', *Harpers & Queen*, May 1979.

255 'Mr Holland has not lost sight': Harvey, 'The Marketing of Tommy Nutter'.

256 'I think the Nutters girls': Tommy Nutter to David Nutter, letter, 11 August 1977. DN.

256 'Savile Row is a fine line': Edward Sexton, quoted in Iain Finlayson, 'The World Meets at Nutters', *Tatler & Bystander*, July/August 1978. Details about the store's physical transformation come from this source.

257 his poppy-red bespoke 'jogging suit': 'Daylight Joggery,' *Man About Town*, 10 May 1979.

257 a pair of pyjamas with a black bow tie: 'Black Tie and Pyjamas!', *Evening Argus* (Brighton), 10 January 1979.

258 'a cross between Cecil B. DeMille and a jockey': Tommy Nutter, quoted in an untitled news item, *Men's Wear*, 7 September 1978.

259 'very me!': Tommy Nutter to David Nutter, letter, 14 November 1978. DN.

259 'very me – won't last dear': Tommy Nutter to David Nutter, letter, 12 December 1979. DN.

259 a series of galas: I consulted numerous sources about the Reid & Taylor events. Some of the most illuminating were 'Flashback: A Night in Venice', *Harpers & Queen*, December 1977; 'Castle Capers', *Daily Express*, 14 February 1978; and 'Russell Harty at John Packer's Big Night', a 1981 film of the Munich gala held by the BFI National

Archive, in London. (Tommy features for a few minutes, gently making fun of John Packer by telling him one of his designs was inspired by a character from *Coronation Street*. Afterwards, he wrote to David about the filming experience and admitted that he was drunk on sherry and came across as 'very camp'.)

259 which could cost more than £100,000: Rhys David, 'Country Style', *Financial Times*, 15 October 1977.

259 'I think the nicest part about the whole jamboree': Tommy Nutter to John Packer, letter, 4 June 1981. JJC.

260 bakery workers to provincial journalists: John Shepherd, *Crisis? What Crisis?: The Callaghan Government and the British 'Winter of Discontent'* (Manchester: Manchester University Press, 2013), 3. My details about the strikes come from this source.

260 'mounting chaos': Ibid., 2–3.

260 'will still eat good food': Tommy Nutter, *My Kind of Music* interview.

260 'there is nothing like a sober suit': Jill Armstrong, 'That Old New Look', *The Times*, September 1980.

261 'officially dead': Tommy's controversial comments caused an avalanche of press, with more than a dozen reports and responses. The best include: 'Changing the Old Guard', *Evening Argus* (Brighton), 12 September 1980; and Anne Simpson, 'The Micro-Chip Chiefs Who Need Advice from Nutter', *Herald* (Glasgow), 10 September 1980 (a syndicated column).

261 'classic, respectable Savile Row jeans': Tommy Nutter, quoted in 'A Message in Their Jeans', *Evening Standard*, 12 May 1980. Later in his career Tommy would apologise for the jeans in *The Times* letters page.

261 'Is there an end to the success': 'The Nutter Numbers Ring in Japan', *Textile Forecast*, August 1980.

261 'Get rid of Are You Being Served? image': Tommy Nutter, untitled notes for Kilgour, French & Stanbury, 1980. JJC.

262 'second helpings of lamb and potatoes': Judy Gould, 'Envied', *Sunday Mirror*, 8 February 1981.

262 Savile Row tailoring would never be quite the same: 'Ready to Wear Invades Savile Row', press release, c. February 1981. JJC.

262 'millionaire-on-the-dole': Ibid. The theme is also discussed in a letter, Bill Tibbals to Tommy Nutter, 13 January 1981; and in 'Tommy Nutter Goes Ready to Wear at Kilgours', *Men's Wear*, 29 January 1981. A good discussion of the collection's strengths appears in 'The Bespoke Path', *Country Life*, 22 January 1981.

264 'Rugged Couture': Tommy Nutter, quoted in 'Points of Sheer Genius', *Men's Wear*, 22 October 1981.

264 'Large cashmere blankets with fringing': Tommy Nutter, 'Press Release: Big Sweep For Men', September 1981. DN.

265 'feeling a little absurd': Liz Smith, 'Blanket Coverage', *Evening Standard*, 8 September 1981.

265 'Meticulously draped or artlessly flung': Melissa Drier and Ruth La Ferla, 'Swept Away', *Daily News Record*, 25 September 1981.

265 'marine blue will be the new colour': 'The Big Sweep', *Evening Standard*, April 1982. I also consulted the original press release, 'The Navy Commands the New Nautical Look'. JJC.

266 'having a bit of fun': Tommy Nutter, quoted in Thom O'Dwyer, 'The World According to Tommy Nutter', *HeLines*, 1991.

266 'may lead to the sale of a substantial part of the group': 'Lincroft Share Halt', *Evening Standard*, 2 July 1981. An earlier indication of financial pressures for the Lincroft Kilgour group appears in an untitled news item, *Financial Weekly*, 21–30 January 1980: 'But turning the fruits of Mr Nutter's labour into profits proved rather more difficult for Lincroft last year, thanks to the rise in VAT which had to be absorbed. On a record turnover of £14.47m, profits halved to £435,000: the first half had already been depressed by the severe weather and lorry drivers' strike.'

266 'boring and old-fashioned': Tommy Nutter to David Nutter, letter, 7 October 1981. DN.

267 'get all those Japanese businessmen': Tommy Nutter, 'Press Release: Mick Jagger's Tailor . . . ', 27 May 1982. JJC. Unless specifically referenced, all details about the Japan trip come from a jumble of letters, notes, schedules, press material and information packs held by the Archive of J&J Crombie Ltd.

267 a fractured arm: 'Far East Lectures', *Men's Wear*, 3 June 1982. Tommy also mentions his injury in a letter to Liz Smith (a journalist with the *Evening Standard*), May 1982. JJC.

267 'Mr Hori – whiskey': Tommy Nutter Rainichi Schedule, 5 May 1982 (with Tommy's annotations). JJC.

267 'part of Britain's great heritage': Tommy Nutter, press release, June 1982. JJC.

267 'never been a megastar': Tommy Nutter, quoted in 'Are the Japanese About to Make Tommy Nutter a Megastar?', *Tatler & Bystander*, June 1981.

268 'Karate in the morning': Charles Pritchard, 'Karate steels IM chief', *Yorkshire Post*, 24 August 1983. Other details about Lewis's character come from my interview with him, and from Gail Counsel, 'Profile: The Recession Player', *Independent*, 5 September 1992.

269 'quite a while' . . . 'waiting for a suitable site': 'Tommy Nutter to Open Shop in Savile Row', *Daily News Record*, 16 August 1982.

269 'I'm getting some of the bright lights back': Tommy Nutter, quoted in 'Fashion Diary: Peter Pan Flies On', *Evening Standard*, 28 September 1982.

Interviews with: Sean Chiles, James Cottrell, Simon Doonan, Catherine Everest (née Butterworth), Timothy Everest, Aldo Fleri, Terry Haste, Wendy Kavanagh (formerly Samimi), Alan Lewis, Ann Mitchell, Joseph Morgan, Eric Musgrave, David Nutter, Thom O'Dwyer.

272 'the sun': Andy Warhol, quoted in Jonathan Kane and Holly Anderson (eds), *Art Kane* (London: Reel Arts Press, 2014). This book offers an excellent overview of Kane's career. I also consulted Art Kane, *Art Kane: The Persuasive Image* (Los Angeles: Alskog, Inc., 1975); and *A Great Day in Harlem*, the 1994 documentary by Jean Bach that was inspired by Kane's iconic photograph.

273 determined to break into show business: David discusses these scripts in his diary, but only vaguely. More specific detail about them and Kane's studio came courtesy of Holly Anderson at the Art Kane Archive.

275 'It began suddenly': Claudia Wallis, 'The Deadly Spread of AIDS', *Time*, 6 September 1982.

279 'Hello there Nutter fans everywhere': Annie Frankel to Tommy Nutter, letter, October 1982. JJC. Reproduced with permission Ms Frankel.

281 'an elegant ocean liner': James Fallon, 'Tommy Nutter Finds His Place on the Row', *Daily News Record*, 23 November 1982.

281 'I wanted it to exude quality': Tommy Nutter, quoted in Ibid.

281 'up-dated traditional look': Tommy Nutter, quoted in 'A Tailor-Made Flagship Store', *Men's Wear*, 20 January 1983.

281 'I wanted customers to be able': Tommy Nutter, quoted in Fallon, 'Tommy Nutter Finds His Place on the Row'.

283 'the suits revolution': Tommy Nutter, quoted in Thom O'Dwyer, 'The World According to Tommy Nutter', *HeLines*, 1991.

284 'The Old Men bought their suits': Patrick Collins, 'Run-Down Built-Up Shoes', *Mail on Sunday*, 29 January 1984.

284 'cutting the buckles and taking the stuffing from a straitjacket': Jay Cocks, 'Suiting Up for Easy Street', *Time*, 5 April 1982. Other good articles on the Armani influence include Suzy Menkes, 'Sex and the Single-Breasted Suit', *The Times*, 15 November 1983; and Ruth La Ferla, 'Sizing Up Giorgio Armani', *New York Times*, 21 October 1990. Other sources are Eric Musgrave, *Sharp Suits* (London: Pavilion

Books, 2013), which has an entire chapter devoted to the Italian influence, and Hardy Amies's *The Englishman's Suit* (London: Quartet Books, 1994), 38–41.

284 'I hate to mention it'... 'Armani came along': Tommy Nutter, quoted in O'Dwyer, 'The World According to Tommy Nutter'.

285 'I don't want to make everything too wild': Tommy Nutter, quoted in Fallon, 'Tommy Nutter Finds His Place on the Row'.

285 'a gentleman never wears vents': Tommy Nutter, undated notes for an autobiography. DN.

285 'Not really': Tommy Nutter, quoted in Rob Ryan, 'Tommy Nutter: Well Bespoke', *Arena*, September 1989.

285 a grey horizontal chalk-stripe suit: There is a small news item in the *Evening Standard* on 19 January 1983. The museum purchase was also announced in a press release written by Tommy, currently held in the Archives of J&J Crombie Ltd. The purchase is referenced in Tommy's obituary in *The Times*, 19 August 1992.

286 'very well-made, but a little other-worldly': Stephen Bayley, 'The Measure of a Man', *GQ*, August 1990.

286 questioned the quality of his finish: On 4 September 2015, Joseph Morgan gave me a demonstration of the differences between a Nutters of Savile Row suit and one of Tommy's suits from the 1980s. The latter, in Morgan's opinion, were vastly inferior. This view was echoed during my interview with Eric Musgrave.

287 'all hung in a gentle arc': Geraldine Ranson, 'Scissor Man', *Sunday Telegraph*, 8 January 1989.

287 1,009,444 black bugle beads: 'Elton's 36th Birthday', press release, 26 March 1983. JJC. This press release also notes the number of hours it took to manufacture the suit.

288 'You never know about romance': Tommy Nutter, quoted in 'Tailor-Made for One Another', *Evening Standard*, 19 April 1983.

289 'HEAVY!!!': Tommy Nutter to David Nutter, letter, 18 October 1976. DN.

289 'very Pink Flamingos': Tommy Nutter to David Nutter, letter, 14 November 1978. DN.

290 'complete surprise'... 'that Elton John would never marry': 'Elton's White Wedding', *Evening Standard*, 14 February 1984.

290 'heard all sorts of stories': Renate Blauel, quoted in Philip Norman, *Sir Elton: The Definitive Biography of Elton John* (London: Sidgwick & Jackson, 1991), 409.

290 'You'd think I was making the wedding dress': Tommy Nutter, quoted in Al Morch, 'Star Grab', *San Francisco Examiner*, 29 May 1984.

291 'immature people [from] making' ... 'long time': 'Elton can marry tomorrow', *Evening Standard*, 13 February 1984.

291 reminded him of John and Yoko: David makes this comparison in Dorian Wild, 'Happy event for Elton not a rush job', *Daily Telegraph*, 16 February 1984.

292 'Good on you, sport': Quoted in Philip Norman, *Sir Elton*, 415.

292 £50,000 reception at the Sebel Town House: Ibid., 414.

293 furious recriminations of theft and grandstanding: The discoveries of – and antagonism between – Luc Montagnier and Robert Gallo are examined in numerous books and articles. Most compelling is Randy Shilts, *And the Band Played On: Politics, People, and the AIDS Epidemic* (New York: St. Martin's Griffin, 2007). More balanced and thoroughly referenced is David France, *How to Survive a Plague: The Inside Story of How Citizens and Science Tamed AIDS* (New York: Knopf, 2016).

294 3,000 Aids cases in the United States: Lawrence K. Altman, 'Fewer Cases Filed at End of '83', *New York Times*, 6 January 1984.

294 a new study conducted in Washington DC: France, *How to Survive a Plague*, 154.

FIFTEEN: HUMDRUM LIFE

Interviews with: Louise Aron, Ian Brierley, Peter Brown, Cheryl De Courcey, Carol Drinkwater, Catherine Everest (née Butterworth), Timothy Everest, Aldo Fleri, Tim Gallagher, Valerie Garland, Brian Gazzard, Tom Gilbey, David Grigg, Stewart Grimshaw, Terry Haste, Wendy Kavanagh (formerly Samimi), Bertram Keeter, Tony King, Robert Leach, Alan Lewis, Ann Mitchell, Joseph Morgan, David Nutter, Thom O'Dwyer, Prince Rajsinh of Rajpipla, John Reid, Tim Rice, Christopher Tarling, Roger Walker-Dack, Judith Wright (née Allera).

297 'the most chic walk ever': Roger Dack, quoted in 'Chic Walk!', *Men's Wear*, 24 April 1989.

297 'nigh on 1,000 people': Pattie Barron, 'Fashion Parade: Walk on the Styled Side', *Evening Standard*, 18 April 1989.

297 estimates varied: The figure of £90,000 appeared in Liz Smith, 'Designer Jumble', *The Times*, 18 April 1989. *Men's Wear* gave the pledge tally as £800,000, noting that the organisers were aiming for '£1 million eventually'.

297 1,116 red balloons: Barron, 'Fashion Parade'.

297 'an American problem': Simon Garfield, *The End of Innocence: Britain in the Time of AIDS* (London: Faber and Faber, 1994), 29–30.

298 'I hope you all get very scared': Ibid., 37.

298 241 cases of Aids in Britain: Alkarim Jivani, *It's Not Unusual: A His-*

tory of Lesbian and Gay Britain in the Twentieth Century (London: Michael O'Mara Books Limited, 1997), 186.

298 refusing to perform the 'kiss of life': Garfield, *End of Innocence*, 43.

298 'leading specialists believe': Thomson Prentice, 'Deaths Could Rise to 10,000', *The Times*, 10 January 1987.

298 swigs from a hip flask: Barron, 'Fashion Parade'.

299 Bill Wyman, for example: Valentine Low, 'Bless Me, It's Mrs Wyman', *Evening Standard*, 6 June 1989.

299 Christie Brinkley had worn: *Playboy*, November 1984.

299 'Divine-sized mannequin': Frank DeCaro, 'Divine's Offscreen Wardrobe Is Strictly Saville Row', *Detroit Free Press*, 25 September 1986.

299 'I guess they came to see me': Tommy Nutter, 'The Man Behind the Joker's Outfits', *Washington Post*, 2 July 1989. When a newspaper printed that Tommy had personally designed the costumes, Warner Bros. issued him with a formal warning. Afterwards, Tommy was very careful to clarify that he had merely tailored the suits based on Ringwood's designs.

299n 'It's common knowledge': Tommy Nutter, quoted in 'Thomas Albert Nutter: Savile Row Tailor', *CUT*, November 1988.

300 'supportive of British fashion': Tommy Nutter, quoted in 'Nuts in Store', *Guardian*, 11 January 1988. See also 'Tailor Tommy Takes Up the Challenge', *The Times*, 12 January 1988. Tommy's first collection appeared in Fortnum & Mason in 1985; see 'Fashflash', *The Times*, 23 April 1985.

300 'I couldn't be doing with all those golf weekends': Tommy Nutter, quoted in Thom O'Dwyer, 'The World According to Tommy Nutter', *HeLines*, 1991.

300 'a relic of the Sixties': 'Tommy Nutter: Well Bespoke', *Arena*, September 1989.

300 'on a level with the best': Tommy Nutter, quoted in *Sunday Times Magazine*, 12 October 1989.

300 'I fall somewhere in between': Tommy Nutter, quoted in O'Dwyer, 'The World According to Tommy Nutter'.

301 still nothing he could do: Tommy notes this himself ('It pains him a little . . .'), in 'Tommy Nutter: Well Bespoke'.

301 Fabric of the Nation: Details about the gala come from the April 1989–March 1990 National Museums of Scotland Annual Report, 7–8.

308 'changing his image': Tommy Nutter, quoted in 'TV Tommy', *Men's Wear*, 6 December 1990.

308 'I suppose it is a lot': Elton John, quoted in Jill Turner, 'Slimline Elton

Packs His Bags', *Daily Mirror*, 2 January 1991. See also 'In Is Out, but "Right Now" Is Right Here', *Daily News*, 8 January 1991.

309 Colour & Design Competition: 'Region's Mills Lay Claim to Three Cloth Awards', *Yorkshire Post*, 3 October 1991. The judging panel was convened at the end of July.

309 'Perhaps a brocade waistcoat': Tommy Nutter, quoted in 'Suited to the Course', *The Times*, 8 June 1991.

309 'dreadful' . . . 'people used to dress': Tommy Nutter, quoted in 'What a State?', *Men's Wear*, 20 September 1991.

309 'Worth Its Weight': Tommy Nutter, 'Worth Its Weight', *Men's Wear*, 17 October 1991.

310 'The move will mean that I will be seen': Richard James, quoted in 'Retail Flocks to Savile Row', *Fashion Weekly*, 2 April 1992. In the article, Angus Cundey links the arrival of young talent like Richard James with 'what Tommy Nutter has done for the trade'.

313 'T. N. in Conduit Street getting inspiration': Tommy Nutter to Barry Grigg, postcard, 28 April 1980. Owned by David Grigg.

318 'Fashion King Nutter Fights for His Life': These headlines come from *Daily Express* and *Sun*, and were on clippings (clipped of their exact dates) given to me by Robert Leach.

318 'Other eyes see the stars': Cilla Black to Tommy Nutter, card, undated, *c.* August 1992. DN.

320 'What really, really makes you happy, Tommy?': O'Dwyer, 'The World According to Tommy Nutter'.

IMAGE CREDITS

SELECTED READING

Aitken, Jonathan. *The Young Meteors*. New York: Atheneum, 1967.

Amies, Hardy. *The Englishman's Suit*. London: Quartet Books, 1994.

——. *ABC of Men's Fashion*. London: V&A Publications, 2007.

Anderson, Paul. *Mods: The New Religion*. London: Omnibus Press, 2014.

Aquilina Ross, Geoffrey. *The Day of the Peacock: Style for Men 1963–1973*. London: V&A Publishing, 2011.

Barnes, Richard. *Mods!* London: Eel Pie Publishing, 1979.

Bennett-England, Rodney. *Dress Optional: The Revolution in Menswear*. London: Peter Owen, 1967.

Binder, Pearl. *The Peacock's Tail*. London: George G. Harrap & Co. Ltd, 1958.

Black, Cilla. *What's It All About?* London: Ebury Press, 2003.

Booth, Stanley. *The True Adventures of the Rolling Stones*. New York: Vintage Books, 1985.

Breward, Christopher. *The Suit: Form, Function and Style*. London: Reaktion Books, 2016.

Brewster, Bill. *Last Night a DJ Saved My Life: The History of the Disc Jockey*. New York: Grove Press, 2014.

Brown, Peter, and Steven Gaines. *The Love You Make: An Insider's Story of the Beatles*. New York: New American Library, 2002.

Buckley, David. *Elton: The Biography*. Chicago: Chicago Review Press, 2007.

Byrde, Penelope. *The Male Image: Men's Fashion in Britain 1300–1970*. London: B. T. Batsford Ltd, 1979.

Cohen, Stanley. *Folk Devils and Moral Panics*. New York: St. Martin's Press, 1972.

Cohn, Nik. *Today There Are No Gentlemen: The Changes in Englishmen's Clothes Since the War*. London: Weidenfeld & Nicolson, 1971.

Cole, Shaun. *'Don We Now Our Gay Apparel': Gay Men's Dress in the Twentieth Century*. London: Bloomsbury Academic, 2000.

Coleman, Ray. *Lennon: The Definitive Biography*. New York: HarperPerennial, 1992.

Crisp, Quentin. *The Naked Civil Servant*. London: Penguin, 1997.

David, Hugh. *On Queer Street: A Social History of British Homosexuality 1895–1995*. London: HarperCollins, 1998.

De La Haye, Amy (ed.). *The Cutting Edge: 50 Years of British Fashion, 1947–1997*. New York: The Overlook Press, 1997.

Edward, Duke of Windsor. *A Family Album*. London: Cassell, 1960.

Epstein, Brian. *A Cellarful of Noise*. New York: Doubleday & Company, Inc., 1964.

Farson, Dan. *Soho in the Fifties*. London: Michael Joseph Ltd, 1987.

Fogg, Marnie. *Boutique: A '60s Cultural Phenomenon*. London: Mitchell Beazley, 2003.

France, David. *How to Survive a Plague: The Inside Story of How Citizens and Science Tamed AIDS*. New York: Knopf, 2016.

Garfield, Simon. *The End of Innocence: Britain in the Time of AIDS*. London: Faber and Faber, 1994.

Gartner, Niko. *Operation Pied Piper: The Wartime Evacuation of Schoolchildren from London and Berlin 1938–1946*. Charlotte, North Carolina: Information Age Publishing, Inc., 2012.

Gross, Michael. *Focus: The Secret, Sexy, Sometimes Sordid World of Fashion Photographers*. New York: Atria Books, 2016.

Haden-Guest, Anthony. *The Last Party: Studio 54, Disco, and the Culture of the Night*. New York: William Morrow and Company, Inc., 1997.

Harrison, Alison. *The Light of Other Days: A Brief History of Friog & Fairbourne*. Wales: Y Dydd Press, 1966.

Hewitt, Paolo (ed.). *The Sharper Word: A Mod Anthology*. London: Helter Skelter Publishing, 2001.

Hibbert, Christopher. *Edward VII: The Last Victorian King*. New York: St. Martin's Press, 2007.

Hogg, James, and Robert Sellers. *Hello Darlings!: The Authorized Biography of Kenny Everett*. London: Bantam Press, 2013.

Holleran, Andrew. *Dancer from the Dance*. New York: Harper Perennial, 2001.

Houlbrook, Matt. *Queer London: Perils and Pleasures in the Sexual Metropolis 1918–1957*. Chicago: University of Chicago Press, 2006.

Howarth, Stephen. *Henry Poole: Founders of Savile Row: The Making of a Legend*. London: Bene Factum Publishing, 2003.

Jackson, Michael. *Moonwalk*. New York: Harmony Books, 2009.

Jarman, Derek. *Smiling in Slow Motion: Diaries, 1991–94*. London: Vintage Classics, 2001.

Jivani, Alkarim. *It's Not Unusual: A History of Lesbian and Gay Britain in the Twentieth Century*. London: Michael O'Mara Books Limited, 1997.

John, Elton. *Love Is the Cure: On Life, Loss, and the End of AIDS*. New York: Little, Brown and Company, 2012.

Kaiser, Charles. *The Gay Metropolis*. New York: Grove Press, 2007.

Kane, Art. *Art Kane: The Persuasive Image*. Los Angeles: Alskog, Inc., 1975.

Kane, Jonathan, and Holly Anderson (eds). *Art Kane*. London: Reel Arts Press, 2014.

Kelly, Ian. *Beau Brummell: The Ultimate Dandy*. London: Hodder & Stoughton, 2005.

Kynaston, David. *Austerity Britain, 1945–1951*. New York: Bloomsbury, 2010.

——. *Family Britain, 1951–1957*. New York: Bloomsbury, 2010.

——. *Modernity Britain, 1957–1962*. New York: Bloomsbury, 2014.

Laurie, Peter. *The Teenage Revolution*. London: Anthony Blond, 1965.

Lawrence, Tim. *Love Saves the Day: A History of American Dance Music Culture, 1970–1979*. Durham, NC: Duke University Press, 2004.

Lewisohn, Mark. *The Complete Beatles Chronicle*. New York: Harmony Books, 1992.

——. *Tune In: The Beatles: All These Years, Volume 1*. New York: Crown Archetype, 2013.

Loog Oldham, Andrew. *Stoned: A Memoir of London in the 1960s*. New York: St. Martin's Press, 2001.

Lord Montagu of Beaulieu. *Wheels Within Wheels: An Unconventional Life*. London: Weidenfeld & Nicolson, 2000.

MacInnes, Colin. *Absolute Beginners*. London: MacGibbon & Kee, 1959.

Melly, George. *Revolt into Style: The Pop Arts in Britain*. London: Allen Lane, 1970.

Miles, Barry. *London Calling: A Countercultural History of London Since 1945*. New York: Atlantic Books, 2011.

Musgrave, Eric. *Sharp Suits*. London: Pavilion Books, 2013.

Neville, Richard. *Hippie Hippie Shake: The Dreams, the Trips, the Trials, the Love-Ins, the Screw Ups . . . The Sixties*. London: Bloomsbury, 1995.

Norman, Philip. *Sir Elton: The Definitive Biography of Elton John*. London: Sidgwick & Jackson, 1991.

——. *John Lennon: The Life*. New York: Ecco/HarperCollins, 2008.

——. *Mick Jagger*. New York: Ecco/HarperCollins, 2012.

O'Neill, Terry. *Two Days that Rocked the World: Elton John Live at Dodger Stadium*. New York: Antique Collectors Club, 2015.

Pang, May. *Instamatic Karma: Photographs of John Lennon*. New York: St. Martin's Press, 2008.

Persson, Hasse. *Studio 54*. Stockholm: Max Ström, 2015.

Postrel, Virginia. *The Power of Glamour: Longing and the Art of Visual Persuasion*. New York: Simon & Schuster, 2013.

Quant, Mary. *Quant by Quant: The Autobiography of Mary Quant*. London: V&A Publishing, 2012.

Reed, Jeremy. *The King of Carnaby Street: A Life of John Stephen*. London: Haus Publishing, 2010.

Robinson, Lucy. *Gay Men and the Left in Post-War Britain: How the Personal Got Political*. Manchester: Manchester University Press, 2011.

Rous, Henrietta. *The Ossie Clark Diaries*. London: Bloomsbury, 1998.

Sandbrook, Dominic. *Never Had It So Good: A History of Britain from Suez to the Beatles*. London: Little, Brown, 2005.

——. *White Heat: A History of Britain in the Swinging Sixties*. London: Little, Brown, 2006.

Scaduto, Anthony. *Mick Jagger: Everybody's Lucifer*. New York: David McKay Company, Inc., 1974.

Sherwood, James. *The London Cut: Savile Row Bespoke Tailoring*. Venice: Marsilio Editori, 2007.

——. *Savile Row: The Master Tailors of British Bespoke*. London: Thames and Hudson, Ltd, 2010.

Shilts, Randy. *And the Band Played On: Politics, People, and the AIDS Epidemic*. New York: St. Martin's Griffin, 2007.

Sigsworth, Eric M. *Montague Burton: The Tailor of Taste*. Manchester: Manchester University Press, 1990.

Spitz, Bob. *The Beatles: A Biography*. New York: Little, Brown and Company, 2012.

Steele, Valerie (ed.). *A Queer History of Fashion: From the Closet to the Catwalk*. New Haven: Yale University Press, 2013.

Taupin, Bernie, and David Nutter. *Elton: It's a Little Bit Funny*. New York: The Viking Press, 1977.

Tippins, Sherill. *Inside the Dream Palace: The Life and Times of New York's Legendary Chelsea Hotel*. New York: Houghton Mifflin Harcourt, 2010.

Took, Barry, and Mat Coward. *The Best of Round the Horne*. London: Boxtree, 2000.

Vyner, Harriet. *Groovy Bob: The Life and Times of Robert Fraser*. London: HENI Publishing, 2016.

Walker, Richard. *The Savile Row Story: An Illustrated History*. London: Prion, 1988.

Weight, Richard. *Mod: A Very British Style*. London: The Bodley Head, 2013.

Wildeblood, Peter. *Against the Law*. London: Weidenfeld & Nicolson, 1955.

ACKNOWLEDGEMENTS

This book exists only because Rebecca Cubitt, my great friend, intuited an untold story behind the figure of Tommy Nutter. Bec was right, and I'm grateful to her for letting me be the one to tell it.

This book exists in its current state only because David Nutter agreed to speak to me about his brother and then opened the gates to his ramshackle memory palace so I could wander around for a few years, during which time I discovered that things were far stranger and more interesting than anyone could have guessed. I feel privileged to call him a friend.

My thanks go to every person who spoke to me during my research period, particularly Robert Leach, who let me bounce ideas off him at all hours of the day and night; Peter Brown, who gave me some crucial early encouragement; David Brescia, who helped me access the J&J Crombie Limited Archive; and Bert Keeter, Tommy and David's second cousin, who lent me his lovely apartment in Grotte di Castro, Italy, where I wrote the first chapter.

My enormous gratitude to Edward Sexton for being so open about the history of Nutters of Savile Row, both the high times and the low. He remains the best cutter working in London today. Thank you also to Dominic Sebag-Montefiore, Edward's business partner, for some invaluable insight into the tailoring trade.

In addition to Grotte di Castro, this book was written in Berlin, London, New York, rural Australia and (briefly) a Botswana game reserve. My gratitude to the best international pit crew ever: Daniel Stone, Elmo Keep, Nicholas Fonseca, Nikita Polikanov, Tony Stewart, Pip Cummings, Laura Smith, Julie Miller, Caitlin Furlong, Melissa Gluck, Timothy Stewart-Winter, Charlie Serotoff and Benoit Denizet-Lewis. In various ways, you all kept me going. My gratitude also to Robert Boynton, who several years ago accepted me into the Literary Reportage programme at NYU, a twist that ultimately led to all of this. Katie Roiphe, my mentor, pushed me further than I knew I could go as a writer. Brooke Kroeger gave me unflagging, unconditional support and introduced me to the sharpest agent anyone could hope to find: Flip Brophy.

My wonderful editor, Tricia Boczkowski, offered constant enthusiasm, lucid advice and a pitch-perfect sensibility, which got me through some existential patches. Bouquets of roses to her, Aubrey Martinson and the whole team at Crown Archetype. I am also grateful to Clara Farmer, Charlotte Humphery and the lovely people at Chatto & Windus – and to Szilvia Molnar for making that happen.

My family – Donna, Murray, Amy, Dwayne, Clancy, Rianne, Emmett, Kaylee, Gloria and Wal (much missed) – makes everything worth it.

My *other* family – Bryan Lowder, Cam McDonald, Charles Kaiser, Joseph Stouter, Rick Whitaker and Chris Davies – has made my New York years the best of my life.

Elizabeth Flock, your voicemails are my Desert Island Discs.

And Theo Milonopoulos, last but most: I love you.

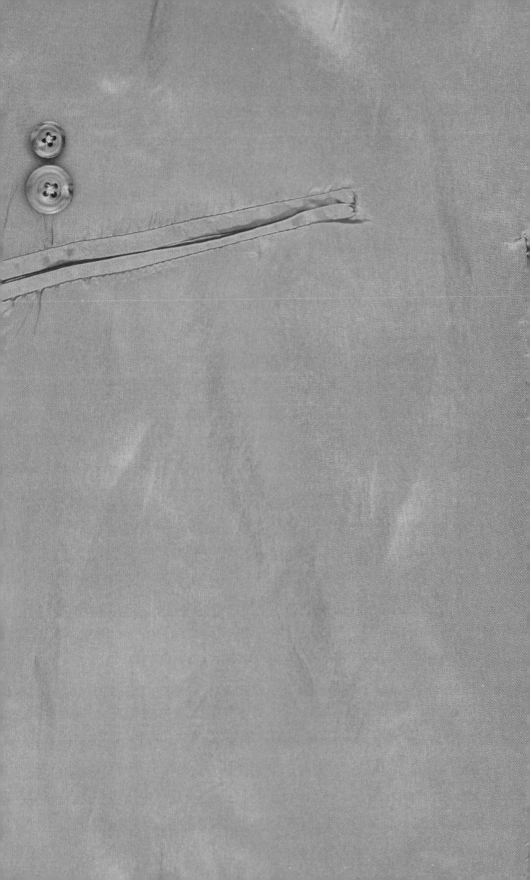